VISUAL & PERFORMING ARTS

SWITCHING CHANNELS

VISUAL & PERFORMING ARTS

SWITCHING CHANNELS

Organization and Change
in TV Broadcasting

RICHARD E. CAVES

with

KAREN GUO · CATHERINE O'GORMAN
MATTHEW S. ROSENBERG · RICHARD J. WEGENER

Harvard University Press
Cambridge, Massachusetts
London, England
2005

Library of Congress Cataloging-in-Publication Data

Caves, Richard E.
Switching channels : organization and change in
TV broadcasting / Richard E. Caves.
p.   cm.
Includes bibliographical references and index.
ISBN 0-674-01878-8 (alk. paper)
1. Television broadcasting—Economic aspects—United States.
2. Television broadcasting—United States.   I. Title.

PN1992.3.U5C34 2005
384.55′1′0973—dc22   2005040345

Contents

Preface

This book follows upon previous research on the organization of the arts and entertainment industries—published in *Creative Industries* (2000). That volume argued that economic analysis can do a surprisingly thorough job of explaining why creative activities are organized the way they are: how deals are done, how collaborations are organized between creative personnel (artists) and the humdrum folk who work with them, how competing firms in creative industries prepare, distribute, and promote these goods. While *Creative Industries* drew ad lib on a number of arts and entertainment industries, it omitted the TV program sector. Keeping that book's length manageable was a key consideration, reinforced by the complexity of TV programs' distribution channels (the proximate selectors of programs). Those channels embrace traditional broadcast networks, their owned and affiliated local stations, cable networks that distribute their signals through local cable systems and direct broadcast satellites, syndicators who distribute individual programs rather than packages, and the public broadcasting system (a complex of nonprofit and governmental organizations). Furthermore, the industry was in the throes of major structural change.

This study addresses how the bedrock properties of creative industries affect the organization and economic performance of TV production and distribution. We investigate not only the dealings between program suppliers and distributors, but also the patterns of transactions between the networks (packagers of programs) and their distributors, including local broadcast stations, cable systems and multi-system operators (MSOs), and satellite distributors. These "downstream" dealings are strongly shaped by the properties of creative goods and industries, as is the distribution of cinema films and trade books, even though the employees and organizations downstream may be free of any *art-for-art's-sake* motives.

Previous economic research on broadcasting is abundant, but it exhibits two shortcomings. Much of it is somewhat dated, having appeared mostly in the 1980s. More important, it focuses on public policy rather than behavioral questions, asking why the sector works as it does. The broadcasting sector indeed is heavily influenced by public policy, which has shaped the sector's structure through its allocation of the broadcast spectrum resource and the rules it has imposed on the market's various participants. These rules are economic in their substance. They are mainly motivated, however, by First Amendment or freedom-of-speech considerations, not conventional economic welfare. Economists have long recognized, however, that broadcasting is subject to market failures, because its public-good character can cause profit-maximizing broadcasters to provide programming of too little diversity. Scholars based in schools of communication have shown more interest in how programs are prepared, acquired, and scheduled, but opportunities remain for further inquiry. The behavioral research opportunities that lie open are important for filling out our knowledge of how this market works, which in turn is necessary in order to get the policy-oriented research right.

Opportunities for research in the broadcasting sector embrace both formal quantitative and more general descriptive approaches. This study mainly follows the latter course. Its predecessor, *Creative Industries*, found a large gap to be filled by showing how the distinctive properties of the arts and entertainment industries shape their industrial organization—the evolving nexus of contract arrangements and market structures. This book aims at the same synthesis for broadcasting. It also exploits the same strategy of developing its economic analysis at a relatively simple level, to provide access for readers interested in how broadcasting operates, but without more than introductory training in economics. Some attention is paid, however, to quantitative research projects of the students who are listed as collaborators in this volume.

Databases unsurprisingly tend to be in short supply in the creative industries. While broadcasting is better served than most, our interest in contract terms and deal structures requires reliance on trade publications—an information source that gets little respect from most economists, presumably on grounds of the inaccuracy and misinterpretation that can trip reporters lacking much training in economics and working to tight deadlines. When several competing trade publications are followed over a run of years, however, these defects can be considerably reduced by cross-checking—watching for temporal inconsistencies and divergence between the information appearing in different periodicals. Another valuable source of information is the studies prepared for proceedings on various policy questions before the Federal Communications Commission (FCC).

TV broadcasting is a moving target for the researcher. As of mid-2004 the digital revolution was under way but moving much more slowly than policymakers had expected. In 2003 the FCC relaxed several of its rules: one limiting the proportion of U.S. TV households that could be reached by TV stations with any given common owner; others permitting some common ownership between TV stations and newspapers. This brought a storm of protest from First Amendment supporters, who succeeded in forcing some rollback, and in 2004 a court decision threw the local ownership changes into uncertainty. We hope that the structural patterns shown in this study will aid understanding of this "creative industry" even as unforeseen future market conditions and policy changes assault it.

SWITCHING CHANNELS

Introduction

This book is about the market for TV programs—how it is organized, why it works the way it does, how it has responded to certain major changes in market structure and public policy. It is not an exercise in social or aesthetic criticism. Whether one's preferred entertainment is the Public Broadcasting Service, *Seinfeld* reruns, or professional wrestling, it is important to understand why this sector is organized the way it is and delivers the programming that it does. Unlike most previous research on the broadcasting industry, this book is not about the regime of policies imposed on or advocated for broadcasting. Still, understanding why market forces cast up the array of programming that they do is vital for projecting the consequences of any policy change.

Broadcasting's Key Organizational Features

Broadcasting is treated here as one of the arts and entertainment industries, or creative industries. While one might casually suspect these sectors to have escaped the humdrum economic laws that govern the run of industries, the creative industries have been found to show a clear common logic in their organization, apparent in similarities to one another and differences from humdrum indus-

1

tries. Central to this book's agenda is determining how fully TV broadcasting shares the organizational logic of its creative brethren.

By the economic logic of broadcasting (or any creative industry), we mean the following. Broadcasting puts before viewers some stream of programs that vary in their character and style—what is on view at any given hour or over the day or week. The shows in this stream also vary in quality. We always speak of quality in the nonjudgmental sense of the resources and talents poured into making a program and/or the size (and perhaps the demographic mix) of the audience that the broadcaster expects or hopes to attract. This program stream emanates from a group of networks—a few transmitting over the air, many via cable and (increasingly) satellite. They launch their transmissions through deals with many distributors—local broadcast stations and cable systems. The program streams then result from a skein of interrelated deals. Deals with program suppliers and the talents they recruit proximately determine what the audience can see. Deals with advertisers yield the revenue that covers the cost of producing and distributing programs—all of it for over-the-air broadcasters, part of it for cable and satellite channels, which can charge viewers for access. The networks and distributors making deals with one another represent groups of firms that vary in important ways—ways that the field of industrial economics finds important for all industries. These include how numerous are the buyers and sellers, how easily newcomers can enter and unsuccessful incumbents extricate themselves, how closely the competing programs that they offer are substitutes for one another, what deal terms the networks deploy as they compete with one another—price, program type and quality, new versus repeated programs. The bilateral dealings between networks and distributors are particularly complex: the parties at the bargaining table often are few in number, and the bargaining range over which the parties can haggle sometimes is large.

A question that is commonly asked about an industry's structure is why firms are integrated across several markets. The familiar term "media conglomerates" alerts us to the need to understand why TV firms develop multi-market operations as they do. Each broadcast network owns and operates a group of big-city stations, known as its O&Os. Ownership links also exist between cable networks and the firms that operate many local cable systems (multisystem operators, or MSOs). The broadcasting networks have been rapidly increasing their ownership of the prime-time programs that they broadcast, and motion picture studios (Fox, Paramount, etc.) that have been major suppliers of programs have integrated forward to control broadcast networks. Broadcast networks and studios have made substantial investments in cable networks. Independent broadcast stations have been banding together in chains, as have the individual cable systems. These forms of integration might be propelled by any of several economic mechanisms that can explain why they are profitable, but their significance for economic welfare is problematic. Integration can produce profit by either increasing efficiency or reducing competition.

How all this works out depends in part on public policy, which has largely determined the number of local broadcasting stations and thereby (indirectly) the number of over-the-air networks. It long called the shots on how the supply of prime-time broadcast programs was organized. It imposes decency standards on broadcast but not on cable or satellite programs. It has limited the extent of common ownership of TV stations and has stepped in to referee the terms under which cable systems carry the signals of local broadcast stations. The effects of these many policies run deep, and recent changes in several of them indeed present us with lab experiments.

The imprint of public policy on the industry has been actively researched and is not hard to find. More elusive and less noted is the role of fundamental structural features identified in the other creative industries.

TV Programming among the Creative Industries

This study holds that we can learn much about the organization and deal structures of TV by fitting it into the category of creative industries. Many of its organizational features can be well explained by bedrock properties common to other creative industries.[1] It also draws on the analysis of an overlapping category of industries, the "information industries," embracing "anything that can be digitalized."[2] The creative industries include entertainment industries—cinema films, music recording—that bear an evident close relationship to the production and delivery of TV programs. For an example, in the 1920s and 1930s the Hollywood movie studios kept many of their actors and other creative talent under seven-year option contracts, for reasons clearly associated with the studios' need for an incentive to invest in developing talent. It is equally clear why these contracts largely disappeared as the film industry adopted "flexible specialization," with a different team of inputs recruited afresh for each project. TV dramatic programs, however, continue to employ long-term option contracts, an evident response to the multi-year life spans in first-run production of successful sitcoms and dramas.

This illumination draws upon relatively simple tools of economic analysis, in particular the theory of contracts and the line of reasoning that economists have developed to explain the scale and scope of the firm (large or small? vertically integrated or dealing at arm's length? using one-shot transactions or long-term contracts?). These concepts and models and the essential structural features of the creative industries are glued together by a series of simple concepts that identify fundamental features of tastes and technology. Those dictate the deal structures and organizational arrangements most satisfactory for the participants as a group. Here are the key concepts.

Nobody knows. The outputs are invariably "experience goods," in that the consumer's valuation is unknown until a good is actually consumed or experienced. Nor is one consumer's valuation necessarily a good predictor of another's response. This property implies a high level of uncertainty for producers of creative goods. William Goldman pinned this adage on the movie industry: NOBODY KNOWS ANYTHING.[3] As he explained, industry executives know a great deal about what has succeeded and failed in the past. They constantly seek to extrapolate that knowledge to nascent creative products at hand, but their forecasts improve little on the roll of the dice.

Sunk costs. Amplifying the problem of uncertain valuations is the requirement that all costs of a creative or information product be incurred and sunk before an informative test of consumers' acceptance becomes possible. If an unsuccessful creative good could be melted down and part of its cost recovered, the hazard of uncertain acceptance would be reduced accordingly. If pre-testing prototypes or first drafts were somewhat informative, likely turkeys could be culled from the flock. Suppliers of movies, music recordings, and so on employ some such concept as a "stiff ratio," the (high) proportion of products that fail to generate enough sales revenue to cover their direct costs. For such uncertain products to be commercially viable, the producer must wring enough revenue from the average winner to cover the losses on six or seven stiffs.

Fixed costs. Information goods and many creative goods share the property that their costs of production are largely or entirely fixed. The marginal cost of serving another consumer accordingly is zero or proportionally tiny. Hence marginal cost (the touchstone for setting prices in standard economic models) provides no guidance at all, and sellers must find some way to quote prices to various buyers that are no greater than the buyers' reservation prices yet cover the producer's fixed costs. That extraction process is eased by the fact that creative goods are commonly not sold or licensed anonymously: their owner (licensor) knows enough of the licensee's economic circumstances to predict the licensee's reservation price with some accuracy. Or the license contract can be written so as to extract more revenue from high-value licensees. Furthermore, information products are durable. That helps the owner/licensor to separate buyers on the basis of their time urgency: the most eager buyers (and/or the licensees serving them) pay through the nose.

Quality choice (endogenous fixed costs). The costs of producing creative goods are fixed (independent of the quantity produced), but they are discretionary or endogenous with respect to the product's quality. Astutely spending more on a cinema film or TV sitcom series increases its quality (in the nonjudgmental sense of raising consumers' willingness to pay). The fixity of cost (zero marginal cost) makes the output a proprietary public good to the producer. The producer therefore decides what quality to provide by comparing the extra cost incurred for quality improvement to the sum of additions to the willingness to pay of all prospective customers. The market's size then becomes fundamentally important to the producer's choice of quality. If $1,000 spent to improve quality raises each customer's valuation by ten cents, the outlay results in a crushing loss when 1,000 customers are served, a break-even with 10,000, a bonanza with 100,000. A profit-seeking producer spends to raise quality until the last dollar fails to raise net profit (marginal revenue falls equal to marginal cost). Hence the large market will be served better quality than the small one. John Sutton attached the banner of "endogenous fixed cost" to this mechanism.[4] It will prove fundamentally important for investigating the reactions of over-the-air broadcasters and cable networks to the exogenous shifts in the sizes of their respective market segments within the overall market for television programs.

A-list/B-list. A reason why the producer of creative goods enjoys discretion in selecting quality is the perceived variation in quality (proficiency, charisma, whatever) of the inputs of talent themselves. Communities of creative workers commonly share a consensus on the ranking of their various members, based on assessments of their performance in previous projects. These assessments seem to depend on professional criteria for the prowess of performance. One is not judged to be an A-list player solely because one's last project made a profit. The standard economic term for quality rankings is vertical differentiation. The property has direct implications for how distinctive creative talents are paid: not on their opportunity cost (waiting tables?) but on the basis of the cash flows generated by their participation in a project. A sitcom star can in principle demand a paycheck equal to the gap between the show's earnings when she heads the cast and the same show's earnings with an uncredentialed (but competent) actor. In economic terms this surplus is a rent. The principle also applies conspicuously to a popular professional sports team or league.

Infinite variety. Creative goods exhibit pervasive product differentiation of the "horizontal" variety—that is, consumers discern differences in the attributes of the product's available varieties but diverge in their preference rankings for comparably priced varieties. An important distinction in creative industries is between the potential variants on a basic program style (sitcom, action-adventure drama), which are effectively infinite, and the number of actual varieties that appear on the market. The market picks some equilibrium number, depending on the fixed costs of production interacting with the size of the potential audience and the diversity of their tastes. The actual number might be small even when the potential varieties are infinite. It also depends on how vigorously the suppliers of rival varieties compete on price. Here *infinite variety* exerts another effect: it softens price competition among rival producers and allows them to sustain prices higher than their (zero) marginal costs, even when their competitors are numerous.

Ars longa. Creative industries' outputs either are durable themselves, or they involve some durable template on call to yield a consumable good. Like cinema films and sound recordings, some TV program series enjoy long economic life spans during which they can earn rents from exhibition in a succession of venues before different audiences. These uncertain but potentially large flows lend importance to what ownership arrangements were selected when the program first reached the screen. The importance stems from the size of the returns that may ultimately accrue to the owner, but those ultimate rents depend in turn on early decisions about how the program is produced and promoted. Hence, getting decision rights into the hands of a party able to furbish the program for maximum long-run rents can make a large difference in its value.

Art for art's sake. An important structural feature of creative industries is the tastes of creative talents, which affect what terms of employment they will accept. Artists get utility from performing creative work, which implies a low reservation wage. More important for organization, their tastes embrace the way in which their creative work is done and the degree to which they control creative decisions. Organizational arrangements and deals hence are likely to turn on issues of the allocation of decision rights among suppliers of creative inputs.

The Big Picture: Summary

The organization of the broadcasting sector is complicated: programs are commissioned or prepared by national coordinators (networks) or local distributors (stations, cable systems). The distribution channels include over-the-air, cable, and satellite technologies. This structure provides many nooks and crannies in which to search for the attributes of creative industries. This book is organized in three major parts, each one yielding a lesson (or a group of interrelated lessons) about TV program distribution as a creative industry. In the balance of this introduction we summarize these lessons. The book closes with an epilogue sketching their application to the changes currently swirling through the industry.

Acquiring and Scheduling Programs

Broadcasting's closest contact with other creative industries occurs in the market where networks (program distributors) acquire their shows. It shares several key properties with markets for cinema films and music recordings. Individual TV programs or series are creative goods subject to *infinite variety*, producible in potentially limitless styles and contents. Viewers have heterogeneous tastes for the various styles and types of content that might be provided. Furthermore, the size and composition of the potential TV audience varies temporally, especially with the hours of the day. Broadcasters know what size and type of audience is likely available, but they know little about how popular a new program series will prove: *nobody knows,* yet all the production costs must be incurred before viewers' evaluation is known. Finally, the costs of providing a program are almost entirely fixed (not varying with the number of viewers or showings), yet their magnitude is discretionary (endogenous) for the producer and network. How much quality (better or better-known stars, better writers, opulent production values) is built in to the show is a mutual decision of network and producer. Since quality is a fixed cost, the quality worth achieving increases proportionally with the size of the show's potential audience. Because that audience varies with time of day and week (apart from long-run changes), the shows sought in the program market vary greatly in quality (but because *nobody knows,* a show's quality may be only weakly correlated with the actual audience it attracts).

The market for prime-time (roughly, 8 to 11 P.M.) dramatic programs (sitcoms, dramas) has long functioned as the top tier of vertically differentiated programs. For reasons addressed in Part Two of this book, it is now threatened by reality programs, but it continues to show in full measure the features of the program market. Producing a single program (a special program or made-for-TV movie) is a small-scale artisan process undertaken by teams of creative personnel and technicians. Such programs are supplied by small and transient firms. At the opposite pole, scripted prime-time shows need a more complex organization, for two reasons. The higher production values require more infrastructure. And their financing needs are larger and more complex—because they cost more initially, and because their expected cash flows include syndication revenues that may arrive years in the future. Supplying prime-time scripted programs thus requires teamwork between the creative workforce and an organization (such as a Hollywood film studio) to provide overhead facilities and finance. As these needs have grown, the writer-producers who "run" prime-time shows have increasingly made alliances with film studios and (now) the broadcast networks themselves.

Within this organization, the process of preparing programs is governed by contracts structured similarly to those in other creative industries. Because *nobody knows,* programs are prepared in steps that allow periodic reassessment of the project as it develops. An idea gives rise to a sample script; if the script pleases the network buyer, a pilot episode is prepared; the pilot competes with other pilots for a spot on the network's schedule; once the program is scheduled, the network orders a number of episodes that increases with its faith in the show's success. Contracts also lock in key personnel from the moment when an actor first reads for a part. The duration of this lock-in reflects an important trade-off: too short, and the network has little incentive to develop and promote the show; too long, and the talent (actors, producer) get no cut of the revenues from a successful series. The compromise on five years means that the network has that long to collect rents on a successful show before they can be bargained away by the producer and actors whose talents are necessary to the show's unique value.

A network's stock of programs in hand must be scheduled by season, time of day, and so on, in order to maximize the net revenue from advertisers and (for cable networks) subscriber fees. This process takes place in several settings. In prime-type broadcasting a stable pattern long existed of matching oligopolistic moves: all networks launched the fall season the same week, programmed for competitive advantage by hour and day, and so on. The entry of new broadcast networks and declining profitability of the incumbents have tended to diffuse this tit-for-tat interplay. Increasingly each network goes its own way with much-reduced attention to rivals' moves.[5]

Scheduling decisions occur, however, in a broader context than that of network prime time. Broadcast and cable distribution each involves both national networks and local transmitters. In either channel the selection of program schedules could be made entirely at the national level (as cable networks do). Or it could be made entirely at the local level (stations and cable system operators selecting from program suppliers' libraries), a model approximated by public broadcasting stations. Or the scheduling task could be split between a national core scheduler supplying a block or blocks, to be filled out locally in light of local tastes. The last model describes the arrangement prevailing in over-the-air commercial broadcasting. An economist from outer space might imagine that this mixture of scheduling systems is efficient overall, with each system giving the best performance (cost-effective, consistent with viewers' tastes). An economist closer to home would recognize that each system is "path dependent," having emerged from public policies and program-distribution technologies that prevailed in its formative years. Chapters on the syndication market and the public broadcasting system (Chapters 2, 3) address the deal-making processes that occur between à la carte commercial and public program suppliers and their station customers.

Shifting Audiences and Program Quality

In the past quarter-century the delivery channels for TV programs have been transformed by the expansion of cable systems and (recently) satellites. While these improved the quality of over-the-air signals received by many viewing households, they also made room for a large number of new networks competing for viewers' attention and advertisers' funds. The cable networks hold a formidable economic advantage over broadcast networks, in that they can charge viewers for access to their programs as well as collect revenue from advertisers; over-the-air broadcasters supply a public good and can gather revenue only from the advertisers. The second section of this book traces the effects of this transformation, which are driven by the mechanism of *endogenous fixed costs*. Quite simply, the broadcast networks' best response to this exogenous loss of viewers was to reduce the quality (costliness) of their programming, while the cable networks symmetrically upgraded theirs to serve their exogenously expanded audience. The broadcasters' downgrade took, or may have taken, a number of forms—some of which have competing explanations. And certain factors, chiefly the premium that some advertisers pay for the broadcast networks' nationwide coverage, have helped to preserve their position.

The broadcasters' most conspicuous response was to shift their prime-time programming from its traditional scripted forms to unscripted game and "reality" shows. Although each type can be produced with high or low quality and production values, industry observers place the cost of typical unscripted programs at around one-third the cost of the traditional sitcoms and dramas. Against this cost advantage stand two partial offsets on the revenue side. Advertisers pay less per thousand viewers of unscripted programs; and reality programs suffer in terms of *ars longa,* for popular reality shows have little syndication value, while the most successful sitcoms earn a fortune (though the majority earn nothing). Another complicating factor, evident from the considerable success of some reality programs, is that many young viewers may actually prefer them to scripted programs. Other forms of economy programming such as news magazine shows have also proliferated.

A program stream's average cost to a network can be greatly decreased by repeating episodes, which reduces the potential audience but not necessarily by a lot. Networks have expanded their traditional repeats of prime-time shows, broadcasting at different times over different outlets (including affiliated cable networks). Programs' revenue has been expanded by increasing the minutes of a program devoted to advertising and public-service messages. In the 1990s this "clutter" during prime-time hours increased by one-quarter or more. Ads and program were intermingled by product-placement strategies and even the writing of commercials into the program's script.

The squeeze on the traditional networks was partly relieved by their position vis-à-vis advertisers, who lack other media that can allow them to reach simultaneously a large proportion of U.S. households. Not only do the broadcast networks enjoy a demand premium, but also their supply of advertising spots is inelastic: prime time cannot be extended, clutter has its limits, and new broadcast networks do not readily enter.

The cable networks symmetrically responded to the exogenous growth of their audience by upgrading their programs in many dimensions. These upgrades came close on the heels of growth in the cable networks' revenues from advertising and subscriber charges. Cable's upgrading also enhanced the variety of programs offered. As the number of channels that cable systems could carry increased, new cable networks emerged to fill (small) empty niches or enter (large) occupied niches with programming differentiated from its incumbents, showing the force of *infinite variety*. Some welfare problems arise because cable systems offer only selected bundles of networks to their subscribers, which indirectly undermines the cable operator's bargaining power against subscriber fee increases by the networks.

This shift of viewership from broadcast to cable networks naturally shunted profits away from the broadcasters. That loss soured the relationship between the broadcast networks and their affiliated stations, which had long enjoyed their own rents owing to the scarcity of channels in the larger-city markets. A continual transfer of profit from networks to stations had long resulted from their respective rents and bargaining power. In the 1990s the Big 3 networks (ABC, CBS, NBC) set about stanching this profit flow—a campaign that was upset by the entry of new broadcast networks and an increase in the turnover of station-network affiliations. Much of the (still continuing) retrieval effort involved the networks' exploiting the many forms of incompleteness of the network-affiliate contracts, such as dividing ad spots and sharing the costs of expensive sports programming. The last section of this book deals with other forms of small-numbers bargaining taking place within the setting of creative industries' structural traits.

Bargaining Tables and Media Conglomerates

Economic analysis employs a standard approach to markets with very few parties on each side—bilateral monopoly, at the limit. The traits of creative industries—fixed costs and uncertainty *(nobody knows)*—increase the friction and transaction costs that can arise and make the parties reach out for various analgesics. In broadcasting this process was exposed by a major change in U.S. government regulation, which in 1995 eliminated a long-standing prohibition on networks producing their own prime-time programs (other than news and sports). The networks that broadcast programs and the producers (often Hollywood movie studios) each make numerous decisions that affect a show's quality (popularity), laying open the question who should own the program's cash flow (in particular, syndication rights).

The policy change was followed by markedly increased integration taking several forms: more joint ownership of programs by producer and network, much-expanded production of programs by networks, and the occurrence of mergers that brought studios and networks under common ownership. Some statistical evidence suggests that ownership by a network gained favorable treatment for a program and raised its value in off-network syndication. In some cases, however, joint ownership stemmed from holdups by networks, not from the efficient management of assets.

Vertical integration also occurred in more comprehensive forms, with network and studio coming under common ownership through control changes (e.g., NBC and Universal), or studios integrating forward by starting their own networks (Fox, UPN, The WB). While all these forms of integration swept across the industry, network officials kept declaring the desirability of an open market for programs with many participants, to realize the value of *infinite variety* and make the best defense against uncertainty *(nobody knows)*. Nonetheless, the logic of foreclosure put each party in the classic "prisoner's dilemma": if it did not pursue integration, somebody else would tie up the available partners.

Another festering nexus of bargaining is the interface between local broadcasting stations and their program suppliers—networks and syndicators. Stations are numerous nationally, but each holds a property right (license) to a segment of the airwaves in its local market. Associated with relaxation of the Federal Communications Commission's limits on a station group's size, the observed groups are homogeneous with respect to sizes of member stations' markets. Groups of stations located in small cities simply centralize administration and pare administrative costs. Recent increases in the chain membership of small-market stations, unleashed by a change in public policy, confirm the apparent extent of scale economies. Groups of large-city stations pool members' interests in dealing with networks (usually most of a group's members are affiliated with the same network). Station groups' dealings with their networks, though contentious, show significant internalization of benefits to the network and affiliates as a group. Networks are still constrained by regulation from owning as many of their affiliates as they would like, but the bargaining frictions that support this attitude seem to stem from issues of compensation and clearance rather than stalemates with station groups. Bargaining power against syndicators may provide a substantial advantage to the group, owing to the syndicator's need to achieve substantially nationwide coverage for viability.

Cable systems and networks face each other in a setting that lacks the "small numbers" alarm bells of other interfaces. Each multi-system operator (MSO) transmits many networks, at least some of them close substitutes for one another. A cable network can be viable if it reaches only part of the national market, even though it still confronts the ever-present fixed costs. MSOs, however, have become quite concentrated as buyers of networks' program streams, opening the door to bilaterally concentrated dealings between MSOs and the highly differentiated networks.

MSOs (frequently more than one) own equity shares (typically minority) in basic cable networks. Ownership stakes are also held by media companies and "content producers." The incidence of these ownership stakes has been increasing over time. The important stakes in networks that succeeded were taken early (first movers). Although investments in novice networks continue, our evidence says that MSOs' carriage of networks has been decreasingly tied to ownership links. This is consistent with the foreclosure mechanism, because both of them rely on sunkenness and *nobody knows*, the difference being whether uncertainty breeding this behavior entered at the start-up phase or (owing to regulatory policy) in a mature but constrained market. MSO-network minority stakes and their periodic purchase and sale suggest investment-type motives for the acquirers that do not depend on operating control. So does the finding that carriage of owned networks is not substantially associated with the exclusion of competing networks.

PART ONE

TV PROGRAMS
AS CREATIVE GOODS

CHAPTER 1

The Market for Broadcast Network Programming

This chapter outlines the organization of the supply and demand for TV programming with the focus on the suppliers of prime-time (evening) dramatic programs and the broadcast networks that license them for exhibition. The suppliers show many traits common to creative industries, along with some distinctive features. One of those is the prevalence of series programs, which require a contractual commitment to keep the coalition of inputs (creative talent) together. Another is the economic durability of successful series. As with any long-term investment, its owner will likely need to endure negative cash flows for years before the series is boosted into profitability by revenues from off-network syndication.

The market for prime-time series programs is in truth part of a larger program market. In addition, broadcasters acquire programs for other times of day ("day parts"). The numerous cable networks also acquire series programs in a submarket that increasingly interpenetrates with that for prime-time broadcast programming. Still, the latter provides our best starting point. It represents the top end of the vertically differentiated supply of TV programs—quality in the nonjudgmental sense of the highest fixed cost incurred by networks in pursuit of the largest audience.

When the broadcast networks select and license programs for exhibition, they perform the primary gatekeeping function. They do

19

this in the context of their long-standing pattern of oligopolistic rivalry, which affects not just the mix of programs selected but also their intended quality—the amount of fixed costs that the networks choose to incur in their quest for viewers and (thus) advertising revenues. The process of recruitment and packaging of programs described here has been in place for some time, but it is now changing in response to increased competition for the networks—a looser oligopoly of broadcast networks and a horde of cable networks that are edging into competition with the broadcast networks as buyers of programs.[1]

Organizing to Produce TV Programs

Organization and Endogenous Quality

Broadcast networks and cable TV consume an enormous amount of program material. During the 1950s, as television shifted rapidly from live to filmed production of programs, program suppliers migrated from New York to Hollywood. By the 1960s, three-fourths of Hollywood's workforce was said to be employed in turning out products for television.

The series TV dramatic show—think of the situation comedy (sitcom)—is the traditional prototype. A continuing series of episodes has a great cost advantage over an equal number of unique programs. It requires only one basic creative formula that can be codified and serves to frame successive scripts by a passing parade of writers.[2] It employs the same small, regular cast performing on a few simple sets. Each script is structured the same way: a series of "acts," each reaching a climax at the commercial break.[3] In a week, an episode can be rehearsed, recorded twice before live audiences, and a final cut assembled with minimal retakes. Ancillary talents such as studio musicians adjust to these quality specifications.[4] This economizing in TV production is not in all respects the enemy of quality and originality. The speedy pace of production and the large volume of script consumed in TV series provide an opening for innovation and experiment in plot development.[5]

These "efficient" aspects also appear in the development of a series. A new series program starts with a core concept that originates with or reaches a writer-producer. This entrepreneur oversees the sequential development of the concept through several gateways until (with great good fortune) it is licensed by a network for production and exhibition as a series. Production of the series involves a managerial ("show runner") task of writing or commissioning and editing episode scripts, recruiting episode directors, and supervising other housekeeping tasks.[6] Production also requires a finance function for prime-time programs with potential long lives in syndication, and therefore subject to sustained initial spells of negative cash flow. Contracts (their duration related to the best-case life span of the show) need to link the network, the writer-producer, the core acting talents, and a movie studio or other such organization equipped to provide the housekeeping and finance functions. (Contract practices are discussed subsequently in this chapter.)

The entrepreneurial writer whose series plan is picked up by a network usually becomes the managerial producer, writing or editing scripts and supervising the preparation of each episode. The episode scripts become the vehicle for sustaining continuity, and accordingly many producers have worked into their jobs from that of writer. Directors in contrast are hired for individual episodes and mainly direct traffic. Flexibility and time to explore relationships in the filming, important sources of creativity in making cinema films, here are forgone luxuries. Directors must be well organized prior to and during the shooting, as little post-production editing is undertaken. The Directors Guild, the talent union for directors, holds out for a first-cut privilege for TV episode directors, but many pass it up, so as a result, this task falls under the producer's supervision. Producers tend to use different directors from episode to episode of a series, to gain an element of freshness.[7] Like other personnel in TV production, cinema film and TV directors come from the same labor pool. B-list directors share the common aesthetic preference for working in cinema films, but choose between the steady pay and employment available in TV and the intermittent employment offered by movies.[8] While budgetary control is a thorny issue in the production of cinema films, the door remains open for a delay or cost overrun that brings aesthetically successful results, but TV production eschews costly inspirations.[9]

Viewers identify regular actors in a TV series with the characters they play. Replacing them is risky for the viability of the series, and this gives them substantial property rights in their roles. They get some say on the dialogue they recite and the script's consistency with the basic qualities of the characters they play.[10] Hence the script may get modified during an episode's production, and TV writers (like writers for cinema films) lack Broadway playwrights' authority over changes.[11] Writers who advance to producer-writer status thus gain not just the usual benefit of job promotions but also increased control over the creative process, a widespread preference of creative workers *(art for art's sake)*.[12] Writers have traditionally worked their way up the ladder writing episode scripts, to the point where they can hope to originate and run a program series. With program supply increasingly lodged in large organizations (networks and studios), one might fear that this dues-paying routine would rigidify. The economic squeeze on prime-time broadcasting (Chapter 4), however, has instead seemingly opened the doors for any novice clutching a sufficiently hot speculative script.[13]

Tasks and Types of Supplying Firms

The production of TV program series has been organized within two quite different types of firms, the large Hollywood cinema-film distributors such as Paramount, Twentieth Century Fox, and

Warner Bros., and much smaller firms organized around individual series producers or partnerships. This diversity responds to the disparate tasks and organizational requisites mentioned previously. While cinema films ceased a half-century ago to be produced in assembly-line fashion on studio lots, that mode of organization remains congenial to the production of TV programs. It fits with their serial structure and their usual reliance on simple studio sets. The studio maintains functional specialist departments that can supply services to a group of continuing programs. It also performs a vital financial role, discussed subsequently. Another group of producers is the broadcast networks themselves. Although long (from 1970 to 1995) forbidden by law to hold a financial interest in the primetime programming that they show, they have now come to produce more than half of it. Because the program market remains organized in the arm's-length mode, we address this renewed vertical integration in Part Three.

The other business unit is the proprietorship or partnership associated with the writer-producer. This organizational unit tends to be only as long-lived as its successful program; over their careers successful producers create several profitable and long-lived series, along with some flops. A producer may have more than one series running at a given time, or perhaps none at all. Fewer than a dozen producers have had more than one big hit, and each of them has turned out flops. This uncertainty is understood in the industry, and no once-successful producer is rendered unemployable by a flop.[14] But no producer's long-term output of shows is steady enough to keep a production facility regularly utilized. The individual writer-producer is thus not the sort of entity that readily sustains a large-scale and enduring business unit with fixed production facilities and administrative staff. Besides, some successful producers simply prefer to spare themselves managerial tasks that can be shunted to a studio.[15]

While independent producing firms therefore tend to be short-lived, some have demonstrated sustained creative prowess. In the 1970s and 1980s MTM launched *The Mary Tyler Moore Show* and a number of other successes. It served as the base for several strong writers, who in turn attracted promising newcomers able to benefit from their seniors' mentoring. Yet the pressure of increasing demand for programs from new broadcast and cable networks squeezed MTM's collegial approach to the gradual development of new writing talent. Among other independent producing firms, only Carsey–Werner has recently stood as that sort of coalition of top writer-producer talent.[16] That firm was started by writers at the ABC network, who upon leaving could not retain most syndication rights to their successful shows. Lacking that source of funding, they arranged a deal with the entertainment conglomerate Viacom (owner of Paramount and cable networks) for financing that sustained their current series in exchange for signing over some domestic and international syndication rights.[17] Other successful independents have levered some advantage or other. Big Ticket Television was started by a distribution company to attract high-quality writers while making available channels for the distribution of their program output.[18] The Canadian firm Alliance Atlantis built on its prowess in producing miniseries, its position in Canada's programming market, and its financial skills.[19]

Financing Program Investments

Fusing the immediate task of the producer with the organizational requisites of the movie studio or TV network is made urgent by the need to finance prime-time program series. For a program to be produced, the present value of the revenues expected to flow from all of its future uses must at least equal the production cost of the series. TV series can be shown in different venues and geographic markets, like cinema films though with fewer "windows" available. A series that survives for a few years on network television can look forward to substantial additional revenue in the syndication market, in which off-network episodes are licensed as a block for re-broadcast on TV stations and cable networks, perhaps including some abroad. Syndication revenue can make a successful series extremely profitable, and the expectation of this large though highly uncertain income source influences the supply and pricing of TV series in their first exhibition on prime-time network television. The equilibrium license fee for a prime-time series therefore covers much of its cost of production, but not all. Someone must finance the unrecouped production cost until the syndication revenue arrives. Since a successful series might accumulate as many as one hundred episodes over five years before its syndication revenue begins to flow, the program supplier needs ample working capital to finance an asset devoid of salvage value and subject to the high risk of cancellation during its prime-time run. Cancellation after three years would greatly devalue an asset with unrecouped costs of sixty or more episodes (Chapter 7). Bearing this risk is not a congenial task for commercial banks and similar financial institutions that rely on the comforts of collateral. Independent production companies are ill suited to the task. The successful independent production company MTM sought to gain publicly traded status in order to finance its program holdings, and sold itself to another company when this failed.[20] Independent production companies seem to have receded during several periods when syndication rents were increasing, and along with them the cost of financing long-lived shows.[21]

The need for financing thus joins the physical requisites of TV series production in calling for some collaboration between a writer-producer and a studio. This could in principle take several forms. The producer might become the studio's hired hand, with the studio holding all the financial risk. Or the producer might organize and manage production but sell off equity and debt positions in individual series to a studio (or some other body of sophisticated investors and lenders). Actual arrangements are distributed between these extremes. Some successful producers or partnerships of producers have maintained independent companies over sustained periods of time, often working out joint-venture arrangements with studios that rely on the latter for finance as well as for ancillary services. The successful producer may make a housekeeping arrangement with a studio (these are common for cinema film producers as well) that funds the producer's efforts to develop new series in exchange for a "first look" by the studio at each project that comes to fruition. If the studio buys, it becomes the site for the program's continuing production. Top-ranked producer David E. Kelley in 1995 entered into a five-year deal with Twentieth Century Fox Television to produce shows for the ABC and Fox networks. Each agreed to take two series. If one network passed on a project, the other got first refusal. Kelley retained full creative control.[22] At the same time, John Wells (producer of the successful drama *E.R.*), operating since 1986 from a base at the Warner Bros. studio, extended his producing agreement with the NBC network. NBC committed to take up to five series. Wells got to produce one thirteen-episode series without a pilot, and a reward for a successful series (in his first two tries) was another such automatic commitment from NBC.[23] Twentieth Century Fox Television recruited three movie directors, including John Woo, on development deals, committing them to direct the pilot of any program that came to fruition but not to manage any ongoing series. This arrangement puts to good use the downtime that cinema directors have between movie projects.[24] Greenblatt–Janollari's partners formed this new independent producing company in 1998, successfully launching three TV series on that year's prime-time schedule. Their firm was lodged within Fox TV Studios, an umbrella organization associated with the Fox network and separate from the Fox film studio's much larger Twentieth Century Fox Television.[25] These alliances vary in the cash flowing up-front from the studio to sustain the producer and the ownership stakes in any program that is developed.[26]

Patterns in Supply Organization

Research by Bruce Owen and Steven Wildman documented the extent of joint production arrangements in the late 1980s. The Hollywood studios and other major suppliers then held a 46 percent share of the prime-time market when shares were calculated on the basis of major-partner status in each deal; they held only 30 percent when shares were allocated proportionally to each partner.[27] When the broadcast networks started their own production departments (Chapter 7), they similarly hastened to make collaborative arrangements with successful independent producers. A bidding war broke out for comedy writers as the studios sought to guarantee their talent supplies with (mostly) four-year deals in anticipation of the networks' entry into that market.[28] Examples of such moves to pin down talent also occur among the entities producing for day parts other than prime time.[29] Over the years there have been substantial fluctuations in the prevalence of independent writer-producer firms as well as turnover among the firms themselves, which experience the heavy turnover that is usually associated with uncertain outputs in creative industries. Furthermore, good track records suffer a built-in erosion, as the more capable producers take on more projects, spreading their talents more thinly and pulling down their averages.[30]

The thinning out of independent firms in recent years has been the occasion for hand-wringing over the threat to creativity. This distress may be misplaced, however. First, the trend toward concentration applies much more to broadcast network prime-time dramatic programming than to material for other day parts and distributors. Second, in prime-time programs the writer-producer's creative role seems to depend little on whether that party's name appears on the door of the sheltering enterprise. For example, the independent program supplier Imagine Entertainment was started by three persons highly regarded for previous work in writing, producing programs, and assembling projects. The three pilots that the firm prepared in its first year were all picked up and all succeeded. Imagine worked with other writers only on a per-project basis, and its partners were hands-on with all projects. Imagine made a point of drawing talent from film as well as TV. The partners had prior relationships with the Disney studio, which held a financial stake in Imagine and provided a studio home.[31] Brillstein–Grey was similarly an entrepreneurial TV producing firm, rooted in the agent business and talent management. It had co-ownership deals on individual projects with several studios and networks and was for a time half-owned by a studio (Universal). It depended heavily on a deal with the Sony studio's Columbia Tri–Star Television Distribution to finance the deficits on Brillstein–Grey shows in exchange for rights to market them in syndication and take a share of the distribution fees.[32] These and similar cases illustrate that the functions of developing programs and providing overhead facilities can come together in diverse ways.

New entrants into program supply can be either entrepreneurial show-runner firms or overhead-intensive organizations such as the movie studios. Scale and overhead economies in the distribution of cinema films have long kept the latter population stable, and the main class of entrants is the TV networks, which until 1995 were excluded by the FCC's financial interest and syndication rules (Chapter 7). Agents and talent-management firms make up another class of entrants. Indeed, in TV's infancy the large talent agency MCA became one of the first major independent suppliers of TV programs. Creative Artists Agency (CAA) later thrived on packaging diverse talents for TV series or cinema films, and other talent agencies have sought specialties in types of TV talent such as comedy writers.[33] Michael Ovitz, the founding impresario of CAA, later launched Artists Television Group as an entrant into program supply, but after some initial successes the venture failed.[34] Other alliances come and go. For example, in 1995 major advertiser Procter

& Gamble had an ongoing agreement with Paramount Television whereby P&G paid 50 percent of development and production costs for shows produced under the alliance, getting in return product placement opportunities and a share of all revenues. The NBC network then joined this alliance, getting first look at the resulting programs (for unreported considerations).[35]

The logic of this fungible organization of prime-time program supply is confirmed when we consider the full population of TV program production units. Those supplying prime-time network television series represent the top layer of providers of vertically differentiated programs, with other tiers supplying made-for-TV movies and lower-cost programs that appear on daytime or late-night network television, individual TV stations, and cable networks. A good deal of specialization occurs, with different suppliers for each type of daytime show (game shows, soaps, etc.). There is also specialization by quality level; daytime serials' cost per minute is around one-fifth that of prime-time programs.[36]

Programs other than prime-time generally have little prospect of syndication or other long-lived revenue streams. They thus lack the financial imperative to link with a studio, and instead can find other partners, such as the overseas distributors who commonly contribute to the financing of "action-adventure" series of hour-long dramas in exchange for exhibition rights.[37] They need no studio-type facilities for successive episodes (soap operas excepted). Producers of such programs thus can operate efficiently as simple individual proprietorships or partnerships. The ABC network, for example, was reported to obtain all of its made-for-TV movies and miniseries from individual producers or partnership shops. Talent agencies such as International Creative Management take part as packagers.[38] Even in made-for-TV movies, one large firm has prospered. Hallmark Entertainment financed producer Robert Halmi's ancient-legend films, budgeted much above usual made-for-TV levels but profitable thanks to the high audience ratings they win and their large earnings abroad.[39] Some independent firms specialize in the efficient supply of low-cost programs for special-interest cable networks and TV broadcast outside of prime-time hours. Gold Coast Television Entertainment, for example, is a production company known for inexpensive, offbeat, reality-based programs. It started as an equipment rental firm, a line that provided cash flows to support investments in programs.[40]

Networks and Demand for Program Series

The broadcast TV networks, long three in number (ABC, CBS, NBC), were widely believed to hold substantial market power as packagers of programming and sellers of ads. The entry of new networks (Fox, UPN, The WB) and intensifying competition with cable TV channels as program packagers have greatly reduced their market power. The original three networks' share of the prime-time viewing audience declined from around 90 percent in the 1970s to below 50 percent by 1996–97.[41] The concentration of networks (broadcast and cable, syndicators) as buyers of programs has also declined to a moderate level.[42] Nonetheless, the broadcast networks still compete in close oligopolistic fashion for the viewing audience at prime-time hours. While the networks' waning market power is diffusing this rivalry, it has long dominated the process that generates the schedule of shows offered at each prime viewing hour. Oligopolistic sellers select their instruments of rivalry. TV networks do compete intermittently for the affiliation of local stations, but their central rivalry is for audience attention (which then determines the prices they can charge to advertisers).

Acquiring and Scheduling Programs

The common ground of rivalry since the 1960s has long been a slate of new and renewed series programs for prime-time viewing hours in the new season that opens in the fall of each year. The series that are introduced then have their genesis in pilot programs prepared by program suppliers (who now include the networks' own production arms). As with other creative products, *nobody knows* their prospective reception by viewers. Deep uncertainty about consumers' response to a new program interacts with large costs that must be wholly sunk before the answer is known.[43]

A gambler's-luck approach might be pursued: take a chance, and economize on ex ante efforts to predict the result. Like cinema film distributors, however, TV networks expend considerable resources trying to cull losers from winners in advance. At least two major strategies are used for this purpose. First, currently successful programs are screened for possible spin-offs—a new show built around a secondary character, or a different use of the successful show's general category (NBC's *Law and Order* family).[44] Second, the risks of a new program are moderated by developing it in steps, with several options to quit built in to the sequence. An idea for a program series is insufficient to warrant a network's commitment. A script is not enough. Deciding whether a show is promising enough to merit a major investment usually requires that a pilot episode be shot and viewed. An industry rule of thumb holds that four pilots yield only one series suitable for broadcast.[45] Finally, the pilot can be tested on a specially recruited audience. This is the option-contract structure, common throughout the creative industries, under which costs are sunk in stages, with the party next in line to sink a contribution taking an option to review the venture's prospects and either continue or quit.

The number of pilots ordered by a network fluctuates with its current competitive position. ABC cut back to a few while its prime-time schedule was dominated by the game show *Who Wants To Be a Millionaire,* then sprang for twenty-nine in 2002 when that show's ratings collapsed.[46] While pilots underpin most of the networks' decisions for scheduling dramatic programs, many series bought on the basis of pilots still fail to attract audiences and get cancelled.[47] Even audience tests based on pilots yield little useful information. On the one hand, pilots are often better produced than the episodes that will follow. On the other, novel programs tend to test badly and, if nonetheless picked up, require patience until they find and acclimatize their audiences.[48] Both networks and program suppliers constantly screen new ideas for programs and pursue promising ones to the stage of pilots. One observer guessed that of some three thousand ideas floated in a year, one hundred go to scripts, and twenty-five become pilots.[49] For the 1997–98 season, the networks spent about $120 million for forty-nine drama pilots and used fourteen in their schedules, of which only one returned for a second season.[50] The industry appears to be on the cusp of dropping the pilot for a shorter screen test of the actors. The consideration that on balance seems to preserve the pilot is its value for establishing the show's basic character, whether the actors are right for their parts, and so on.[51]

The networks commission pilots from program suppliers for delivery in May for the season beginning the following September. On delivery the networks review the programs and engage in their game of scheduling the selected series. They make sequential decisions about which incumbent programs to renew and which pilots to pick up. The process is rendered more stressful by the uncertainty involved *(nobody knows)*. Shows that prove popular with audiences are frequently not well reviewed by critics, and vice versa. A show that ultimately becomes highly successful may languish far down the ranks in its first year or two. When an incumbent series is "on the bubble" (considered marginal for renewal), bargaining chips come into play. A marginal program's chance of renewal is better if the producer's past track record makes the network eager to preserve goodwill; if a talent agency is involved, the network's future access to personnel under contract to it (such as writers) may influence the decision.[52] These "political" gambits are economically rational, in that recurrent, heterogeneous deals among the same parties leave lumps of rent here and there, making credible a deal partner's promise to supply (or threat to withhold) cooperation in some future interchange.[53] The process of selecting programs causes serious organizational stress for the competing suppliers. The producer of a marginal program has trouble retaining its writers and other specialized personnel not under long-term contracts.[54] The same goes for talents committed to marginal new projects who might, with a timely rejection, be able to scamper after a deal with another program supplier. One might expect stalemates to occur in bargaining over price, at this point, because network and supplier have both sunk substantial resources and closed off many alternative opportunities. Nonetheless, suppliers themselves seem to agree that the determination of license fees remains competitive, basically keyed to the cost of producing each episode and common expectations about a program's likely syndication value.[55] This pattern pays tribute to the force of repeated interactions and settled customs of renegotiation. Repeated interaction involves, among other factors, efforts that networks make to sustain relationships with successful producers, despite the frequency with which once-successful producers suffer flops the next time around.[56] The only apparent exception to this tranquillity is holdups over ownership stakes following the demise of the financial interest and syndication regulations—a major change in the rules of the game (Chapter 7).

For a pilot's preparation, the network pays a fixed sum that typically covers the program supplier's budgeted cost. The supplier (including the producer and principal actors) has a powerful incentive to create a successful pilot and plan for a series. A successful pilot wins an order for a certain number of episodes, and it also opens the chance that the series might run long enough to accumulate the ninety to one hundred episodes needed to make it viable in syndication—renting the series for rebroadcast on TV stations or cable networks (Chapter 2). The license fee paid by the network is by custom determined as a fraction of the supplier's cost of producing the program. The reservation price for a (risk-neutral) supplier would be its cost of production minus the present value of its expected net revenues from syndication. A sample of eighty-six prime-time entertainment programs broadcast around 1990 indicated a mean license fee of 83.8 percent of the production cost (standard deviation of 8.8 percent).[57] Ratios of fee to cost seem to vary among programs in expected ways, with high values for programs either unlikely to hold much syndication value or promising enough to elicit a high competitive bid from the network. The ratios also vary over time, with the average rental realized on the off-network syndication market. These rentals were rising rapidly in the later 1980s, lowering license fees and raising the suppliers' costs of holding episodes for syndication.[58] The distribution of expected returns for the program producer is thus quite unusual: breakeven if the pilot is not picked up, possibly a serious loss if it is selected but falls off the schedule too soon for syndication, a large windfall if it survives long enough to be viable in syndication. Work on pilots hence involves the strong motivation of a shot at the syndication prize. It thus poses a daunting risk even for a major movie studio; in the decade before it (temporarily) exited from the industry, Sony Corporation's Columbia Tri-Star Television Distribution made two hundred pilots, but only five reached syndication. The risk also implies a strong incentive for the program supplier to exert its best effort.[59] This incentive prevails despite the *nobody knows* property, which leaves the program supplier with little more objective knowledge of its product's sustainable quality than anyone else, when the suppliers all fly east for the annual May scheduling period.[60]

While the pilot represents the template for a series, once it is picked up by a network, developmental effort does not cease when the production of regular episodes begins. Networks engage in various forms of "trading up," making deals with actors, writers, and/

or producers who were previously unavailable owing to commitments to other shows.[61] Critical input continues from the network (as well as from the production studio) as episodes come to life, in such forms as "notes" on episode scripts before they are filmed.[62]

This description of the market for prime-time programming pertains to practices that prevailed for a quarter-century but now are in the throes of major changes, most obviously the newfound popularity of "reality" programs. The bases for this popularity, considered in Chapter 4, certainly include their low cost and simplicity of production, which has attracted new, independent producing firms. These entrants specialize in the creation or adaptation of formats and the recruitment of participants.[63] Numerous precedents have aired on European TV, and indeed many U.S. reality shows' formats were licensed from their developers abroad. Reality shows require no sequential option-based development, so they can be readily produced either by the networks themselves or by independent contractors.

Networks' Scheduling Rivalry

The networks then make their scheduling decisions, which embrace the interrelated problems of which shows to pick up and when (day of the week, hour) to schedule them. Perceived audience tastes define a general level of demand for sitcoms, hour-long dramas, and other types of shows, with considerable attention paid to the demographic (age, sex) composition of a show's audience—which strongly influences advertisers' willingness to pay. Scheduling is also driven by the tendency of viewers to stick with a particular network or channel once they have tuned in to it. Although the TV set's remote control has surely weakened this propensity, it remains central to schedulers' thinking, and they have adopted a number of techniques to shorten breaks between programs or cause them to overlap in order to suppress the temptation to switch channels.[64]

Each network holds an inventory of new and renewed programs and a set of prime-time slots to fill, and each moves its pieces on the scheduling board in an attempt to maximize the value (to advertisers) of the audience that it attracts.[65] Apart from the public's yet-un-revealed judgment on their quality levels, the programs generally eschew innovation and do not differ much from their competitors and predecessors. Programming executives recognize that they play on a board with a small number of different tiles, and the main search is for small but effective variations on the established canon (*infinite variety* and the closeness of substitutes). Innovative programs tend to be born more from desperation than inspiration. Successful shows quickly beget imitations.[66]

Much attention is paid to leveraging the popularity of successful incumbent shows in order to capture audiences for new and/or struggling programs. For example, a new sitcom is scheduled immediately after a successful one that is being renewed. A strong established program may be "exported" to a different night of the week to anchor what the network hopes will be a block of successful shows. Each of a network's moves on the scheduling board takes account of what it expects its rivals will do. Broadly speaking, a network has two strategies for selecting a program to place opposite the show scheduled by its rival. It can match the rival with a program that will appeal to the same audience, hoping to seize a large share of this group. Or it might "counter-program" with a show appealing to a different audience. The latter pattern suggests "soft" competition or a cooperative approach to scheduling. A network, however, could counter-program for lack of a show that stands a chance against the competition. Or it could match its rival's program style simply because that serves the preferences of most viewers. Without more information, we cannot link the mix-or-match pattern of programming to the sort of market equilibrium prevailing among the networks. The problem proved rather intractable for scholars until recent research by Ronald Goettler and Ron

Shachar, who used information on how viewers' characteristics are associated with their program choices to measure the closeness (matching) or distance (counter-programming) in networks' choices.[67] They concluded that networks' prime-time schedules involve too little counter-programming to maximize viewers' welfare. Another distortion results from too little homogenizing of a network's programs to serve the tastes of viewers prone to stick with one channel throughout the evening. Both of these distortions plausibly reflect entrenched patterns of scheduling rivalry. Goettler and Shachar also concluded, however, that significant welfare losses flow from the networks' habitual treatment of the 8–10 P.M. (East Coast) block differently from the 10–11 P.M. block—a practice without obvious competitive significance.

In the annual scheduling game, each network wishes to make the last move and optimize its schedule after its rivals have locked up theirs. Indeed, over the years this effort pushed the scheduling period from February to May, leaving the producers minimal time to film the episodes once a series has been ordered. That slippage of lead time and the resulting haste in preparing the fall season's programs was perhaps associated with an increased incidence of unsuccessful shows that led to mid-season rescheduling. This congestion fosters several forms of inefficiency in the program supply industry. All pilots are being cast at around the same time, so an actor wanted for show B may be tied up with a prior commitment to show A, a long-run option contract that will remove her services from the market if A is picked up.[68] The chances are high, though, that A will not be selected. It follows that the average pilot is made with more second-choice actors and writers than if pilots were developed more evenly around the calendar year.[69] Even before the pilot-making crush, about a year before a new season, comes a quest for drama scripts. Early purchases lock up writers whom a network considers strong, but the network knows little then about what its programming needs will be the next season.[70]

Some participants suggest that the seasonal programming crush is really driven by its advertising-market component.[71] Once the networks have announced their fall schedules in May, a period of intense bargaining opens with the buyers of advertising time on network programs. After a week or so of haggling, this "up-front market" clears overnight in an orgy of deal-making that commits a variable but majority proportion of the ad spots available for the coming year.[72] Ad spots not sold in the up-front market are later sold piecemeal in the "scatter market."[73] The difficulty of devising a way to market advertising time as efficiently as in the up-front market is a strong force sustaining the scheduling game, and it seems likely to continue as long as enough advertisers will pay a premium over other media (including local broadcast and cable TV) for network television's national reach.[74]

Competitive shuffling of programs resumes once the season has started and audience reactions to the various new series become known. Attempts are made, but seldom can a program be reconfigured effectively once the season has begun; a number of episodes have already been produced, and weak ratings (as usual with creative products) transmit little hard evidence on what is broken or how to fix it.[75] Each network normally saves some shows that were also-rans in the May scheduling game as possible replacements for series cancelled during the season. With or without replacements, programs may be shunted between days and hours in order to maximize the carryover of audience between a network's shows. Combative and predatory scheduling does occur. One network may attempt to disrupt a rival's efforts to build one evening's programming. A network may show an important cinema film at the hour when a rival is introducing a prized new show ("stunting").[76] The networks vary in their propensity for head-to-head scheduling rivalry because of the differing overlaps in their target demographic audiences. CBS traditionally was strategically distant from ABC and NBC, drawing older and less urban audiences.[77] CBS, however, has lately sought to distance itself from senior citizens, whom advertisers largely shun, thereby reducing its strategic distance from ABC and NBC and the new competitors. Meanwhile, ABC has backed off from its unsuccessful attempt to match NBC in pursuit of a young, sophisticated audience, settling for more blue-collar viewers instead.[78]

A major locus of oligopolistic rivalry has long been Thursday evening, which NBC first came to dominate in 1984. Enjoying a combination of luck with new programs and skill in scheduling, NBC managed to preserve that dominance through the life cycles of *The Cosby Show, Cheers, Seinfeld, Friends,* and *E.R.* One might expect other networks to concede this turf and counter-program. Yet assaults have been mounted repeatedly: Fox with *The Simpsons* and *The O.C.,* CBS with *Survivor II* and *C.S.I.* What makes Thursday the battleground is advertisers' high reservation prices for Thursday spots, greatly exceeding those for other nights of the week. Movies open on Friday night. People tend to buy autos and make other major purchases on weekends. The supply of Thursday spots is inelastic, so advertisers pay enormous premia. Observers conjecture that NBC earns more advertising revenue on Thursday night than the other six nights combined.[79] Therefore, a small entrenchment on this turf or a small chance at a large share makes an attractive if risky investment for other networks. In late 2004, however, it appeared that NBC's winning streak with its Thursday night shows might have ended.[80]

Another factor disturbs the ongoing schedule rivalry: the phenomenon of "sweeps months." Audiences for network programs are measured (sampled) daily, and those for individual stations in the fifty largest U.S. cities monthly. Beyond those cities, however, lies 40 percent of the market, in which stations' audience ratings (the basis for pricing their advertising) are measured in only three months—November, February, and May. Networks upgrade their programming in these months, seeking to lift the ratings of their local affiliates and their ad prices for the next three months. Ambitious specials and miniseries appear.[81] The continuous rivalry over scheduling regular series is bent to the task of attracting viewers during the sweeps. Series programs broadcast new episodes. Of the twenty-two episodes of a series typically ordered each year, twelve first appear in the sweeps months and another five to seven at the start of the fall season, so the viewing audience must subsist mostly on reruns for the remainder of the year. While the sweeps rivalry is due to Nielsen's technology for measuring small-city audiences, it operates like a dysfunctional form of imitative oligopolistic rivalry.[82]

Oligopoly rivalry among the networks may wither away along with the broadcasters' potential profits. Program diversity has naturally increased with the entry of several new networks (Chapter 7).[83] If each network must nowadays take five rivals' likely moves into account, their sundry reactions may grow so uncertain, and the expected value of incurring costs to meet them so small, that the scheduling game may no longer be worth the candle. That is, each network's scheduling may come to take the interdependence of its own programs into account but largely ignore its rivals' moves. Each year brings more departures in scheduling from the old pattern of a thirty-nine-week season starting in September.[84] Programming during the summer has grown more competitive. The older networks once routinely filled their prime-time summer schedule with repeats from the preceding season. Some cable networks took advantage of this by introducing new program series in the summer, and recently some of the broadcast networks have replied by running new reality programming in the summer months.[85] As cable networks upgrade their programs enough to enter into the reckoning, that change grows all the more likely (Chapter 5). There is some evidence of eroding head-to-head competition associated with (what market participants see as) a reduced frequency of "breakout hits." With a larger number of alternative programs catering to diverse audience tastes, the most successful program grows less likely to achieve any given high rating or share of the market. This proposition is strengthened if the total audience size is inelastic with respect to the perceived average quality of programs, and any program offered attracts at least some devotees.[86] Another constraint is the supply elasticity of high-quality or promising programming, discussed subsequently.

The whole oligopolistic lockstep routine of the September seasonal introduction and the preceding up-front ad market is probably dissolving. Networks keep finding reasons—of their own, or responding to rivals' actions—to shift some program introductions away from early September. Many reality programs have natural life spans of less than a year, and are thus suitable for introduction at any time. Also, nothing prevents the broadcast networks from imitating the cable networks' practice of short-run dramatic series.[87] Eroding season-based oligopolistic rivalry among the networks undermines the May scheduling season and with it the up-front ad market. Advertisers have reason to welcome its demise, because it forces them into an auction, notably efficient in extracting surplus from buyers. And the increased uncertainty of the next season's programs reduces the value of firm commitments to the advertisers (who chafe at the capricious course of pilot-less and free-wheeling reality programs).[88]

Contracts and Rents to Talent

With the basic supply-demand properties of the prime-time program market in hand, we can consider the deal structures that govern these transactions. The series format on which much dramatic programming relies raises some distinctive issues for structuring contracts between network and program supplier parallel to those between producer and actors. Each series rests on a plan conceived by its writer-producer (individual or team), embodied first in a prospectus or sample script, then in a pilot, then in successive episodes. As the episodes roll on, the actors bring the plan to life in the audience's perception. Important cast members are not easily replaced without threatening the show's ratings, so they acquire a compelling claim on its rents. Much in the market's operation rides on the efficiency of the employment contracts and their subsequent enforcement. Since each program is unique, and teams of inputs naturally change from project to project, one might expect to encounter a litany of contract failures (negotiation, haggling, monitoring costs, etc.). In fact, the prevailing impression is of a widespread acceptance of standard contracting practices and a strong role of reputation to support their enforcement. Contracts are often formalized only after projects are under way, on the basis of deal memos and an understanding that "we'll do this deal like the last one." This procedural consensus seems to extend to renegotiation of deals that do not turn out as expected, such as series subjected to early cancellation.[89]

The option contracts usually employed in creative industries are standard in TV.[90] A pilot is commissioned, with the network holding the option to order a certain number of episodes at an agreed price if the show joins its schedule. Standard practice has long been for the network to hold options for four years of renewals, after which the contract must be renegotiated, and any rents flowing to the network from a successful series are ripe for picking by the talent (actors and writer-producer).[91] The worth of the purchase option to the acquiring network depends on the originality and attractiveness of the program's concept but also on the producer's expected proficiency in turning out episodes, fleshing out and enriching the plan. Both elements have been sources of significant rents to shows' originators. Increases in the numbers of both broadcast and cable networks have raised the demand for these skills and at least temporarily created large rents for experienced producers regarded as dependable for developing and sustaining a series. The networks' inauguration of their own production studios occurred at the same time, augmenting and sustaining this demand increase. The stock of experienced human capital cannot be freely increased in the short run, so the inflated flow of rents persisted.[92] The same applies to writers skilled in preparing individual episodes.[93] Some shows are contracted not from a writer-producer's script and pilot but by recruiting an established cinema or TV star as the principal character in a new series. These deals, signed without a scripted plan or an experienced producer in place as "show runner," cost the networks heavily in compensation that transfers the star's expected rent, and they impose risks when commitments are made without these important elements in place.[94]

Actors in TV series are committed to a program by option contracts from the moment they read for a part. The producer gains an option to renew them in their roles for five to seven years with built-in raises (e.g., 8 percent a year). Shares in syndication revenues are of course an important form of compensation for producers and principal actors; details on these seldom become public, but producers apparently claim up to half of net profits, principal actors up to 10 percent.[95] Another source indicates that a holder of any essential element of a program—star actor, writer, producer—gets 3 to 5 percent of the license fee and 10 percent of syndication revenue.[96] As with the Hollywood studios' one-time contracts with film actors, such deals may leave large rents for the producer and the network if the show is a success. But contracts cannot compel excellence in performance and cooperation on the set. Renegotiation with actors in successful series becomes very likely, as both producer and newly minted star have strong incentives to keep the revenues rolling in.[97] The renegotiation of a highly successful program hence transfers copious rents to its core talent. Before the sitcom *Seinfeld* was terminated in 1998 (an aesthetic choice of its talent), its producer-star had been earning more than $1 million an episode, and was offered $5 million per episode to renew for another season.

Each of its other stars had earlier renewed for this final season at $600,000 per episode.[98] The popular drama *E.R.* was renewed for a three-year period at the price of $13 million an episode (increased from $6 million). Earlier, the Warner Bros. studio (which owned the show) had offered NBC (which broadcast it) a two-year extension of its extant four-year contract for an increase from $2 to $4 million an episode (the two did such a deal on the show *Friends*), but NBC declined, and Warner put the series up for bid with NBC holding only a right of first refusal.[99] Financial analysts' assessments of these deals agree with the theoretical expectation that networks on average can only break even on these programs after renewal.[100] Indeed, these payments clearly exceed the ad revenue that the renewed show might bring in. They embrace the additional profits due to the audience retained for programs that follow in the schedule, and also the network's extra time to develop a "hot" replacement.[101]

Actors in successful series programs find their compensation under the original contract puny relative to the cash generated by the show, making a holdup tempting. Renegotiations often follow with the show's star, or with the principal actors as a group if they sustain solidarity (the *Friends* cast and *Seinfeld*'s co-stars). Principal actors' base contracts commonly give them a share of the show's profits, including future syndication, a strong disincentive to rock the boat. This does not deter lesser players on straight salary. A strategy commonly used, however, is to threaten to write their character out of the series—frequently a credible threat.[102] Negotiations over rents tend to be bitter, because of their zero-sum property, and also because rents may be hard to measure. Consider the voices of the cartoon characters in Fox's program *The Simpsons*, deadlocked in 2004 with the Fox network: Fox avowed they were replaceable; the actors bet they were not.[103]

The duration of talent contracts in series programs raises an interesting problem for the parties to find a mutually best deal.

Lengthening the period of commitment postpones an actor's access to rents from a successful program—bad for the actor. Yet it warrants more generous initial investments by the network in promoting the program and possibly sustaining it at a loss until it catches on—good for the actor.[104] Too long a duration leaves little expected life span for the program during which the actor has full access to her rents, encouraging holdups. The five-year contract thus might yield the maximum (discounted value of) compensation to TV series' talents as a group, if not for actors in standout successes. This practice has been contrasted to the two-year commitments standard for British TV actors, which are said to inhibit the development of costly, venturesome series.[105]

A seeming corollary to the uncertainty surrounding programs' success is that networks should be observed to trade established programs with one another. A given network's need for new programs varies with the unpredictable fates of all its current programs. The composition of a new program's audience is uncertain, though less uncertain than its size. Hence, at any given time some networks should be able to benefit from purchases or swaps. Programs do migrate between networks, but the movements nowadays are infrequent. In TV's early days (1948–1957), advertising agencies were the main suppliers and owners of programs, and they moved their shows quite freely from network to network. That mobility plummeted, however, during the period when the financial interest and syndication rules transferred ownership to the studio suppliers; it picked up again when the new networks entered.[106] One type of switch occurs when a successful program's contract expires and its license comes up for bid. The program's owner naturally tries to foment an auction and sometimes succeeds, as when The WB gave up its hit *Buffy the Vampire Slayer* rather than match UPN's bid.[107] Other shifts occur without the trigger of a lapsed contract, when another network simply values a program more highly than its current licensee. That can occur because the program better suits its new licensee's style, because it possesses a style to which the new licensee aspires, or because the new licensee holds a more optimistic view of the program's future trajectory in its life cycle.[108]

Program Selection and Welfare

Although this book focuses on the behavior of TV broadcasting rather than its welfare implications, we offer a few suggestions about the linkage between the two. The problem of welfare economics that has preoccupied most economists' research on broadcasting is that small audiences for a differentiated product with a fixed cost may be underserved. If 24 percent of the audience prefers a detective story and 76 percent sitcoms, three competing networks will choose to offer homogeneous sitcoms (each drawing on average 25.3 percent of the audience) and none will show a detective story.[109] The problem nowadays lacks the urgency it held when three networks seemed joined in a tenacious oligopoly, and cable networks and direct broadcast satellites lay far in the future. Furthermore, the problem as formulated neglects the fact that a broadcaster can offer a portfolio of programs over a period of time, so that any "excess" homogeneity of programs offered at a given time might be offset by the diversity of each channel's offerings over time.[110] Nonetheless, the rivalry of the networks retains enough of its oligopolistic form that further erosion of the scheduling game could desirably raise the incidence of counter-programming.

The preceding review of the prime-time programming market has suggested something of the current state of this welfare problem, with imitative programming still evident (the Thursday night wars) but counter-programming on the rise with the loosening of oligopolistic rivalry. With cable subscribers now enjoying access to dozens of cable networks, the program-diversity problem seems transformed into two rather different issues. The first is the appropriate reformulation of the program-diversity problem with broadcast and (especially) cable networks becoming more numerous. When products are differentiated *(infinite variety)* and their costs are at least partly fixed, the set of goods provided by the market may not be the one that would maximize welfare. The most obvious distortion (but not the only one) is the absence of goods (programs) with high fixed costs but sufficient appeal to some consumers that they would be willing to pay access fees sufficient to cover these costs. Unlike over-the-air broadcasting, cable networks and the public television network have mechanisms for collecting these fees (Chapters 3, 6).

The other welfare issue concerns the use of ad revenue to finance over-the-air broadcasting. Suppose that the networks' ad revenue is proportional to the program's number of viewers, and viewers choose freely from a large number of differentiated programs *(infinite variety)*. The resulting program service has its attractive features, since the broadcaster's fixed outlay is keyed to attracting the most viewers at a price (marginal cost) of zero. Advertisers' willingness to pay, however, increases with those demographic traits that make the audience likely to purchase goods of the sort advertised. The advertiser thus seeks the largest zero-price audience prone to purchase the advertised product rather than the maximum zero-price viewers overall. Broadcast TV, with an appeal broader than that of the competing distribution media, is thereby constrained to pursue relatively broad demographic groups, most notably nowadays young adults aged eighteen to forty-nine (the age brackets are conventions employed in the industry's standard audience-sampling procedures). The premia that advertisers pay for viewers in this category are impressively large. In 1999 the teen-oriented program *Dawson's Creek,* with 5.25 million viewers, was reported to bring $200,000 for a (thirty-second) spot, while *Nash Bridges,* watched by 13.4 million viewers significantly older than the *Dawson's Creek* audience, commanded only $105,000.[111] The CBS network long suffered because its traditional audience base was older and more rural than its competitors': both features depress advertisers' willingness to pay.[112] Another discrepancy between body-count viewership and ad revenues lies in advertisers' regard for the critics' reaction to a program. Advertisers will apparently pay more (i.e., a higher cost per thousand, or CPM) for a program that is critically well regarded. They will pay less for unscripted "reality" programs. By implication, advertisers assume that viewers' utility from watching a better program extends to goodwill toward the product advertised, a positive signal of that product's quality, or some such spillover. Advertisers also value programs that appear to catch vanguard public interests and social patterns, with large CPM differentials for programs about urban singles and their problems over family-oriented shows.[113] These patterns may create some linkage between the intensity of viewers' program preferences and the revenue captured by advertisers, if ads enter into consumers' utility functions and effect a tie between the utility gained from the program and the goodwill extended to the advertiser's product.

CHAPTER 2

Syndication

This study of the organization of the TV programming market has so far emphasized the long-serving broadcast networks—their acquisition of program series bundled with advertising messages for distribution through their affiliated stations. TV programs, however, reach their audiences through other channels as well. This chapter focuses on the syndication market, in which individual program series prepared by syndicators are licensed to stations and station groups for broadcast. After placing syndication in the context of the total supply of programming, we describe the participants in this market and the organization of their dealings with the broadcasters. These contractual arrangements exhibit some creative ways for coping with programs' uncertain reception *(nobody knows)*. They have undergone major changes as the broadcaster-licensees have coalesced into station groups, thereby altering bargaining power and lowering transaction costs in the syndication market.

Scope of Syndication

In principle, TV programs can be assembled in different-sized bundles to exploit any available economies of scope. Obvious economies arise in supplying programs as a series of episodes, featuring the same presenters or characters (actors) and sets, rather than

49

styling shows individually. Beyond that lies a range of bundling strategies. The efficient choice among them is given by two basic properties of creative goods—*fixed costs* and *infinite variety*. Each differentiated program incurs its own fixed cost; because *nobody knows* what program will please until after its cost is sunk, a trade-off necessarily prevails between the variety available and the total cost. There is another important fixed cost, however, of selecting and transmitting bundles of programs with maximum appeal to viewers (the number of viewers weighted, in commercial broadcasting, by their responsiveness to advertisers' messages). Tastes can differ in several distinct ways. They can differ among individuals dwelling in each geographic area, or among typical viewers in different areas. Tastes can differ among types of programs, or only among times of day when given programs are desired. Depending on the height of selection costs and the dispersion of viewers' tastes (How much do they differ? How big a premium do they bestow on their first-choice programs?), any of several selection mechanisms might prevail. A highly centralized system might offer one national around-the-clock menu of programs. Or a number of networks might offer differentiated bundles (different mix of programs, or different times of their broadcast). This is the pattern of cable networks, and it can accommodate high levels of non-geographic heterogeneity in tastes. At the opposite extreme, every local program distributor (station) might compose its own bundle of programs, or its own time schedule of those programs—a large aggregate amount of managerial effort, giving rise to high selection costs. The public broadcasting system (Chapter 3) operates largely on that model. The long-established commercial broadcasting system splits the difference in accommodating local diversity of tastes: it supplies a common nationwide feed of programs during the majority of the day, but stations may acquire programs à la carte or produce them locally for the remaining hours.

Syndicators provide the stations with individual program series or program blocks to fill out the networks' feed. The syndication market deals in both newly prepared programs (first-run syndication) and wide-ranging vintages of previously licensed programs (off-network syndication). First-run programming is diverse but shares certain traits relative to networks' prime-time offerings. It is functionally differentiated to appeal to different audiences: action-adventure dramas, quiz and game shows, talk shows, children's programming, how-to programs. Much of it is also differentiated vertically: low-cost entertainment that can be broadcast profitably even at times when few people are watching.

Off-network syndication deals in program series previously shown on networks (usually prime-time). The fixed costs of these series—the negligible costs of repeat showings—encourage syndicators to license them in what may be a lengthy series of repetitions. This commerce is further encouraged by the goodwill these series retain with former viewers in first run and the substantial new audiences they can attract. A program's off-network syndication licenses usually cover its whole stock of episodes, including any yet to be produced (the first round of a successful program's syndication is generally licensed while the show's first run remains on the air). If the rerun episodes are shown weekly with repeats, a syndication license will lock in the parties for a number of years. A series might be licensed for successive cycles, perhaps winding up on niche cable networks that reach small audiences and have little willingness to pay. These cycles of exhibition of a TV series, like the successive windows of exhibition of cinema films, can be spaced out over time; a series that has "rested" can attract enough viewers to justify the syndicator's wait for the additional cash.[1]

From its basic functions, we might expect syndication to be a diffuse market with many participants and much turnover. Off-network material suitable for syndication can turn up in many hands: programs owned by the networks that first showed them, programs owned by the other suppliers of network programs described in

Chapter 1, cinema films, cartoons, and other movie industry cre-
ations. This stock of material churns slowly as aging series lose
their appeal and new programs come onto the syndication market.
In first-run syndication the unit of transaction is the single program
series. It is unclear whether economies of scale and scope support
any advantage for large-scale organization, and whether considerations of governance and incentives push syndication into integrated organizations.

The syndication market was long affected by the Federal Communications Commission's Prime-Time Access Rule (PTAR). In
1970 the FCC ruled that the Big 3 networks (ABC, CBS, NBC)
could not supply network programming in the fifty largest metropolitan markets for broadcast during the hours of 7 to 8 P.M. (East
Coast time). This rule was intended to attract other program suppliers to the market, and also to improve the relative position of
independent local broadcast stations (which would not have to
compete against network programs during that relatively popular
viewing hour). The rule nullified the networks' efficiency advantages in preparing "quality" programs for a mass audience, causing the major-market affiliates to depend instead on whatever they
might choose from the syndicators' menu. While diverse local tastes
might have been better served under PTAR, the fragmentation of
the market implied a reduction in the average quality of the programming offered—another implication of the mechanism of *endogenous fixed costs,* and likely a reduction in consumers' welfare.
Indeed, there was some evidence that viewership during the time
period declined after PTAR went into force.[2] No changes attributable to PTAR occurred in the overall concentration of program
types, but the mix did shift. Public affairs and children's programs
were squeezed out of the networks' feed.[3] The syndication market
responded to this created demand with low-cost game and entertainment news shows suited to the audience available in the access

period. The PTAR was repealed in 1995, raising the value of off–Big 3 sitcoms in syndication (discussed subsequently).

Organization of the Syndication Market

Diverse organizations supply and distribute programs in the syndication market, and the assortment is in flux. Independent syndicators market program series prepared by others or handed off for distribution in different outlets. Specialized producers of various types of first-run syndicated programs may distribute their own products. Producers of content suitable for syndication secondhand start their own branches for off-network distribution. Successful individual producers of syndication programming form alliances with production and distribution organizations, as in the development of network prime-time programs. Coalitions of content producers and distributors form joint ventures to develop and market syndicated programs. Participants in the market are numerous and entry is fairly easy, although the market has been growing more concentrated as the entertainment conglomerates have extended the scope of their activities toward syndication.[4] First-run syndication has evolved into a core of large units integrated into the media conglomerates, surrounded by a fringe of independent firms providing low-cost shows for specialized niches.[5]

The present-day syndication market emerged in the 1980s as the number of TV stations was greatly increased, raising the demand for syndicated programming. The Big 3 networks already had affiliates in all the larger markets, leaving the Fox network as the only source of bundled network-supplied programming for these new stations. Program license fees were bid up. The mechanism of *endogenous fixed costs* did its work: suppliers tended to raise the quality (and price) of first-run syndicated programs in order to make them more competitive with popular off-network series such as $M*A*S*H$. Casual evidence suggests that the mix of prime-time programs can be affected by sufficiently large disturbances in the syndication market.[6] The Paramount studio's Paramount Domestic Television accounted for a number of market innovations. It co-founded the entertainment news program *Entertainment Tonight* and developed miniseries and other innovative types of programs for syndication.[7] It guaranteed to licensees the total number of episodes of an off-network series that would come available even if the program were dropped by the network. It built a first-run syndication operation around the revival of the space-adventure program *Star Trek,* presenting the series in various outlets ("windows") of both domestic and foreign broadcasting. It put shows up for bid by the stations and otherwise enlarged its revenue stream from the stations' increased demand.[8]

Vertical Integration

Several broad patterns are evident in the changing population of syndicators. First, there is a strong movement toward vertical integration between the production and marketing of programming suitable for syndication. Unintegrated marketers have traditionally taken a 35 percent commission, with incentive-loaded variants. For example, the marketer might hand over all revenue to the production firm up until a threshold per episode was reached, with 65 percent of revenue over this threshold going to the marketer.[9] With or without incentives, these commission rates apparently struck program producers as high enough to warrant undertaking the marketing function themselves, once they had on hand enough programs suitable for syndication. A major independent producer of prime-time network programs, Carsey–Werner, developed a full-service marketing organization for off-network syndication of its flow of successful network programs. It spent heavily to retrieve rights to some of its shows that had been marketed by Viacom's syndication branch, and it successfully sought syndication business from other producers.[10] It is easy to see why interests can diverge between the owner or producer and the marketer of syndicated programs, encouraging integration. Program series can be long-lived in syndication; successful sitcoms earn rents that commonly increase in successive rounds of syndication—negative depreciation.[11] The contract between syndicator and licensee is incomplete, with the syndicator concerned with revenue over the program's whole economic life span, the broadcast outlet only with the life of the current license contract. Maximization of the long-run value of a program series calls for continual surveillance and lobbying by the syndicator to obtain the exhibitor's best time slot, most effectively organized local ad sales, and so on, both at the beginning of the contract and as an off-network series is played off in syndication over a period of years. Stations showing a long-lived series tend to drop their promotion after several years, when the contract's end comes in sight, curtailing spillover benefits to the syndicator.[12] In order to exert optimal effort to maximize the value of a series, the syndication marketer needs to "own" at least the marginal component of its whole cash flow.

Networks' Syndication Branches

A second move toward integrated syndication involved the Big 3 networks, once freed from regulatory restrictions on producing their own prime-time programs. They set up their own syndication operations as they increased their ownership of suitable first-run programs (Chapter 7). ABC became linked to a syndication organization, Buena Vista Television, when the network was acquired by Disney.[13] ABC soon found itself wondering whether the $45 to $50 million annually paid by its owned-and-operated stations (O&Os) for top shows for the "access" period from leading syndicator King World could be profitably displaced with in-house product.[14] CBS started several syndication divisions which it reorganized into one producer of first-run syndicated programming (CBS Enterprises) and one distributor (Eyemark Entertainment). Later it acquired King World and folded Eyemark Entertainment into it.[15] NBC had a small international syndication unit—permitted under the financial interest and syndication ("fin-syn") rules—but not until 2000 did it accumulate an ownership interest in enough prime-time programs to warrant the fixed cost of a domestic syndication organization.[16] In several ways the networks' chains of O&Os proved valuable for establishing first-run syndicated programs and maximizing their license revenue.[17] Evidently, off-network syndication involves some economies of scope and scale.

The broadcast networks indeed represent just one type of firm producing (or possessing) program content that could yield cash flows in syndication. The movie studios' vaults contain cornucopias of feature films, cartoons, short subjects, and early TV series that can be packaged for both broadcast stations and cable networks. Each film studio continually offers packages of its feature films, differentiated vertically by quality and perhaps horizontally by subject matter. Old short films may be bundled in two-hour blocks. The Columbia studios' Screen Gems offerings provide a vigorous example.[18] Made-for-television movies, modestly budgeted and prone to address subjects of current (and transient) interest, are candidates for syndication packages.[19] Even packages of early television programs can receive a warm welcome from some of the cable networks.[20]

Alliances and Joint Ventures

For a third form of integration, temporary alliances and joint ventures to produce first-run programs for syndication have developed between station groups and content providers. Large station groups have emerged in the past decade or so (Chapter 8), and their newly achieved scale allows them to consider supplying their own program needs. A common approach has been to ally with some content provider. Thus, in 1995 the New World station group made a $30 million investment in TV producer Stephen Cannell's firm, obtaining ownership of all new projects and the rights to distribute uncommitted shows in Cannell's 1,200-episode library for fifteen years. Cannell, who shared the profit flowing from these transactions, was concerned with access to distribution facilities at a time when distributors were being consolidated in large firms—the foreclosure problem investigated in Part Three.[21] In 1997 the sixteen-station Tribune group entered a multi-year joint venture with NBC's syndication arm and an independent producer (Peter Engel Productions) to supply teen-oriented sitcoms to Tribune and for syndication to other stations and groups.[22] In 2000 a similar development and distribution alliance was formed between NBC and the Gannett and Hearst–Argyle station groups. The station groups sought programs suited to particular time periods that they needed to fill. Also, acquiring ownership interests in their daytime programs would allow capture of the spillover value of promoting programs broadcast on these groups' own stations when the programs were aired in syndication by other stations.[23] Some alliances of this sort occurred incidentally to content providers' acquisition of station groups. Entertainment conglomerate News Corp.'s purchase of the New World stations (Chapter 7) allowed Twentieth Century Fox Television to market the programs of New World Communications Group (*Highway Patrol, Access Hollywood*) with little increase in its own costs, and to enjoy a scale economy in coupling *Highway Patrol* with its own *Cops* in a one-hour block of the two stripped half-hour programs (a "stripped" series is broadcast an episode each weekday).[24] The first-run syndicator marketing a new program enjoys a considerable advantage in having a captive station chain to launch the vessel, as we show subsequently.[25]

Alliances and joint ventures in general risk the emergence of conflicts between their partners, and the uncertainties associated with "creative" products only enlarge this risk. For instance, in 1984 syndicator King World began distributing producer Columbia–TriStar's successful syndicated shows *Jeopardy!* and *Wheel of Fortune.* Their agreement did not allow King World to syndicate another game show for the early evening time period. In the early 1990s King World acquired rights to the revived game show *Hollywood Squares,* stating that it would subcontract distribution in order to avoid violating the 1984 deal. Columbia objected, and countersuits were brought. They were settled out of court by giving Columbia a share of the *Hollywood Squares* project.[26]

A complex case illustrates governance problems with joint ventures but also the competition among them. It involves the entertainment news program *Access Hollywood,* a joint venture of NBC and the New World station group. The program competed with the long-established *Entertainment Tonight,* itself a joint venture between Paramount Domestic Television and the cable operator Cox Broadcasting. It suffered strategic disadvantages relative to the popular *Entertainment Tonight,* whose managers pressured stars and their handlers not to appear on *Access Hollywood* at the risk of quashing their future invitations from *Entertainment Tonight.* It also competed with Warner Bros. Domestic Television Distribution's *Extra;* that show's broadcast clearances (i.e., agreements to run it) depended heavily on NBC O&Os, which would be lost to *Access Hollywood,* and Warner had to reformat *Extra* and give NBC an equity share in order to preserve clearance on the O&Os. *Access Hollywood* faced a problem when News Corp. acquired the New World station group and Twentieth Century Fox Television became NBC's partner. *Access Hollywood's* clearances wilted (were not renewed, or were downgraded to less popular times) as the New World stations' affiliations were switched to the Fox network, leaving the program securely cleared only with the NBC O&Os. Under the standing contract the program was profitable for the O&Os but not for Fox (News Corp.) or for the NBC network taken by itself. Furthermore, NBC now depended on a competing network for its program. The deal had to be revised, with Twentieth Century Fox Television retaining only a minor position and NBC shopping the program to other syndicators.[27] Paramount soon followed suit and acquired full control of *Entertainment Tonight*.[28]

In sum, the organizations and deal structures in the syndication market respond to the standard features of creative goods—fixed costs, durable rent streams *(ars longa),* and pervasive differentiation *(infinite variety).* The wide bargaining ranges faced by owners of assets with large sunk costs push them into organizational links and alliances. These seek to avoid uncertainty and holdups that potentially threaten their revenue streams, but they encounter their own governance problems.

Placing New Syndicated Programs

Decline of the Central Marketplace

The producers of new syndicated programs face a marketing problem that has only grown more vexing over time—yet another outgrowth of programs' wholly fixed costs. Episodes of an hour-long action-adventure drama cost at least $1 million each to produce, and even the more popular among them obtain quite small ratings (the fraction of TV households watching). Therefore it is necessary to clear a program (that is, obtain distribution) in a large proportion of potential U.S. metropolitan markets in order to generate enough revenue to cover the fixed cost of production (we ignore for the moment cash flows from repeat broadcasts and foreign markets). This task has been strongly affected by the coalescence of stations into groups, the result of both economic forces and progressively relaxed FCC curbs on group ownership (Chapter 8). Syndicated programs, both new and off-network, were formerly marketed mainly at the annual convention of the National Association of Television Program Executives (NATPE), where individual station managers made their deals with syndicators. Station groups were capped by the FCC at seven members, so the syndicators dealt with buyers numerous enough to make a common marketplace efficient. Programs were licensed for cash, and the deals involved no substantial ongoing relationship between syndicator and licensee. With stations gathered into larger groups, fewer clearance decisions are made, and for the syndicator, more rides on each decision. The station groups have gained bargaining power against syndicators, shown by their ability to demand equity slices in programs that they clear.[29] Reciprocally, large syndicators seem able to impose tied offers that ride on bargaining power that could be countervailed.[30] For reasons explained subsequently, negotiations with station groups have come to cover a more complex set of issues, including the slot in which the stations will run the program, the duration of the contract, and the like.[31] Station groups do not wholly centralize their programming—station managers retain considerable authority for selecting what their stations show—but key clearance decisions are commonly made at the group level. On the one hand, this change reduces the number of transaction costs that the syndicator must incur. On the other, more is riding on the individual deal, increasing the uncertainty for the syndicator and the scope for holdups.

This marketing process has many ramifications. Although a good deal of business is done at the NATPE convention by individual stations and small groups, and also by international licensees of U.S.-made programs, the convention's reduced role causes syndicators to question whether their substantial fixed costs of attending and mounting an exhibition are warranted.[32] This market for small transactions may be in danger of unraveling.[33] Station groups rely for their program needs less on the spot availability of suitable offers and more on alliances and joint ventures with networks and their syndication arms, smaller independent syndication firms, and the like. Each party opting out of the spot licensing market reduces the number remaining in the pool, increasing the associated uncertainty and pressing the rest to defect to long-term contractual arrangements. On the one hand, this process is limited by the widespread recognition that *nobody knows,* no program supplier is infallible, and a substantial option value resides in access to a wide range of suppliers.[34] On the other hand, the reduced number of deals and deal-makers may facilitate the informal renegotiation and multi-period reciprocity that seem to lubricate the market for prime-time network programming, giving the parties some insurance against deeply unsatisfactory deals.[35]

Station Groups and Clearance

The prevalence of station groups and alliances strongly affects the task of establishing a new syndicated program. (The situation for off-network syndication is different because the fixed cost of preparing a program series is sunk, which reduces but does not eliminate the entrant's problem of scaling a clearance threshold.) The first step in the process—devising a program—is easy for entrants, because ideas for syndicated programs, especially a new twist on an established type (game show, talk show, action-adventure drama) spring up readily, and the needed inputs are easily assembled. Successful programs beget hordes of imitators. The success of *Judge Judy* brought seven syndicated court shows to the NATPE meeting in 2000. The talk show *Ricki Lake* (1994), with its distinctive appeal to young adults, prompted a talk-show race with thirty-four contestants counted by 2000, but only one clear success *(Rosie O'Donnell).*[36]

Thus, in any one clearance season (the months leading up to the NATPE convention), several programs of any given type (action-adventure dramas, talk shows, etc.) contend for clearances, each seeking the mass of potential viewers critical for attracting national advertisers and thereby making the program's production profitable. A distinct threshold exists for the share of U.S. households that must have access to a program in order to attract national advertisers, often cited as 80 percent. The advantage to the syndicator of an affiliated station group lies in providing a base commitment that puts this threshold within sight. Programs that reach the NATPE convention with clearance near or over 75 percent are commonly propelled by commitments from corporate siblings (a network's O&Os) or affiliated station groups.[37] An example is the (off-network) one-hour drama *Dr. Quinn, Medicine Woman,* owned by CBS Productions and relying for clearances on the CBS network's O&Os. These stations cleared the program when it was first marketed in syndication, with the understanding that any CBS station would give up the show if competing stations in its market later offered the syndicator a better time slot.[38] There appears to be a correlation between the ratings achieved by a program entering into syndication and the size and strength of the syndicator's affiliated station group.[39] Even programs that ultimately fail benefit from the ability to launch on an affiliated station group, where a program can be tuned and polished once it is on the air.[40] Overall, the failure rate of new first-run syndicated programs is very high—according to one industry source 85 to 90 percent.[41] The also-rans often reach national coverage of 45 to 60 percent but then stall (abandoned, or perhaps diverted to the cable market).[42] While room is constantly being made for newcomers as underperforming incumbents drop out, an entrant's shot at the best time slots is blocked by popular incumbents that show little sign of attrition (this turnover is discussed subsequently).[43] With the market's acceptance of a new syndicated program so uncertain, syndicators keep their up-front investments as low as possible, to one pilot program at the most.

Structures of Syndication Deals

Cash versus Barter

The deal between a syndicator and a broadcast station or group embodies a number of choices that affect the returns to both parties—the form of payment and associated distribution of risks, the duration of the contract, degree of exclusivity given to the licensee, and so on. The chosen method of payment is central. The licensee may simply pay a cash fee to air the program, then sell the ad spots it contains either locally or through a national representative. The broadcaster seeks a profit in the excess of ad revenue over license costs (more exactly, a larger profit than it could obtain on any other program available for the same slot). In addition to or instead of receiving cash, the licensor may retain some ad spots, which it then sells and pockets the revenue—a practice called "barter." A program may be sold for cash, barter, or any combination of the two. The choice has several important effects. The rationale for barter stressed in the trade press is to ease cash-flow constraints on stations—plausible when the syndicator is an "entertainment conglomerate" and the station is an independent small business. A shift from cash toward barter terms for a program lowers the licensee's exposure to risk and raises that of the syndicator, who likely has better opportunities to pool it. Both hypotheses—capital constraint and risk—are consistent with the observation that barter deals, all things being equal, are more profitable for the syndicators.[44] Syndicators' preferred method of payment, however, depends not on the licensee's finances but on the program type—a fact pointing to other influences. Barter also gives the syndicator a way to make credible its confidence in the program's success. In first-run syndication it provides an incentive for the syndicator to sustain (not degrade) the quality of the episodes that it continues to produce. It probably lowers the cost of selling ad spots for syndicator and licensee taken together, as the syndicator (a large national organization) can sell national ads at lower cost than the local station (which must work through a representative). Barter, however, involves complex coordination, because all stations clearing the program must broadcast it at the same hour so that the national bartered ads air at contractually committed times. As licenses expire and the economic life of a series nears its end, at some point national sales of bartered ad spots becomes infeasible. A station paying cash for a program series can schedule at its discretion—hold it in reserve or rest it for a period of time.[45]

Information on syndication deals tends to confirm these propositions. Barter was apparently first employed in two contrasting but consistent cases—one where the syndicator offered a program of dubious quality (a failed NBC drama, *Fame*), and one where the syndicator offered a highly promising off-network program *(The Cosby Show)* with an asking price that ran up against limits in stations' willingness to commit cash.[46] Barter became entrenched in large part because syndicators discovered considerable interest among national advertisers in the stronger syndicated programs, so that the syndicators could realize more profit by dealing directly with the advertisers than by leaving the task to the stations. In another setting, Warner Bros. Domestic Television Distribution was leaning toward purely barter deals in syndicating two somewhat unusual shows styled for young audiences; the stations were prone to pay less cash than Warner thought the shows were worth, and accepting barter allowed Warner to bet on its hunch.[47] Among similar shows sold for barter, there is a clear pattern of the syndicator holding out for a larger share of ad spots in the more popular shows. In a group of (hour-long) action-adventure dramas, the most successful was sold for nine minutes of national ad time, five minutes local; less successful shows were offered for eight and six minutes, seven and seven, or six and eight (one case).[48] Certain types of programs are more likely sold on a cash-plus-barter basis, others on pure barter. Off-network sitcoms that face relatively predictable levels of viewer interest are offered on a cash-plus-barter basis, while (for example) first-run syndicated weekly programs usually sell for barter. The latter's appeal is more uncertain; furthermore, a program's quality is an ongoing decision to be made by the syndicator, whose incentive to sustain quality increases with its share of the ad spots.[49] Similarly, packages of A-list cinema films able to attract substantial audiences are usually bartered, while B- and C-list packages are licensed for cash.[50]

Bargaining Power

While a syndicator sets its distribution strategy by choosing the form of the compensation arrangement, the exact payment it receives (or expects to receive) still depends on bargaining in each local market. The syndicator hopes to foment an auction among stations in the largest cities, using the base thus established for quoting prices in smaller markets. Barter contracts of course automatically align the syndicator's expected cash receipts with the market's size and hence advertisers' willingness to pay. Licensees in the largest markets (New York and a few others), however, enjoy leverage that often allows them to extract from syndicators side payments outside the standard deal. The station's bargaining power stems from several sources. They include the near-impossibility of crossing the threshold for national syndication of a program without serving the New York market (7 percent of national TV households) and the spillover of promotional value from a program's airing in the major media capital. That promotional value is shown in advertisers' reduced willingness to pay (per thousand viewers) for programs not broadcast in New York. Also, syndicators may make side payments to guarantee that the program is scheduled in a choice time slot.[51] Some side payments to New York stations allegedly come from syndicators of relatively weak programs that seek to infuse credibility into asking prices suited to their more successful brethren.[52]

Large station groups also wield enough bargaining power to elicit side payments from syndicators. A station group may simply obtain a discount from what individual stations would pay, or the group may demand a kickback from the syndicator for accepting a barter deal expected to bring a bountiful ad revenue to the syndicator.[53] Side payments can occur within an ongoing syndication relationship. Syndicator MGM Worldwide Television paid CBS O&Os to keep two MGM shows alive for two more years (MGM was caught in a bind by the Fox station group's failure to renew them). Syndicator Rysher Entertainment gave a small equity stake in a program cleared by a consortium of four medium-size station groups. Syndicator New Line Television gave the Tribune Broadcasting Group an implicit equity in its program *Lost World* by assigning barter ad sales to Tribune's marketing organization.[54] The Sinclair station group tried to invert the auction process used by the syndicators by putting up blocks of weekend time on its stations for bids by syndicators, who could then broadcast whatever programs they saw fit and collect the ad revenue. This "barter minus cash" arrangement left the syndicators with no prospect of profit in Sinclair's medium-sized markets, and the plan got no takers.[55]

The local market's size matters because of the importance to syndicators of national coverage. The only likely syndication customer in a small market, however, has substantial bargaining power against a syndicator with a zero reservation value. The removal of two of four independent stations from the Cleveland market lowered the price the survivors paid for movie packages by 50 percent and for sitcom episodes by 43 to 71 percent.[56]

Turnover of Syndicated Off-network Programs

Timing of Syndication and Programs' Life Cycles

First-run dramatic programs undergo natural life cycles (Chapter 1), and these in turn raise substantial issues of timing in the syndication market. This section shows how these dynamic processes work themselves out. Off-network programs normally need to accumulate at least four years of episodes for successful syndication.[57] The syndicator can negotiate the deal earlier, however, guaranteeing a minimum stock of episodes that will be available when the licensee is ready for them. The licensor faces a decision about the optimal time to open a program in syndication relative to its primary network run. Too early, and the reruns may compete for viewers with the first run; also, the syndicator and potential licensees face an elevated risk that the program's first-run ratings might falter or some mishap take it off the air. Too late, and the present value of the syndication revenue shrinks owing to its postponement. Syndication licenses are long-term agreements that lock in the licensee for a period of typically three and one-half years but that can last much longer because of automatic extensions.[58] Even when a program's ratings in syndication wither, the contract continues to run.[59] These lock-in problems and the modest number of prime-time programs that achieve high levels of success mean that the syndicator's choice of timing depends strategically on both the cycle stages of programs now in syndication and the age distribution of competing programs still in their first runs.

Examples in the sitcom market illustrate the process. In 1997, *3rd Rock from the Sun* and *The Drew Carey Show* were both sold to open in syndication in the 1999–2000 season. Both went to the market a year earlier than is customary, in order to avoid a crowd of weaker programs likely to come up for syndication the next year. The deal for *3rd Rock* was particularly profitable, yielding expected revenue for the licensor (not counting bartered advertising) of $2.8 to $3.2 million per episode (comparable to sums derived from top sitcom successes—$3.1 to $3.5 million for *Home Improvement*, $4 million for *The Cosby Show*).[60] Similarly, CBS's syndication arm, Eyemark, heeded the large number of mid-tier sitcoms on the market for fall 2000 and offered *Everybody Loves Raymond* for fall 2001, expecting revenue per episode of $2.5 million. *King of the Hill* would also open in fall 2001, but it had been sold early during its second broadcast year in order to exploit its strong sophomore ratings. (Twentieth Century Fox Television sold *King* first to a sibling organization, the Fox network O&Os, which provide coverage of 40 percent of the national market. This is another illustration of the facade of arm's-length negotiations between jointly owned business units that nonetheless seemingly achieve a credible lock-in.)[61] At the same time, plummeting first-run ratings for two shows already in their first year of broadcast syndication caused them also to be licensed to a cable network, in order to harvest the available revenue from a foreshortened lifespan.[62] Sitcoms usually are licensed for cash plus barter, with the syndicator's rents from successful shows taken partly in larger cash payments, partly in a greater national share of ad spots. Rents can flow to the syndicator without any substantial increase in risk imposed on the licensee.

When a program first enters off-network syndication, a deal is usually made for its later appearance on a cable network. In 1995 *Friends,* only in its second year on the air, was sold for fall 1998 to Tribune Broadcasting Co. and other station groups, with a window to follow on cable network TBS in fall 2002.[63] NBC's *Profiler* was opened in broadcast syndication in fall 1999, with NBC retaining the right to syndicate it on cable in fall 2000.[64] A program typically is licensed exclusively to broadcasters for its first three years off-network, then concurrently to cable networks after that.[65]

Timing and Conditions in the Syndication Market

The time when a program opens in syndication may depend on developments in the syndication market. The values of programs in the syndication market are correlated, though imperfectly, with their first-run performance (ratings and longevity). An important reason for discrepancies is that the stock of programs competing in off-network syndication at a given time may be large or small relative to the stock in first run. *Sister, Sister,* an indifferent success in first run, did well in the syndication market for lack of competing programs with strong appeal to teenagers (national advertisers would buy into such a show even with national coverage under the conventional 80 percent).[66] So did *Buffy the Vampire Slayer,* because in its first run on the infant WB network it found relatively few viewers.[67] Such considerations have important effects on the timing of when programs are marketed for syndication. Columbia TriStar Television Distribution advanced the syndication of *News-Radio* by one year to fall 1998 because the fall lineups of several station groups had unfilled holes at congenial times of day. This program, not particularly successful on the network, obtained clearance in 75 percent of the market by means of a straight barter deal (syndicator and licensee splitting the ad spots fifty-fifty) for a fixed interval of two years, rather than the conventional open-ended commitment that depends on the duration of the program's prime-time run.[68] (The open-ended contract exposes the station to substantial risk, as it may be locked in for five or six years when a show proves long-lived in its first run during prime time, yet nothing guarantees that its ratings in syndication will remain strong.)

A major stimulus to the off-network syndication market was the abolition of PTAR, allowing affiliates of the Big 3 networks in the fifty largest markets to broadcast network-originated programs during the early evening hours. The most popular off-network sitcoms earn considerably more profit for licensor and licensee than the syndicated game and entertainment news shows that provide the best alternative. Thus, the rule had been a blessing to the independent stations and Fox affiliates.[69] Conversely, its departure raised the demand for off-network sitcoms and pushed the weaker entertainment news programs into less popular slots (and, in some cases, out of the market).[70] Locked-in contracts for game shows delayed the market's adjustment to the policy change.[71] Nonetheless, the foreknown policy change affected the decision to syndicate *Mad About You* in fall 1996 (rather than fall 1997), as did the paucity in the 1996 market of sitcoms competing closely with *Mad About You.*[72] Another condition in the syndication market affecting timing decisions is the recent licensing of a highly popular program that adduces large cash bids from the stations and depletes their bank accounts for other programs.[73] On first glance this assertion seems fallacious, since a high bid for a hot show presumably reflects the larger audience and till-filling ad revenues it will bring. Yet the stations may rightly regard the demand for local advertising as inelastic: a hot program that captures many viewers for local advertisers erodes their willingness to pay for additional access to the local audience with ads on other programs.[74]

Developments that affect syndication decisions also include the entry of new networks (Chapter 7). Networks and syndicators compete in supplying programs to stations. The larger the bundle of programs obtained from the network, the fewer programs the station demands from the syndicators, driving down the prices realized for off-network syndication and causing the supply of first-run syndication to shrink. Furthermore, the new networks themselves soon augment supplies of program series for the off-network syndication market.[75] The Fox network's entry in 1986 indeed coincided with a dip in the syndication market (falling prices, fewer exhibitors at NATPE). This was due only partly to Fox's supply effect. As the number of independent U.S. TV stations increased from 100 in 1979 to 310 in 1987, syndication prices were bid up sharply, sometimes in stations' strategic efforts to starve their local rivals. Fox's entry then pricked a bubble.[76] There are, however, qualifications to the relationship of substitution between network and syndicated programming. When the Pax network entered, it bought off-network syndicated programs to fill out its own schedule, and The WB similarly needed off-network syndicated programs to fill out the schedule for The WeB, its cable-based system for delivering its signal to small markets outside the topone hundred.[77]

Overall Turnover of Syndicated Programs

One useful perspective on the syndication market is in the overall dynamic character of its churning set of programs. Each enters at a particular moment, perhaps flourishes for a period of time, but sooner or later gets cancelled (exits). While on the air it may only eke out marginal profits in unpopular viewing hours, draw crowds of viewers that give it claim to the best time slots (yielding the most ad revenue), or fall somewhere in between. The trade regards popular and entrenched syndicated shows as a barrier to entry by new programs. That view is correct, but in a sense that needs careful interpretation. Off-network syndicated programs' costs are sunk; the gradual turnover of the TV audience continuously provides new viewers; and the human relationships on which their plots turn do not become dated. These properties add up to a strong barrier to displacement, reflected in the ability of top sitcoms to earn steady or even growing streams of rent in their second and subsequent rounds of syndication.[78] Competing on price with an entrenched off-network program with its costs wholly sunk is a most unattractive prospect.

Consider a somewhat softer target for displacement by entry— the first-run syndicated program which continues to incur production costs. Any new program must be styled for maximum attractiveness to some particular audience and viewing time, so its owner in effect selects its competition among the shows currently running. The entrant might target a weak incumbent which, owing to its weakness, probably plays at an unpopular time; the entrant's chances against a weak incumbent may be good, but the prize is small. Conversely, an entrant's assault on a top show is unlikely to succeed, but *nobody knows,* and even a small chance at a large prize provides strong temptation. The paradoxical-sounding result is that entries are attempted where the barriers to entry appear the greatest. Especially if program suppliers are risk-neutral or even risk-loving, it becomes plausible that "hit" programs are longer-lived than run-of-the-mill ones, despite facing (and dispatching) more entrant rivals.[79]

This discussion of turnover has stressed the "creative industries" properties—the uncertain reception of new goods, the prevalence of vertical differentiation (*A-list/B-list* property). Turnover or its absence sometimes depends simply on whether the typical incumbent is profitable (that is, the conventional supply-demand balance). For example, few hour-long action-adventure dramas have been profitable lately, and as a result, few entrants are tempted.[80] The problem for these programs is not a low rate of successful entry into competition with profitable incumbents, but rather revenue failing to cover cost because no contender can enthrall enough viewers. As recently as 1997, when the syndicated dramas *Hercules* and *Xena* still flourished, nineteen out of twenty-four adventure dramas achieved ratings high enough to sustain them. One survival strategy is to license these programs to cable networks more or less simultaneously with their broadcast airing.[81]

International Market

Throughout this book we generally treat the U.S. market for TV programs as if it were separate from the rest of the world, because that is a fair first approximation. In recent decades the United States has exported a large number of TV programs as well as cinema films, with several consequences worth noting.[82] Markets abroad welcome certain types of syndicated programs, chiefly action-adventure dramas and cartoons, both of which are easy to dub into other languages. Also, the dramas' high (fixed) production costs make the foreign market important to their commercial viability. Action-adventure programs hence have often been produced with overseas collaboration or with clear expectations of foreign license revenue.[83] Such programs, costing $1 million an episode to produce, may elicit bids of only $200,000 to $300,000 on the U.S. syndication market. The European market for them at times has been large enough to cover the balance. Co-production deals to serve this market are common, though at hazard of efforts to accommodate various national quirks in joint-venture production.[84] With international support, such a program can stay in production long enough to be recycled profitably in the syndication market.[85] U.S. made-for-television movies are good candidates for syndication abroad.[86]

These patterns have some effect on the firms participating in the U.S. program market. Specialists in adventure dramas and TV movies and miniseries maintain international connections (Hallmark) or are based outside the United States (Alliance Atlantis).[87] Britain's Pearson PLC acquired a U.S. syndication firm specializing in game shows, with more than ninety of them already licensed at home and/or abroad. These were pooled with Pearson's own large library of games and soaps. The combined company also planned to become more active producing action-adventure dramas.[88]

This international market has in fact been declining.[89] In part its scripted programs are giving way to less costly unscripted programming, just as in the networks' own prime-time schedules. More broadly, the expansion of commercial TV abroad for a time got ahead of local capability to supply programs, but the development of European production has now restricted the demand for U.S. exports.

The U.S. syndication market includes some imports from abroad. It is cheaper to license and dub Japanese cartoons than to produce new ones in the United States, and some other types of Japanese programs have proved adaptable for the cable market.[90] Reality programs involve a brisk international trade taking the form of format licenses rather than dubbing of shows made abroad. Also, a U.S. subsidiary of the Dutch producer Endemol has established itself supplying domestic versions of programs devised abroad.[91]

CHAPTER 3

The Public Broadcasting System

Markets for creative goods may fail to deliver the best mixture of outputs for reasons well known in the theory of differentiated products. When the property of *infinite variety* applies literally to the potential supply of creative goods, only a limited number of the potentials are actually produced, and some of the wrong ones can get left out. That is because the revenue generated when they pay the producer's asking price fails to capture enough of the consumers' surplus to cover the producer's fixed cost. The market's best way around this problem is usually the "two-part price": buyers pay a variable price for each unit they consume (ideally, equal to its marginal cost) and also a fixed charge or membership fee that covers the product's fixed costs. Two-part prices are commonly found in the economy. In creative industries, with their predominance of fixed costs, two-part prices are often implemented by nonprofit organizations—the performing arts (season tickets), museums (memberships), and so on. Good reasons have been advanced to explain why these appear where they do.[1]

Over-the-air broadcasting faces this problem acutely because it is a pure "public good": non-payers cannot be excluded from tuning in. Only advertisers' willingness to pay for viewers' attention saves the day for commercial broadcast stations and networks. Cable systems, satellites, and the networks that they deliver of course can exclude non-payers and evade the problem. The nonprofit organization also appears in broadcasting as a device to implement two-part prices, in the guise of public television (PTV) in the United States and government-run or funded TV networks in other countries.

To add perspective to this study of the organization and reorganization of commercial TV broadcasting, we provide a brief comparative treatment of PTV. This book's focus is behavioral rather than normative: Why does the broadcasting industry provide the amount and style of programming that it does? Many people evidently believe that market forces select something other than an ideal set of programs; witness the prevailing choice of most foreign countries (until recently) to confine broadcasting within the public sector. In the United States, PTV emerged without a coherent plan as a collection of nonprofit enterprises and organizations. PTV bears some resemblance to the commercial broadcasting networks —a central assembler of programs linked contractually to a collection of local stations. PTV faces the same squeeze as the commercial networks from the audience's migration to cable networks. It suffers an additional squeeze from the continual shrinkage of the funds flowing to it from the federal government—from nearly 24 percent of its total revenue in the early 1980s to less than 15 percent more recently. Subventions from state and local governments have similarly declined. The falling governmental share forces reliance on other sources (grants by corporations and foundations, syndication and related revenues, and viewers' donations) that are not readily expanded.

We first provide a brief sketch of PTV's complex organization as it has emerged from various governmental decisions. This leads directly to the pressures that have befallen PTV to find non-governmental sources of revenue as the supply of public funds has withered. A discussion of the goals apparently pursued by PTV decision makers leads to a review of how PTV programs are developed and selected. PTV is shown to face a threat from cable at least as dire as that to commercial over-the-air broadcasting, and it lacks ready routes of reorganization to address its problem.

Structure of Public Television

The Organizational Units

The components of the public television system sprang from several public policy decisions.[2] In 1952 the Federal Communications Commission set aside 242 TV channels for educational use; aside from denying them advertising revenue, the FCC articulated no specific mission. The local franchises were picked up by a variety of organizations. As of 1998, 136 stations (90 licenses) were in the hands of nonprofit community organizations, 85 (82) universities, 8 (8) local governments, and 123 (26) state governments.[3] At the outset each station was left on its own to prepare and acquire programming. The Ford Foundation took an interest in conjoining them into a decentralized system of educational broadcasting, making available a substantial number of grants to fund stations operated by community nonprofit corporations. They were obligated only to exchange programming with one another and to join a programming consortium.

PTV's central components emerged in the 1960s in the wake of a report by the Carnegie Corporation that contemplated a system organized as a network with dedicated public funding, such as a tax on the sale of television sets. In 1967 Congress passed legislation creating the Corporation for Public Broadcasting (CPB) to receive U.S. government funds and distribute them to cover the system's costs of programming and operations. Its basic task was to facilitate the development of educational programming of high quality. Congress declared that the public interest would benefit from supporting the development of creative programming that addresses the interests of unserved and underserved audiences. CPB was also to assist the development of the local stations and arrange for their interconnection. Interconnection of the stations (then a much larger cost than today) was nonetheless not to compromise the stations' independence in scheduling programs. Nor was CPB to produce programs itself. The legislation put CPB squarely under the governmental thumb, requiring it to seek annual appropriations (no dedicated funding) and to be governed by a politically balanced board of directors.[4]

With CPB in place, a great deal nonetheless was left unsettled. Who was to produce PTV's programming? Decentralized program production appealed to many, and a small group of stations took on the task—WGBH in Boston, WNET in New York, WETA in Washington, and a few others. In this role they faced resistance from other stations that sought equal opportunity to become program producers for the system. In 1969 the Public Broadcasting Service (PBS) was created as the central operating arm for PTV, assigned to manage interconnection, arrange for the preparation of programs (though not itself allowed to produce programs), and make them available to the stations. PBS selects the central pool of programs prepared for broadcast by the stations, but it is not an autonomous scheduler like a commercial network. It functions as a cooperative organization of the member stations, governed by a board consisting of station heads and outsiders. Since 1996–97, station representatives have held 50 percent of the seats on the PBS board; they are elected on a one-station/one-vote basis, and so tend in a sense to overrepresent the interests of small stations and markets. PBS collects dues from the stations as well as funds from CPB to cover the cost of programs that it commissions or acquires, and it organizes these programs into a schedule. Whether a station should broadcast that network feed as received or treat it as a library available for its own scheduling decisions is a much-disputed question, similar to that of clearance of commercial TV programs by network affiliates (Chapter 6).

Shrinking Government Funds

This organization has not fundamentally changed in three decades, but it is under constant strain for lack of a regular and settled source of funds. Table 3.1 traces the recent history of PTV's sources of revenue. The federal government's contribution has shrunk steadily as a fraction of the system's resources. The share of funds from state and local governments has also withered, gradually but substantially, and the system has had to raise the share of revenue that it digs from private sources from 41 to 61 percent. The increase has come partly from corporate sponsorships but mainly viewers' donations and "other private sources," which prominently include videocassette sales and other such spin-offs from PBS programs and associated products.

The federal funds received by CPB are passed along to the stations and to PBS. CPB's direct grant to each station, mandated by Congress, comprises three components: a fixed sum ($385,000 in fiscal year 2002), a payment related to the potential audience reached by the station, and an incentive component related to the funds raised from other sources by the station itself.[5] Data on individual stations are not reported, but those reaching small audiences apparently depend much more heavily on federal funds than those in large markets (as the grant's fixed component implies).[6] Funds then flow from the stations to PBS as dues to support the cost of preparing programs for the national system. PBS in turn receives funds from several sources. In fiscal 2001 it obtained 45 percent from member stations' program and service assessments, 11 percent from CPB grants, 7 percent from U.S. Department of Education grants, 17 percent from sales of educational products, and 20 percent from royalties, license fees, investment income, and other sources. Programming and promotion absorbed 73 percent, member and educational services 17 percent, satellite distribution and technical support 6 percent, and general and administration 4 percent.[7]

TABLE 3.1 Public broadcasting system revenues, selected fiscal years, 1982–1999
($ millions)

Source	1982	1986	1990	1994	1997	1999
CPB	$172	$159	$229	$275	$260	$250
Other federal	26	26	38	55	62	51
All federal (%)	23%	16%	17%	18%	17%	14%
Local governments	42	51	60	56	66	57
State governments	167	213	262	272	299	298
Colleges, universities	105	141	183	208	213	221
Foundations	22	38	71	97	112	123
Businesses	100	171	262	301	278	315
Subscribers	142	246	341	399	472	550
Auctions	20	23	23	21	21	17
Other private	49	65	112	111	150	265
All private (%)	41%	50%	53%	53%	55%	61%

Note: The "all private" percentages include private colleges and universities, which are
pooled with public colleges and universities in the line above.
Source: Current Web site, www.current.org/pbpb/statistics/totalrevs.html.

The system has been gradually privatized as an outcome of recurrent battles with political and social conservatives. In its drive to
nourish unserved audiences, PTV's eye frequently alights on groups
arguably short-changed for social justice or untethered to conserva-
tive morality. This focus has fomented three major campaigns to
terminate federal government funding of CPB, by President Nixon
in 1972, by Congress under the Reagan administration in the early
1980s, and again by the Republican Congress in 1995.[8] While each
move to "zero out" CPB was repelled, the real value of the federal contribution has been ratcheted down, as shown in Table 3.1.
Equally unsuccessful, however, have been pro-PTV attempts to provide it with an assured and politically insulated trust fund so as to
regularize its federal funding. This quest naturally founders on the
question of whose cash will endow the fund. Suggestions of a share
of government proceeds from broadcast spectrum auctions or a

tax on proceeds from sales of commercial stations carry the virtue of economic efficiency (little or no distortion of the affected parties' incentives) but also the political defect of imposing lump-sum charges that induce the victims to resist mightily.[9]

These entities and provisions render decision making in PTV, even in the eyes of its stalwarts, a cumbersome process.[10] The uncertainty of the congressional appropriation process precludes CPB and thereby the whole system from engaging in long-term planning with confidence about its access to resources. Although non-federal revenues are more predictable, the stations and central organs of PTV share the same problem of all non-profit cultural organizations: they lack a slice of equity capital to absorb adverse cost and revenue shocks in the short run. The 349 stations are independent, separately licensed entities that function something like a pure democracy in making group decisions. PBS and CPB have their own organizational interests related to their functions within the system, but neither is "in charge" of the system or able to form a coherent policy and make it stick. As a result, PTV pursues federal government support not with a unified request but as a clamor of discordant interests, with CPB only nominally in charge. The stations seek guaranteed levels of federal funds to be passed through CPB to them (more than half of CPB's appropriation is passed through to the stations). To a degree they have profited from CPB's political misfortunes, since conservatives object less to public support for local stations than to the heretical programs distributed by PBS.[11] The independent producers of PTV programs sought and got their own earmarked guarantee of federal funds, which reached a maximum of 8.6 percent of the CPB appropriation in fiscal 1986.[12] Interest groups that had locked up their own slices of the pie (funding or policy commitments) then could withdraw while CPB continued to fight the main battle.[13] In addition to the strife over federal funding, decisions made within the system are never final; there is no titular authority to declare an issue closed and settled.

New Funding Initiatives

The long-run erosion of government funding and especially the 1995 trauma forced PBS and the stations to seek new sources of funds in the private sector. Donations from viewers are avidly sought by the stations in periodic pledge drives decked with special programming, auctions, and other devices. These drives now occupy enough of the broadcast year that expanding them further might yield little additional net revenue. PTV stations seem poorly suited to exploit the donor-supported nonprofit organization form common in the performing arts. Service on public television boards may lack the festive character of performing arts events and the public approbation that comes to those who support them generously.[14] Nevertheless, a few big-city stations have made some progress in embracing this model.[15]

With viewers' donations thus limited, PTV reached out for commercial sources of revenue. This proved an uneasy venture, because PTV has sustained a distaste (discussed subsequently) for commercial activity and what one might call sharp business practice. Nonetheless, necessity nurtures invention. The historic distaste for money-grubbing is shown by PBS's passive stance toward acquiring valuable rights in the programs broadcast on PTV. PBS has broadcast many series that possess substantial residual values—toys and books from children's programming, videos and syndication revenues from prime-time programs and miniseries (compare the commercial networks' quest for rents). Only in 1993 did PBS reserve the right to condition program funding commitments on obtaining institutional and home video rights.[16] PBS made the toy figure Barney famous without (until recently) demanding a share of the rents. More aggressiveness is now visible: PBS has come to seek residual rights in programs it broadcasts and to take part in entrepreneurial ventures with its suppliers aimed at capturing residual values.[17] Such deals include the syndication of PBS programs such as *This*

Old House and the marketing of videocassettes, compact disks, and related merchandise through retail outlets and catalogues.[18] PTV's nonprofit organizations are of course not well suited to such entrepreneurial activities, and they have sought partnership deals that spare them from having to supply equity capital or managerial services.[19] Apparently the producing stations and PBS hold concurrent rights with no formal allocation of usage between them. Each might pursue back-end revenues, potentially in competition for the same revenue stream.[20] In 1995 PBS promised the stations that copyrighted programs in which PBS held the relevant back-end rights would be available for their derivative use. Because those rights had not been routinely obtained, however, the value of this promise lay in the future.[21] While PBS reports substantial increases in gross revenues from derivative uses, the costs of obtaining them are not reported separately, leaving profitability uncertain. At least some miniseries such as *Jazz* have yielded substantial gross profits.[22]

Much controversy has occurred within PTV over commercial initiatives. Some stations have allowed commercial sponsors to lengthen their messages from the traditional fifteen seconds to thirty, and to tread somewhat closer to advertising their products rather than just stating their corporate identity.[23] This incremental tolerance for sponsors' messages might be expanded, but PTV manifestly lacks the organizational capability to sell national promotion in the manner of the commercial networks, even if its scruples were overcome.[24] Product-placement revenues provide a temptation: the chef in a cooking show must wield *some* brand of implement.[25] PTV's problem with program sponsorship is in a sense worse than that of commercial television. A commercial sponsor cares mainly about the number of viewers attracted to a program and their demographic and economic traits (although critics' ratings do matter). Its ad is its own message. When a corporation sponsors a PBS program, however, its message to viewers *is* the program, and the sponsor must inevitably care about its consistency with the image that the firm seeks to cultivate. While PBS has sternly resisted input by commercial sponsors into programs' substance, the need for sponsorship makes it impossible for PTV fund-raisers to ignore the match between a proposed program's form and content and the image that potential sponsors will wish to signal.[26] Finally, these quests for revenues bring objections from guardians of traditional PTV virtues, who assert that trolling for new revenue sources will destroy the system's access to private contributions and federal subventions.[27] There is, however, no way to measure those potential offsets without actually performing the experiment.

Since PTV's revenue squeeze is clearly a long-run structural problem, it will inevitably continue its quest for commercial revenue. It has come some distance in making the best of a (self-perceived) bad situation. For example, the four most active producing stations have formed a consortium to coordinate their approaches to potential commercial sponsors. The consortium can offer a portfolio of projects rather than competing for sponsorship of individual projects in an uncoordinated way.[28] PBS has also come to weigh program candidates with more concern for their potential to generate merchandise sales.[29] International co-productions of programs have been structured with more attention to their back-end value to PBS.[30]

Goals of PTV Organizations

A quest to understand the behavior of nonprofit organizations necessarily starts with the question of what goal or goals they pursue. When decision making is decentralized, the answer may not come easily, as individuals' tastes and their organizational domiciles may be diverse. There is widespread agreement that PTV seeks to fulfill unserved broadcasting needs. "Unserved," however, is hardly an objective status. Needs can go unserved because they are rarely or weakly felt, specialized, or ignoble. Satisfaction comes to PTV participants from serving needs that in substance are deemed worthy and meritorious, and that provide scope for creative work—originality and high production values. The latter property translates into a preference for "quality" programs that will win approval from other program producers and critics—*art for art's sake*.[31] When choosing the program substance that merits quality treatments, PTV decision makers tend to march under two different banners. One group pursues social justice—reporting on the state of disadvantaged groups and probing the practices and institutions that appear to sustain their deprivation. The other focuses on education and high culture as a terrain unserved by commercial broadcasters. Sophisticated inquiries into public affairs, science, and the arts then hold attraction.[32] The objective of meeting unserved needs has the paradoxical effect of deflecting concern with audience ratings. A built-in excuse for low ratings relative to the commercial networks is the charter objective of serving interests that the networks have ignored. Nobody knows the potential size of such neglected audiences, so no one can summon evidence to indict PBS for underserving them.[33]

Along with these leanings, and consistent with them, come more specific objectives that bear directly on the policies of PTV's various organizations. Stations hold the system's basic franchises—their broadcasting licenses. The independent decision-making power that these franchises confer on station managers clearly is a source of utility to them. Symmetrically, they seem to suffer little regret when their exercise of local preferences impairs PBS's function. The same goes for the decision-making costs and the inability to fix responsibility arising from the exercise of "station democracy."[34] The stations see themselves raising substantial fractions of their revenues and making large payments to PBS for programming, yet the national organizations have no way to save them if their revenues fall short of costs.[35] These attitudes have fostered chronically difficult relationships between the stations and PBS. As the system's program coordinator, PBS naturally seeks some of the efficient properties of a network—a common schedule of suitably composed programs that spreads their high fixed cost and allows for the efficient promotion of new programs, specials, and so on. PBS has lately grown concerned for the audience "flow" from program to program that obsesses the schedulers of commercial networks' prime-time programs. But if the stations are insensitive to ratings, how much will they value flow? PBS managers are regularly called upon to grovel before the stations and deny any ambitions to centralize programming decisions in the manner of a network or initiate policies such as alliances with outside commercial entities.[36]

Another attitude evident in PTV might be called "abhorrence of commerce"—disutility from managerial choices that involve purchase and sale transactions. PBS and the program producers incessantly beg for donations from viewers, foundations, governments, but these pleas appeal to high-minded motives of the donors and not to greedy urges for goods or services obtained for cash.[37] As noted previously, PBS long neglected to seek equity or ownership rights in the programs it acquired and showed, apparently from a distaste for mercenary thinking about how to maximize the residual values that these programs might have in syndication or other such uses. Offering videocassettes and other merchandise based on PBS programs puts PTV stalwarts in mind of Disney figurines flogged in fast-food establishments, and they apparently gain no solace from the thought that people buying this merchandise part willingly with their cash and presumably regard themselves as better off.

The preference of PTV for "quality" in programming leaves the question of who decides what constitutes quality. Commercial broadcasters generally equate quality with that which enlarges the audience viewing a program (although unpopular programs that draw favorable reactions from critics are cancelled with a tiny tear). PTV could in principle follow the same course and base its standards on ratings (the number of viewers attracted—or the number attracted from the unserved audiences addressed by PTV). Or PTV managers could apply their own subjective tastes, which seem to embrace high production values and freedom for the producer to pursue a project to full aesthetic satisfaction. To make a rough judgment, PTV's interest in ratings seems mainly associated with its need to justify government subventions. Particular programs' ratings appear to get little attention, for purposes of replacing or refurbishing them. Indeed, PBS program planning seems to eschew the commercial networks' policy of routinely holding an inventory of replacements for programs whose ratings falter, which could be regarded as another excuse for ignoring ratings.[38] The decision in 2002 to appoint a new and more powerful programming coordinator at PBS was accompanied by some step-up in the attention paid to ratings.[39]

The importance of these policy preferences is underlined by the conditions of employment for PTV decision makers. Many of them serve out lengthy careers within the system, for which they may be paid well, though less than their counterparts in commercial broadcasting.[40] It is natural for them to regard the exercise of policy preferences as compensation due for a short ration in the paycheck.[41]

Program Supply

The suppliers of programming to commercial broadcast and cable outlets form an extended common pool, marked by vertical differentiation and with the major film distributors active in bankrolling series with syndication value (Chapter 1). PTV chooses to go it alone, drawing for its principal (prime-time) shows on a different set of suppliers. These are the producing stations (listed previously) and a group of independent producers of nonfiction educational and documentary programs.[42] The dramatic programs that have been the mainstay of commercial prime time are represented largely by syndicated off-network British sitcoms and dramas and jointly produced dramatic programs (also mostly British). Like commercial TV, PBS has relied on series programs, with formats loose enough that episodes can be gathered à la carte from numerous sources. PBS also favors miniseries and has been quite successful with high-profile documentary series made by producers such as Ken Burns. Locally originated programs have high status in the stations' scale of values, but the inefficiency of preparing programs with high production values for small local audiences presses heavily enough to squelch the preference. Local programs draw little corporate sponsorship. Hours of local programming on PTV dropped from 12 percent in 1974 to 4 percent in 1997.[43] As to functional types of programs overall, a tabulation of all PBS programs in fiscal 1993 recorded 46.1 percent public affairs, 17.3 percent children's programs, 16.7 percent cultural programs, 7.4 percent how-to shows, 6.1 percent each of science and nature programs, and 0.2 percent sports programs.[44]

These series and episodes are selected through a complex process in which the stations voice their preferences, and PBS assembles the pieces. Between 1975 and 1991 programs were selected through a voting procedure in which a station that favored a program committed itself to contribute to its cost. Since the contribution declined with the number of other stations selecting the same program, the arrangement provided a strong incentive for the stations to reach consensus. But it also provided an incentive for clinging to incumbent programs rather than taking a chance on new ones.[45] As a result, the major PBS program series have soldiered on for many years. In 2002 *Mystery* was twenty-two years old, *Frontline* twenty, *Nova* twenty-eight, and *American Experience* fourteen. A struggle persisted through the 1990s between the partisans of stations' autonomy and those who saw the advantages of network-like coordination. These advantages include the efficient promotion of the program schedule (no "check your local listings"), the ability to guarantee sponsors the broadcast times for their programs, and the ability to fix responsibility for the success or failure of programming decisions. In 1990 a single executive was placed in charge of programming and promotion at PBS, and by mid-1995 a good deal more commonality had been achieved among the stations' schedules.[46] In 1995 the pendulum swung, however, and the programmer resigned upon being saddled with a competing program supplier set up within PBS to offer a library of alternatives to the stations.[47] In 2000 another strong programming executive was hired (from the TNT cable network), this time also holding the title of PBS president. The trade press by then was referring to the PBS schedule as "like Stonehenge, an odd assortment of pillars that have stood longer than anyone can remember."[48] The new program head was soon at war with the producing stations over her efforts to lower the average age of the PBS audience (typically fifty-five to sixty-five, white, and female).[49] In particular, an eruption occurred over an attempt to modernize the program *Wall $treet Week* by putting its long-time host out to pasture and reformatting the program by means of a *Fortune* magazine connection.[50] This effort incidentally brought PTV into some contact with the commercial program market. PBS picked up *American High,* a series commissioned but quickly cancelled by Fox, and it was developing a Latino family drama prepared as a pilot for but passed by CBS.

Program Selection by PBS

PBS programming decisions center on the selection of documentary and investigative programs to fit into long-standing portmanteau series (*Frontline, P.O.V.*) or run as independent programs or miniseries. PBS gatekeepers screen large numbers of projects and proposals at various stages of development, coming from independent producers, member stations, or collaborations between them.[51] Around 95 percent are rejected. Projects slotted to established series get guaranteed financing but also fall under the editorial control of the series producer. The producer of a freestanding program retains control but must forage for financial support, backed perhaps by an advance from PBS against a license to broadcast (four times over three years), perhaps by nothing more than an expression of interest from PBS.[52]

Independent Producers

The quest for financing is commonly a large part of the independent producer's work. The established writer-producer Jon Else, preparing a program on water and politics in the U.S. West, filed 307 applications for support and ultimately drew funds ($2.7 million) from twenty-one sources.[53] Clearly, this system of financing programs exacts crushing transaction costs. Programs have suffered from being stale on completion owing to protracted delays for obtaining financing.[54] It is not clear to what extent these transaction costs are passed on to PBS or absorbed by the independent producers with *art for art's sake* tastes.

As noted previously, the independent producers in 1988 succeeded in diverting their own mandated rivulet from the stream of federal funds flowing to CPB. It supports the Independent Television Service (ITVS), another instance of PTV's conflicted objectives. When mandated funding was first obtained, the organization used it extensively to support experimental programs. It soon became clear, however, that little of this product would get on the air, as PTV's audience was clearly not ravenous for experimental video. ITVS conceded only grudgingly that its programs' length had to align with broadcasting's standard thirty-minute modules. Eventually it settled down into being a regular program supplier. Over a decade since its founding (1991), about one-third of ITVS-financed films have got onto national programs such as *Frontline,* and another one-third onto PBS's package of optional shows such as *P.O.V.* Remaining films are shopped individually to stations. ITVS programs are also offered to HBO and similar outlets, but any sustained collaboration here has foundered on the insistence of ITVS on producers' final cut, while the commercially driven cable channels demand their own control.[55]

The Producing Stations

Two-thirds of PBS's regular prime-time series are produced by just two stations, WNET (New York) and WGBH (Boston), and the two received about 45 percent of the PBS production budget in 1999. Their program series on PBS's prime-time schedule have enjoyed a long tenure, as have their staffs at the major producing stations that supply them. Descriptions of their operations convey the flavor of established bureaucratic organizations free from immediate budgetary pressures to work to self-defined criteria of quality. Each series has its own budget and staff of producers who take an *auteur* view of their task. As a result, WGBH's continuing series cost around $500,000 an hour, compared to $150,000 for cable networks' documentaries. A special project might reach $1 million, similar to a network drama that generates substantial rents for its talent.[56] This high standard of production by no means disdains service to the audience's interest; the focus falls on how to convert a subject into a story well told in images and words.

The complex task of the producing stations is illustrated by the efforts of KCET (Los Angeles) to become more active in producing dramatic programming for PBS. The station enjoys an obvious locational advantage and has successfully reached out to bring Hollywood talent onto its board of directors. Yet an effort to develop a new dramatic series languished from the difficulty of raising funds to cover its production cost. KCET tends to see a first-mover financing advantage going to WGBH and WNET, but KCET itself has a record of budgetary control problems. The obverse of the fund-raising problem is the gulf between the pay levels to which movie talent is accustomed and what public broadcasting is ready to pay. Film talents commonly will take lower pay for projects of special personal interest, but the premium cable channels HBO and Showtime are already in the game playing that card.[57]

The producing stations carry a considerable burden of drumming up and sustaining foundation and corporate sponsorship and funding for their programs. They take substantial risks in committing expenditures before funds are in hand. Some programs have enjoyed stable corporate support over long periods, but in general, fund-raising entails a high and continuous burden of effort. The burden and the uncertainty are enlarged by foundations' taste for involving themselves with novel initiatives but declining to support continuing projects (no matter how worthy).

Competition between Cable and PTV

PTV faces the same exogenous loss of market as commercial broadcasting (Part Two)—more alternatives available to consumers—and its audience has been shrinking about 2 percent annually (a bit slower than the commercial networks'). PTV has it worse in some ways, because it seeks consciously to address unserved niches, while the advantage exploited by cable networks is exactly their ability to cover the cost of programs that appeal to small, specialized audiences. Thus, PTV finds itself competing with suppliers of programs similar to its own on such cable networks as Discovery, The Learning Channel, The History Channel, A&E, and BBC America. PTV faces at least as much threat as commercial TV from the enhanced quality of cable programming (Chapter 5). Its daytime children's programming competes closely with that of Nickelodeon and at least three other cable networks.[58] Basic cable receives both advertising and subscriber revenues, while premium cable forgoes advertising but enjoys the freedom to present adult subject matter that is denied to both commercial and public broadcasting. Thus the series *Tales of the City* migrated to Showtime when its subject matter brought down conservatives' wrath on PBS. Some types of PBS programs were especially ripe for imitation by cable. Its how-to programs, both inexpensive and politically innocuous for PTV, offered the former virtue to the cable networks.[59] These are easily adapted, as are most program innovations on PTV (witness the quick duplication of *Antiques Roadshow* by several cable networks).[60]

Cable confronts PTV with competition for programs and program talent as well as audience. For example, of sixteen documentary films competing at the Sundance Film Festival, five each were produced by ITVS (for PBS) and by HBO, another by PBS itself, and the remaining five were expected to wind up on either PBS or HBO.[61] PTV managers argue that PBS retains an edge in creative freedom for its producers, and its respect for quality and critical opinion seems to support the judgment.[62] Cable documentaries may be more formulaic and more cheaply produced, but the cable networks spare the independent producer the agonies of fund-raising. Constraints on PBS's funding clearly accelerated the migration of independent producers to cable.[63] PTV may even face some rivalry from cable for advertisers. They are said increasingly to regard support of PBS programs as advertising rather than charitable contributions, which automatically injects the question whether cable networks may offer more cost-effective promotion services.[64]

Issues of Efficiency in the PTV Stations

PTV labors under substantial costs of inefficiency in the organization of its stations. This was the forceful judgment of the Twentieth Century Fund Task Force on Public Television (1993), which lamented the fact that outlays on national programs accounted for only one-fourth of PTV's annual expenditures, with much of the rest absorbed in the operating costs of local stations.[65] Inefficiencies are immediately apparent when one compares features of commercial station networks, notably their chain organization and their vigorous pursuit of "duopolies" (two local stations with a single management). Commercial station chains create value for themselves partly by increased bargaining power with program suppliers—a source of more private than social value, but real economies are evident as well. And common administration of two local channels achieves large economies in operating costs (Chapter 8). A few PTV franchises operate two channels (sixteen duopolies in 1996) or even a statewide chain of local transmitters, but mainly they function as independent units despite substantial overlaps in their signal areas. As of 1995 PTV signals overlapped in fifty-three markets involving 137 (of 349) stations. Overlapping stations reach about 40 percent of U.S. households. While this count embraces channels already under common operation, it correctly suggests that consolidating operations would yield large economies.[66] Their managers' taste for local independence deters consolidation to achieve operating economies. Even in the 1990s the stations showed little interest in exploiting their un- and underused second and third assigned channels, although some have been sold to commercial broadcasters.[67] PBS's efforts to establish a second national feed appealing to a younger audience went nowhere.[68] More subtly, their nonprofit organization keeps anyone from capitalizing the real gains from consolidating stations by buying a controlling equity stock interest, achieving the cost saving, and selling out at a profit. There is thus little incentive for stations to merge except to absorb a failing business. CPB does supply some incentive for the consolidation of overlapping stations by paying only one fixed component of the station subvention per market, so that overlapping stations must share. And there have been consolidations of facilities (master control rooms, towers) affecting at least a dozen stations.[69]

The great disparities between the big-city producing stations and the small-town outlets sustains low-level tensions within PTV. The small stations prefer that PBS slant its investments toward low-cost programming to minimize their dues to the service. The large ones voice their taste for quality. The mechanism of *endogenous fixed costs* implies the existence of an optimal system-wide quality level for PTV as a whole, with each station contributing to its costs out of the "surplus" associated with its own market. The dependence of the system on subventions and grants, however, creates a large gulf between the value created for PTV viewers and the PTV stations' ability to pay for programming.

Even if PTV moved more aggressively to accept advertising, this would not save the skins of the small-market stations. First, the demand for corporate-image advertising congenial to PTV and consistent with its image is weak in small markets. Second, many stations belong to local governments or schools, and these are unable to accept advertising; some others are precluded by their charters.[70]

Two policy options remain for the stations. One is to abandon the local production of programs and the fixed costs of studios and facilities associated with them. The Twentieth Century Fund Task Force regarded national programs as the core source of value in PTV and local programs as an expensive luxury. This judgment grew from a consultant's report which found that local production's fully allocated costs accounted for 35 percent of the system's total outlays but only 7 percent of the average station's broadcast hours.[71]

The second broad remedy is consolidation of overlapping stations. Some consolidation has occurred—notably the absorption by New York's WNET of Long Island–based WLIW (2001), described as the first merger of its kind among PTV stations. Some reduction in personnel would occur, and the consolidation of the periodic drives for donations promises economies analogous to the consolidation of ad sales by combining commercial stations.[72] More consolidation seems likely to be triggered by the conversion to digital transmission, which imposes a substantial fixed cost on each station while giving it the capacity to transmit six channels in the band-width that supports only one analog channel. Mergers between sta-tions and sell-offs of the extra transmission capacity offer ways for PTV stations to cover the costs; either way, the PTV stations face the prospect of a lowered fixed-cost burden.

PART TWO

SWITCHING CHANNELS
AND PROGRAM QUALITY

CHAPTER 4

The Squeeze on Broadcasters' Rents

Over a quarter-century the broadcast networks have gone from being nearly the sole providers of TV entertainment to serving a smaller share (45 percent) than the cable networks (48 percent).[1] In 2000, 96.6 million U.S. households had access to cable lines, and 68.6 million households subscribed (68 percent of all TV households). Table 4.1 shows the fivefold increase in the number of households subscribing to cable over the two-decade period, 1980–2000. While the number of households with TV sets kept increasing, it was near saturation at the outset. Table 4.2 reports the consequences for the average shares of the audience tuned to the various distribution channels. The Big 3 networks, later joined by Fox, lost their share of the viewing audience in mirror image to the gain by basic cable networks. New broadcasting networks and pay cable networks accounted for only a little of the redistribution. In recent years satellites have added another technology for delivering programs. Table 4.1 also presents some information on the changing population of TV stations. Their numbers increased greatly in the 1980s as the Federal Communications Commission (FCC) authorized many new stations. This expanded population of stations needing program material set the scene for entry by the Fox network in 1985, followed by UPN and The WB a decade later, but the growth of stations greatly decelerated in the 1990s. Other things being equal,

TABLE 4.1 Size of broadcast audience and size and turnover of TV station population, 1980–2000

Year	Number of commercial TV stations	TV households (millions)	Cable households (millions)
1980	734	76.3	13.2
1981	756	79.9	n.a.
1982	777	82.0	n.a.
1983	813	83.3	31.4
1984	841	84.9	34.2
1985	883	86.5	36.3
1986	919	87.7	39.7
1987	968	89.2	42.6
1988	1,055	90.9	45.7
1989	1,064	91.6	49.3
1990	1,092	92.1	51.9
1991	1,098	93.1	54.9
1992	1,118	92.1	55.5
1993	1,137	93.1	57.2
1994	1,145	94.2	58.8
1995	1,163	95.4	60.5
1996	1,174	95.9	62.6
1997	1,177	98.0	64.8
1998	1,204	99.4	65.8
1999	1,216	100.8	67.1
2000	1,248	102.2	68.6

Sources: Statistical Abstract of the United States, various years, and *International Television & Video Almanac* (Quigley Publishing Co., various years).

Note: Data on cable households in 1981 and 1982 are omitted because originally published values seem inconsistent with later revised data for adjacent years.

this lost audience translates into lost advertising revenue for the traditional broadcast networks. Other things are not always equal, however. Some advertisers will pay substantially more (per thousand viewers) to reach the broadcast network TV audience than the households contacted by other media. In boom times (such as the 1990s), they bid up the price of broadcasters' ad spots substantially.

TABLE 4.2 Audience share of TV viewing during prime time by
distribution channels, 1984–85 to 1998–99 (percent)

Year	Network-affiliated stations	Independent stations	Public broadcasting system	Pay cable	Basic cable
1984–85	74	16	4	7	6
1985–86	75	17	4	6	6
1986–87	73	18	4	6	8
1987–88	69	20	4	7	10
1988–89	66	20	4	7	13
1989–90	63	21	4	6	16
1990–91	67	14	4	6	20
1991–92	71	9	4	5	22
1992–93	70	10	4	5	23
1993–94	69	10	4	5	24
1994–95	66	11	4	5	27
1995–96	62	11	4	6	31
1996–97	58	12	4	6	34
1997–98	55	12	4	7	38
1998–99	54	11	3	7	41

Source: Nielsen Media Research, *2000 Report on Television* (New York: Nielsen Media Research, 2000), p. 17.

Notes: Prime time is Monday–Sunday 8–11 P.M., and the broadcasting year extends from September through August. The "independent" category includes the UPN and WB networks and superstations except TBS. In 1991 Fox was reclassified from independent to network, and TBS from independent to basic cable. Percentages can total more than 100 because a sampled household with more than one set in use can be counted in more than one category.

In this chapter we identify the underlying factors that explain how the broadcasters respond to their defecting audience. We look for evidence of their predicted responses and then ask whether other explanations also fit the facts.

Source of the Squeeze

The diversion of audiences from broadcast to cable networks stems from two fundamental causes. First, cable and satellite transmission offer generally superior technologies for distributing broadcast signals to households. Second, over-the-air broadcasting is a pure public good, lacking a convenient technology to charge viewers for the programs they watch and exclude those who do not pay. Cable distribution is a private good; the viewer can be charged for programs at little addition to the transaction cost of billing for the distribution service itself. Cable networks thus can pick their preferred combination of pricing their programs to viewers and charging advertisers for distributing their messages. Over-the-air broadcasters have only the advertising revenue stream. While some cable networks choose to rely solely on advertising revenues, others (premium networks) forgo the advertising stream and rely on fixed or pay-per-view charges (Chapter 5).

When in its early days all cable offered its subscribers was improved reception of over-the-air broadcasts, cable's and broadcasters' services functioned as complements. If anything, better viewing conditions over cable caused more households to watch broadcast programs, while more attractive programming from the broadcasters raised households' willingness to pay (WTP) for better reception via cable. But then cable systems started to import distant signals, such as Ted Turner's WTBS "superstation" and Time–Warner's Home Box Office (HBO). As cable networks emerged to offer programs competing with over-the-air signals, cable turned into a substitute for broadcasts. It drew viewers and national advertisers away from broadcast networks' programs, and cable operators began to compete with broadcast stations in selling advertising to local businesses. If households were unwilling to pay a subscription fee for cable programs that differ from those offered over the air, cable would enjoy no economic advantage in competing with broadcast networks beyond its technical advantage in the number and quality of program signals it can transmit. If cable's programs elicit a positive WTP, however, cable gains the opportunity to cover the fixed costs of additional programs, when these costs are less than the sum of viewers' and advertisers' WTP but greater than that of the advertisers alone. Thus, cable's competitive threat to over-the-air broadcasting rests on both technical advantage and pricing efficiency.

Although cable and satellite distribution have done the most damage to the broadcast networks, recent evidence fingers another competing attraction. Young adults, prized by advertisers, have been drawn away from TV in large numbers to video games and Internet-based amusements. With 75 percent of young adult males having Internet access, the potential diversion from TV (broadcast and cable) is large.[2] Furthermore, advertisers are also showing signs of switching some outlays to video games, by getting product plugs inserted into game publishers' offerings or constructing a game around a product and giving the game away.[3] How do the broadcast networks and their affiliates adjust to the shift of viewership to cable, satellite, and the Internet? Standard supply-and-demand economics suggests that this exogenous diversion of demand would reduce the quantity of broadcast programming supplied. Yet the Big 3 networks have kept the hours of programs they distribute essentially unchanged, and the total supply has indeed continued to expand with the entry of new networks and stations (Table 4.1). A major hypothesis of this study is that the key change associated with the shift lies in the quality of programming offered, because of the role of *endogenous fixed costs*. The cost of preparing a program is wholly fixed (and sunk); once this "first copy" cost is incurred, the show can reach additional viewers at little or no marginal cost. Furthermore, the potential quality of the program (although *nobody knows*) increases with the fixed cost that is incurred. As we explained in the introduction, the mechanism of *endogenous fixed costs* then comes into play, and an exogenous increase (or decrease) in the size of audience for a program raises (or diminishes) the optimal fixed cost for its producer to incur. The encroachment of cable on the broadcast networks' audience is therefore predicted to shrink the profit-maximizing quality of broadcast programs and to raise the quality of cable networks' offerings. Of course these induced changes in quality would reinforce the flow of viewers from broadcasting to cable; the key point is that the quality shifts are a consequence of cable's realized technical and economic advantages and not an exogenous cause of the audience shift.

We evaluate this hypothesis in two steps. The first is to document the various ways networks adjust program quality, consistent with the mechanism of endogenous fixed costs. Quality reductions in network broadcasting are considered here, the corresponding increases in cable networks' program quality in Chapter 5. The second is to consider various forces that might have interfered with the link between expanded cable and satellite service and altered program quality.

Endogenous Fixed Costs and Vanishing Viewers

Types of Prime-Time Programming

While the series dramatic program—the half-hour sitcom, the hour drama—economizes on costs of producing TV entertainment, it is clearly not the cheapest format around. Unscripted reality shows, game shows, and news magazine programs can be produced much more cheaply. Many casual comparisons appear in the trade press; they vary depending on just what programs the observer has in mind. An episode of a half-hour reality show such as *Cops* apparently costs around one-third to one-half as much as an episode of a half-hour sitcom that lacks rent-commanding stars. The elaborate reality game show *Survivor* cost CBS 77 percent as much per episode as an hour drama, but quiz shows such as the highly (if briefly) successful *Who Wants To Be a Millionaire* cost about one-third as much as scripted shows.[4] Reality shows suffer a revenue disadvantage, however, in that most of them seem to hold little value for syndicated reruns, whereas even a moderately successful sitcom that accumulates a sufficient library of episodes becomes a valuable property.[5] Nonetheless, in 2004 some reality shows were producing syndication value for their owners, and Fox was planning a cable channel specializing in them.[6] Also, advertisers' WTP is restricted for reasons discussed subsequently, and reality shows' cost per thousand viewers (CPMs) may run 30 percent below the cost of scripted shows.[7] Another type of program alternative to prime-time scripted shows is sporting events, which are traditionally confined to weekend daytimes but can readily be moved to prime time. How cost-effective these prove depends on the presence or absence of star athletes and the network's ability to negotiate contracts that keep the sports enterprises from absorbing all the rents.[8]

Reality shows, game shows, and news magazine programs have all expanded in bursts on networks' schedules since the early 1990s, occupying a large majority of networks' prime-time schedules by 2003. It is impossible to distinguish the effect of their long-run cost advantage from the random inspirations that can swell the ranks of any type of show, but both are clearly evident. News magazines proliferated around 1994 as NBC discovered that its *Dateline* could readily be expanded to fill several slots in its prime-time schedule. Scale economies appeared in the preparation of large numbers of stories, and the program's slant toward "sidebars" and human in-terest angles ensured it an unlimited supply of material. It also could devote a mass of resources to a hot issue, if desired, and sto-ries could occasionally be shuffled among the several weekly broad-casts to match the demographics of their viewers.[9] The 1999 and 2000 seasons brought a burst of quiz shows *(Who Wants To Be a Millionaire)* and reality/game shows *(Survivor)*. These proved to be effective innovations that initially drew immense audiences, espe-cially among the young adult viewers most attractive to advertisers *(Millionaire* averaged 28.5 million viewers). Then came talent con-tests, fronted by Fox's *American Idol.* Cost savings were a minor component of their attraction. Prices paid by advertisers remained lower than for top dramas such as *E.R.*, but total advertising revenues were much greater than for the scripted shows that got displaced. ABC was estimated to have earned $435 million on *Millionaire* in its first year, topped up by enlarged lead-in audiences to other shows ($52 million), increased local ad revenues for the networks' owned-and-operated stations (O&Os, $44 million), and merchandise and Web site activities ($25 million).[10]

This dose of reality soon revealed its self-limiting properties. The recent wave of game-type reality shows *(Survivor, Big Brother)* has employed the wrinkle of a contest running its course; this proved a strong audience attraction for the first few cycles, but it might not support numerous repetitions. Reality and game shows turned out to be only a temporary patch for the networks that relied most heavily on them. The Fox and ABC networks overdosed on reality shows (ABC in 2001 offered *Who Wants To Be a Millionaire* for four hours a week) at times when those networks' scripted shows were seriously underperforming in the ratings. The bonanza permitted the immediate reduction (50 percent in ABC's case) of the budget for developing new programs. In the season of its maximum reliance on *Millionaire,* ABC launched only four other new shows, all of them weak performers.[11] The net revenue gains from reality programs were also threatened by rent seekers among the participants. Some employed no defining and irreplaceable actors, except for experienced producers and support staff who could claim temporary rents. Others found their costs much inflated by securely entrenched rent seekers, such as real estate mogul Donald Trump in *The Apprentice*—surely a man to spot a rent.[12]

It is not clear whether this wave of reality programs implies a speed-up in the networks' long-run retreat from scripted programs. On the one hand, it showed the same potential for self-destruction as other programming fads. ABC expanded *Millionaire*'s airings only to see its audience erode sharply and shift toward viewers over fifty, unloved by advertisers. It faced conversion to a syndicated program and did not return the next season as a network show.[13] The rapid onset of staleness in these shows is confirmed by the fact that *Survivor,* a great success in the United States, performed weakly in the United Kingdom, where several similar programs had already appeared. On the other hand, the greater prevalence of reality shows might indicate a new long-run equilibrium of viewers' tastes and program-making technology. Critics have suggested that reality shows suit the imbued preferences of today's young people, familiar with camcorders and personal computers from their early years but ignorant of the nuances of well-made drama and insensitive to the higher production values of traditional scripted network programs. Also, technological changes in cameras and editing equipment have much reduced the cost of filming and editing on-the-run reality shows.[14]

Repeating Programs: Theoretical Choices

A TV show's episodes can be rebroadcast an indefinite number of times at next to no out-of-pocket cost (although they trigger royalties payable to the talent and affect the value of future cash flows to the owner). The network's basic business is providing packages of programs to fill up a regular and substantial part of the day and week. How much of this package should consist of new episodes not seen before? How much should be repeats, and how should the repeats be timed relative to the first showings? Repeats spare the cost of producing new episodes, so there is room for a substantial loss of audience and advertising revenue before a repeat becomes less profitable than a new episode. The profit-maximizing extent of repetition depends on several characteristics of the broadcast audience and its tastes. We examine these in the abstract, then review the empirical evidence. Consider the demand for viewing a fresh episode of an established series program. A set of viewers will be aware of and potentially interested in watching it. Their opportunity costs vary from hour to hour and day to day, owing to each individual's changing mix of alternative activities (including watching other TV programs). Some will find this opportunity cost too high at the hour when the first showing is scheduled. The number of viewers attracted to a repeat showing will therefore increase with (1) the total number of households interested in the episode, (2) the proportion of those who skip the first showing (because of opportunity cost) but then choose to view the repeat, and (3) the number of enthusiasts who choose to watch both showings. The second category leads to further implications. A low correlation between potential viewers' time-specific opportunity costs will favor repetition. So will differences among potential viewers in their physical access to various broadcast channels or the quality of their reception. This consideration might favor a switch of network, or from broadcast to cable, for the repeat. A different day and hour would likely draw more viewers. Finally, the value to the network of a given repeat audience depends on its demographics as well as its size.

With the revenue potential of a repeat thus determined, the network compares it to its best alternative, which might be a new program that could draw a larger audience, though not necessarily one large enough to cover the additional production costs and consequent license fee. Of course, the owners of the original program (including talents who participate in profits) will likely demand a license fee that increases with each episode's number of showings.

Repeating Programs: Empirical Patterns

Broadcast networks long followed a customary pattern of repeats for prime-time programs, rerunning the preceding season's episodes during the summer, generally in the same time slot and on the same channel. The whole program series got repeated in syndication after a substantial delay (Chapter 2). Made-for-TV movies commonly receive repeat broadcasts; ABC reported little decline of ratings for the second play.[15] The exogenous loss of viewers has induced broadcasters to expand the use of repeats while shrinking the numbers of new episodes ordered. During the 1950s and 1960s the TV prime-time season lasted a minimum of thirty-nine weeks each year. By the early 1970s, however, the season had contracted to thirty-two weeks and the number of original episodes to thirty-two. As competition from cable set in, the contraction proceeded, with the season dropping to thirty weeks and orders for episodes to twenty-six per program in the 1980s, then to twenty or twenty-two for the season in the early 1990s.[16] As a result of the increased proportion of programs that get cancelled, even this number is split into two separate orders (except for star producers).[17] In 2002, with advertising revenue shrunken by a recession, for less popular shows networks commonly ordered thirteen episodes at the start of a season, deciding later whether to acquire the full "back nine" or reduce the order.[18]

The use of repeats by cable networks provides a contrast. They repeat programs much more frequently than broadcast networks, an aspect of the lower quality of their programming, which has receded as they upgrade their program stream (Chapter 5). The contrast to broadcasting rests on another factor, however: the large differences in the average size of first-run prime-time audiences for broadcast and cable network programs. That suggests another mechanism to explain cable's greater resort to repeats. Assume (contrary to the preceding theoretical argument) that cable viewers are not well informed about most of the programs they can receive. As a result, they sample extensively at random. When they select a program they have already watched, they pass. When they draw an unfamiliar program, they either watch it or proceed to sample the next channel. The smaller the audience for a cable program's first showing, the larger the potential audience that might sample and stay with it during a repeat showing. As more repetitions occur, the stock of previous viewers grows but is still small, and the stock of potential viewers remains large. Because the audience grows saturated so slowly, numerous repeats might generate maximum profit for a cable network.

The broadcast networks tiptoed into offering short-term repeats on different channels as well as at different times (the practice is called "repurposing" in the industry). The market for off-network syndication (Chapter 2) of course deals in programs repeated after long delays, but short-delay repeats have occurred mainly in distribution channels that are under the originating network's control. This is not surprising, since the timing of the runs, the delay between them, and the promotion provided all need to be jointly determined. NBC has relied on rebroadcast over its affiliated cable networks MSNBC and CNBC, sometimes fortifying the vintage with related material (such as National Basketball Association post-game shows not carried by the broadcast network). ABC has rebroadcast prime-time shows on cable affiliates such as sports network ESPN, and ABC's acquisition by Disney enhanced these opportunities (Second Noah repeated on the Disney Channel).[19] The Fox network planned to rerun programs on the Chris–Craft stations after that group was purchased by Fox parent enterprise News Corp.[20] Some rerun deals have emerged between unrelated broadcast and cable networks, as with NBC's Law and Order series repeating on USA Network (but the series' producer, Universal, owns a share of USA Network).[21] USA Network's successful comedy-detective program Monk was rerun on the ABC network under a deal foreseen when the program was first produced by ABC's parent, Disney.[22]

In 2004 repeats began appearing on the same network and in the same week as the first run. Saturday night (with Friday, drawing the week's smallest audience) showed signs of becoming a domain of repeats.[23]

The networks have undertaken various transactions to secure

outlets for repeats. NBC's purchase of full control of the Bravo cable network was motivated by the possibility for reruns and other collaborative ventures.[24] ABC established the SoapNet cable network to provide evening reruns of ABC's daytime soap operas. ABC also purchased the Fox Family Channel from its co-owners News Corp. and the children's program producer Saban Entertainment, renaming it ABC Family Channel. ABC could use it extensively as a rerun outlet, thanks to a deal with ABC's affiliated stations allowing it to repeat up to 25 percent of its entire entertainment programming within the week. ABC also wanted the network's extensive operations in children's programming overseas. Fox and Saban had been unable to collaborate effectively, and Fox owned other outlets for reruns on cable.[25] NBC acquired a 32 percent interest in the Pax network, recently emerged as a general broadcasting network from its origin in a chain of home shopping stations. While Pax built its prime-time schedule initially on off-network CBS programs skewed toward Pax's elder and family audience, the NBC transaction contemplated the rebroadcast on Pax of NBC network news and other such programs. In 2002 the Pax deal foundered on the mismatch between the Pax audience and NBC's programming aimed at urban sophisticates.

Licenses to repeat network programs trigger payments because several groups can claim some property rights in the gross profits. Reruns on cable divert some revenue from a network's affiliated broadcast stations, which lose viewers to their local cable competitors. This issue has ensnared the networks' efforts to stem the flow of compensation to their affiliates (Chapter 6) and forced extensive negotiations. CBS eventually reached a deal allowing it to repeat up to five hours of prime-time programming a week, two hours on the UPN network (its corporate sibling) and three on non-broadcast channels.[26] It was also necessary to deal with program suppliers, whose licenses specify the licensee's options to schedule a program. The program's owner holds a valuable asset in future syndication rents for a successful prime-time show. Short-run repeats threaten to reduce rents from repeats in the more distant future, raising demands for compensation from the supplier. Apparently the network commonly shares the profits from the repeat with the program supplier but pays a lower license fee for the program.[27] ABC ordered sixty-six additional episodes of the improv comedy show *Whose Line Is It Anyway?*, getting the option for up to eight additional runs in any day part in exchange for a "potentially graduated" increase in the license fee paid by ABC. The deal also covered the program's back-end syndication (likely small for such a program), thereby simplifying the deal's negotiation.[28] A deal between ABC and program supplier Warner Bros. Television permitted ABC to rerun a program on cable (ABC Family Channel) but protected the value of Warner's off-network syndication assets with a put option that allowed Warner to sell the syndication rights at a price guaranteeing it a profit. (Should a higher bidder appear, Warner and ABC would share the additional profit.)[29] The WB network managed repeats through its affiliated TNT cable network, where they would air outside The WB's 8 to 10 P.M. broadcast hours.[30] The replays would be conditional on deals with the program suppliers.

"Clutter": Expansion of Commercial Messages

Networks' Supply of Advertising Spots

How many minutes of advertising does a profit-maximizing network insert into its half-hour entertainment program? Assume that viewers get less utility per minute of advertising than per (average) minute of program content. (Whether ads are actively disliked is not important for the analysis, if we assume that enjoying the program requires watching the ads.) The intrusion of commercial messages then lowers the number of viewers who will watch a program, by reducing the utility obtained from this use of the viewer's time.

Charges to advertisers for ad spots take the form of costs per estimated thousand of viewers (CPM). The profit-maximizing amount of ad spots then will balance the increment of revenue that the network obtains from the last unit of time devoted to ads against the ad revenue lost because fewer households tune in to the program. Even with the number of viewers held constant, the network might face a downward-sloping demand by the advertisers for ad spots, causing marginal revenue to decline as the number of spots is increased.

The exogenous long-run erosion of broadcast programs' potential audience affects both terms in this marginal relationship, so there is no general presumption how the number of ad spots would change. Some independent factors suggest, however, that the squeeze would lead to expanded ad spots. The FCC has been generally hostile toward the expansion of ads, an attitude hard for profitable stations and networks to ignore. The broadcasters may have been effectively constrained away from the profit-maximizing allocation of time to ads. Also, it is plausible that neither the number of viewers nor the marginal revenue from ads declines much as ad time increases within the observed range. The networks' supply of ad spots is inflexible in important ways. Prime time has long consisted of twenty-two hours per week, while the U.S. economy and the number of advertisers seeking ad time have grown steadily. The entry of new networks is only a modest offset (Chapter 7). An expanding demand for ad spots interacting with a (nearly) fixed supply implies a continuous rise in the equilibrium (real) CPM, even while the total viewers diminish. Real CPMs for prime-time advertising did indeed increase in the 1980s and 1990s, so this consideration supports the hypothesis that small expansions of ad spots in prime-time programs are unambiguously profitable.[31] A dark cloud appears on the horizon, however, in the form of the digital video recorder's ability to delete commercial messages. This threat has led to experiments at writing commercials into the script of a program.

TABLE 4.3 Prime-time commercial minutes and total non-program minutes per hour, by network, selected years

Network	Prime-time commercial minutes per hour			Total non-program minutes per hour		
	1992	1997	2001	1992	1997	2001
ABC	7:22	9:30	9.50	12:46	15:44	15.02
CBS	7:41	8:13	9.15	13:24	14:29	14.11
Fox	8:04	8:54	7.41	14:38	15:54	13.44
NBC	7:38	8:29	9.28	13:18	15:19	14.54

Source: John Consoli, "A Crescendo of Clutter," *MW,* Mar. 16, 1998, pp. 5–6; Louis Chunovic, "TV Clutter Reaches All-Time High," *EM,* Mar. 11, 2002, pp. 1, 29.

Notes: The 1992 and 1997 figures pertain to the month of November, those for 2001 to the whole year. Comparability of the underlying tabulations is assumed but not assured.

If commercial-zapping technology were available to viewers at no cost, and consumers got no utility from ads, the only equilibrium outcome would be no commercial revenue available to broadcasters and TV programs provided only over cable.[32]

Growth of Clutter in Prime Time

Whatever these theoretical conjectures, the evidence is clear that the minutes of non-program material per prime-time program hour— "clutter" is the industry's term—have crept up. Clutter comprises revenue-producing ads, public service announcements, and the network's own promotions. Table 4.3 shows changes over the 1990s, during which the average number of commercial minutes per prime-time hour for the established Big 3 rose by a quarter or more.[33] This change coincides temporally with other putative responses to the demand shift discussed in this chapter. Like them, it also may reflect other changes occurring in the industry. The National Association of Broadcasters code once limited commercials to six minutes in the hour, but a Justice Department challenge ended the agreement in 1981.[34] The increase in clutter thus might be regarded as the gradual erosion of a cartel agreement.

A sidelight is the attempt by some affiliated stations to bring high technology to the expansion of clutter. They invested in the Time Machine, an electronic device that compares each frame of a network TV program to its successor and deletes the latter if the difference between the two falls below some threshold. An hour program can be compressed by two minutes, leaving the station with that much more advertising time to sell.[35]

Other techniques exist for generating more advertising revenue. Ads are no longer clearly separated from program materials, as when network logos and plugs appear at the bottom of the TV screen.[36] Product placement deals (long prevalent in cinema films) also occur in TV programs, as when a fleet of Ford vehicles ferries reality show players to the sites of their back-country adventures. Recently the networks have pursued product placement deals with increased vigor, to make up for a recession in the demand for ad spots.[37] Purchases of advertising may carry product placement perks as well, or the promotional message is sometimes rolled into the substance of the broadcast on daytime programs.[38] In a deal with Ford Motor Company, NBC agreed that Lincoln automobiles would be featured on *The Tonight Show with Jay Leno* in exchange for $9 million of Ford advertising spread across the network's programs. There are some signs of revival of the practice, prevalent in early television, of the advertiser taking full and exclusive control of a program.[39] ABC sold a 50 percent equity position in some of its shows to a major advertising agency, giving it an opportunity at the outset to inject its clients' products into scene and plot.[40] In 2004 product placement seemed to reach a critical mass, bestirring the appearance of new brokers and the reorganization of existing ones (talent agents, advertising firms) to pursue the business.[41]

A special form of product placement pioneered by The WB was

to draw on contemporary record album clips for background music in its hour dramas. The network gets a large discount on the usual license fee when the album is identified by a "card" at the end of the program.[42]

The relationship between advertising demand and the squeeze needs recapitulation. The demand for national TV ads has grown with the economy at large, while the supply of prime-time ad spots has expanded only a little, through the increase of clutter and other promotion-serving devices, and through any net increase in the total network audience associated with the entry of new networks. During the 1990s the advertisers' demand for viewers' attention shifted outward faster than the networks' audience declined, so that advertisers' total purchases of network ads increased. At least temporarily, the downward pull on quality was stayed. Thus, broadcast TV ad revenue grew roughly as fast as GDP during 1990–2000, but cable ad revenue grew much faster (143 percent versus 68 percent).[43]

Other Influences on Quality Choice

If we accept this evidence linking the expansion of cable (and satellite) viewing to the decline of broadcast quality (and the increase of cable quality), strong implications follow for the future. Broadcast networks might ultimately exit or convert themselves to cable networks. Other forces might intervene, however, to interrupt the trend or even cast doubt on the hypothesized causal link. Could the decline of broadcast quality result not from the mechanism of endogenous fixed costs but from some other source, such as a change in viewers' tastes, an increase in the cost of high-quality programming, or a myopic response by the networks to declining profitability? Could other changes—past and/or anticipated future—retard or even offset the adjustment of broadcast quality?

The effect of quality adjustment on broadcasters' revenues depends of course not only on the migration of viewers but also on the associated changes in the real prices paid by advertisers. Here the news for the broadcast networks has been better. Many advertisers are willing to pay more per household reached for ads carried on the broadcast networks than on their cable competitors. Some are attracted by the national scope of network TV and the lack of substitutes to serve advertisers who want to deliver a message simultaneously to the broadest possible set of U.S. households. Others may find such premia justified: delivering the same message through several smaller-scale outlets, each with its own audience, entails wasteful duplication when these audiences overlap. Thus the broadcast networks obtain $43 per thousand for male viewers aged eighteen to forty-nine, while a broad-range cable network such as USA Network gets $19. The differential is similar for other demographic groups, and it has remained largely unchanged for years (cable's discount actually increased by 2 to 4 percent between 1997 and 2001). Some specialized cable networks, however, do earn premia for delivering otherwise hard-to-reach audiences (ESPN, MTV) or for attracting audiences with high incomes and educational levels (Discovery, A&E).[44] The broadcasters fret about the long-run viability of the premium for national scope, and indeed a cumulative process could occur in which shrinking audiences force networks to lower their programs' quality, but the resulting shrinkage of advertisers' WTP leaves the networks with little gain in profits.

The broadcast networks' premium faces a threat stemming from the mechanism of *endogenous fixed costs*. Advertisers pay a premium for "quality" shows that are well reviewed—beyond the CPM for the extra viewers that a well-reviewed show may attract. By implication, advertisers assume that a program enjoyed more by viewers elicits more goodwill for their products. Advertisers also pay less for audiences of "reality" shows than for viewers of traditional scripted programs. Reality programs are sold to advertisers without a pilot, leaving them uncertain about the program's compatibility with their promotional message and target audience. Also, unwelcome surprise events can occur during the runs of unscripted programs, and advertisers discount for these.[45] Thus, the networks' efforts to economize on program costs, if they indeed impair the perceived quality of broadcast programs, may be partly offset by shrinking CPMs.

If national broadcast networks' ad spots command a stable premium, that is good news but does not halt the erosion of quality. It just means that networks' adjustments to the eroding audience proceed on a higher quality trajectory than otherwise. An additional complication is that ad prices appear basically auction-determined and fluctuate strongly with business conditions.[46] Thus, the networks' revenues increased during the prosperous 1990s (almost one-third in nominal terms between 1990 and 1996), then dropped in 2001, but subsequently recovered. The quantity of ad spots that the networks can sell is quite inelastic (as explained previously), so cyclical shifts in demand can produce large fluctuations in ad prices and networks' revenues. How much these fluctuations affect the pace of adjustment to the long-run demand shift is impossible to tell.

Ad prices affect the networks' decisions about the profit-maximizing level of quality to supply. Higher WTP by advertisers raises the networks' most profitable level of quality—to reap the high CPM rates from additional viewers. This calculation is not directly related to the average level of cash-flow profit that a network is earning—so long as it earns enough to stay in business. In fact, during the late 1990s the profits of the Big 3 and Fox networks were approximately zero (except for the substantial rent earned by NBC), although their owned-and-operated stations were highly profitable.[47] Low profits or losses by themselves are neither necessary nor sufficient to accelerate the degrading of quality, but this pattern is suggestive. Profit might, however, be directly linked to quality by another channel.

Squeeze on "Merit" Programming

Public Trust and Private Profit

The broadcast networks have been to some degree diverted from profit-maximizing policies by a vague social contract with the government, implemented partly through the franchises held by the owned-and-operated stations and partly by regulations of the FCC.[48] Because the broadcast networks and stations together long enjoyed monopoly rents, they could pay some heed to these social-contract provisions while retaining reduced but still generous profits. The squeeze has decreased the economic room for this deviation from policies maximizing private value and pressed the broadcasters to defend the commercial bottom line.

Consider this social contract and its incomplete enforcement. Property rights to use the broadcast frequency spectrum are distributed in ways chosen by public policy. The government could leave them to the market's allocation by auctioning off perpetual rights and letting their owners use or trade them as they wish. The actual choice of U.S. policymakers was quite different. Components of the spectrum resource were allocated by the FCC under temporary licenses assigned free of charge to the applicants deemed best suited to hold them. The rationale of this policy held that the airwaves represent a public resource, and their use should be placed in the hands of those broadcasters who pledge to provide programming that supplies maximum benefits to the public. Advocates of this procedure had in mind various "merit good" aspects of broadcast programming that would be underprovided by a profit-maximizing broadcaster. News and public affairs broadcasts, contributing to an informed citizenry and thereby more democratic participation and better public policy decisions, have been a central focus of these concerns. Other merit-good uses could provide education and raise moral fiber (e.g., educational children's programming). And, of course, many people believe that broadcasters should be deterred from various sorts of "demerit programming" such as scenes of violence that would degrade the moral and social fiber of the audience (children especially).[49] Whatever one's attitude toward the principle of governmental regulation of programs' merit, the practical problem is that no substantially complete and enforced contracts ever came into existence between the U.S. government and the broadcast station licensees as to what rules they need to follow in order to retain their licenses. The stations indeed face a dire but rarely exercised threat of loss of license, and so they select their programs for broadcast on the basis of what they see as an appropriate compromise between profit-maximizing and "socially responsible" programming. The networks are not formally involved in this control process. As they are the source of most programs broadcast by commercial stations, however, their self-censorship governs the stations' programming options.

What happens to a network's supply of merit programming when its audience, program quality, and profit all shrink? Merit programming must be presumed unprofitable—otherwise the networks and stations would provide it willingly. These commercial entities must of course at least break even to stay in business. Shrinkage of the commercial market therefore leaves less room between minimum viable and actual profit for "donation" to provide merit programs.

"Minimum viable profit" in economics refers to the sufficiency of revenues to cover costs. For publicly traded corporations, however, there is another constraint: the level of profit below which takeovers are mounted by raiders (individuals or firms) less willing than the incumbent management to forgo profit for merit. This is exactly what happened to the Big 3 networks, whose incumbent managers had honored some forms of merit programming more than their owners thought viable or appropriate to the shrinking profit stream. As their main tribute to this social contract, each network had maintained an extensive news-gathering organization, a badge of "public trust," bestowed on broadcasting by government license and worn with pride by the network news organizations themselves. Surveying this scene around 1990, Ken Auletta observed that the networks' news organizations faced little budgetary constraint. Network officials lacked rudimentary data on the cost or revenue productivity of the news organizations' various activities and products. At NBC, an outside consultant's report identified abundant redundancy in the news organization: many correspondents in reserve for "crisis" events that (by definition) seldom occur, many stories gathered relative to the number used.[50] One might argue that this redundancy was responsive to the public interest in a well-informed citizenry. The point, though, is that no such treaty or judgment existed, and each network's allocation of resources to news gathering and other merit activities was the result of internal decision making (or bargaining). By the late 1990s the networks were evidently economizing on their news operations, with cuts in their news staffs, intensified use of news product in magazine shows, and sharing of news personnel and facilities with affiliated cable networks.[51] In 2002 ABC negotiated unsuccessfully with the (unaffiliated) CNN cable news channel over a possible merger that could much reduce their combined fixed costs.[52]

Changes in Control

The organizational slack in networks' news staffs and elsewhere (for example, the networks' owned-and-operated stations) associated with this wraithlike social contract has clearly been threatened by the squeeze on networks' profits. As often happens when profitable, oligopolistic industries must adjust to major adverse disturbances, incumbent managers were slow to overhaul their business strategies. The stock market thereupon exerted decisive pressure for a profit-seeking (profit-preserving) response. Depressed stock prices attract raiders, leading to changes in the management of the networks. CBS came under the control of Laurence Tisch, ABC was acquired by Capital Cities (a station group), and NBC (as part of RCA) was acquired by General Electric.[53] Each control change was followed by a campaign to lower costs and an attempt (not immediately successful) to stanch the flow of rents from the networks to their affiliated stations (Chapter 6).[54] Subsequent moves to economize by the networks cannot be tied closely to these control changes, but they were clearly a contributing factor. This intensified pressure on the networks to maximize profits could have accounted for some of the moves to reduce quality, thus qualifying the role for the mechanism of *endogenous fixed costs*.

Hard and Soft News

James T. Hamilton provides an ambitious study of how the networks adjusted the quality of their evening news programs in response to various pressures.[55] Many observers have charged that the networks' key evening news programs have undergone a dumbing-down process, shorting international and governmental news in favor of soft news about personalities, entertainment, and sports. One might attribute such a change to a general shift of American cultural interests away from political and business events and leaders to the various branches of the entertainment industry.[56] Hamilton, however, offers an explanation specific to TV that requires no general cultural shift. The elderly (fifty and over, in Nielsen's categories) are proportionally the most numerous viewers of evening news. Advertisers, however, are willing to pay more (per thousand) for younger (and especially female) viewers (eighteen to thirty-four). That target group has a relatively strong preference for soft news. The networks have been under pressure to squeeze more profit (or eliminate losses) from their news broadcasts by reducing the hard news content and increasing the soft. Older listeners would be displeased, but they are in any case enthusiastic viewers of news and would not desert the newscasts, while younger viewers would be attracted. The change would probably increase total viewers and would certainly raise advertisers' willingness to pay. Hamilton documents the softening over time of the content of networks' evening news broadcasts. The explanation for this softening may be pressure on the networks to exact more profit from their news operations, but another factor seems also to contribute. The production of traditional hard news broadcasts, in particular international news, is an expensive operation, requiring far-flung correspondents available to swing into action on short notice. While evidence is not easily provided, soft news would seem less costly to collect—indeed, much of it comes to the newscaster's door. Thus, the softening of network news might be due at least in part to the mechanism of *endogenous fixed costs*. The advertisers' craving for young viewers is a sufficient but perhaps not necessary explanation. Still another possible explanation is competition from cable news networks (CNN, CNBC, MSNBC, Fox News). While these offer various mixtures of news products, they arguably compete more vigorously and effectively at the hard end of the news spectrum.

Declining Audience and Competition among the Networks

This section deals with ways in which the shrinking audience affects competition among the networks and thereby feeds back to influence the rate of decline.

Economizing on Programs' Preparation

Beyond the shift toward cheaper unscripted programs, the networks have sporadically employed a number of cost-cutting measures that add up to endogenous reductions of quality in prime-time programming. These include using unknown actors, employing few sets, and shooting with a single camera and digital tape.[57] In 2002 NBC was casting about for hour dramas that could be produced for a license fee of $500,000 an episode, barely half their typical cost. In 2004 the Fox network created a separate producing unit assigned to explore systematically ways to economize on program costs.[58] Production abroad is one source of savings. Sundry previous attempts at economy programming have produced few hits, however.[59] Other predictable economies have been pursued. The squeeze reduced the number of pilots produced for the new season from an average of forty-five to fifty per Big 3 network to eighty-five for all of them in 1992–93. This amounts to a straightforward reduction in expected program quality, since *nobody knows* which show will succeed, and there is some chance that the next try might produce something better than any preceding pilot.[60] The high cost of pilots coupled with continued high failure rates for new programs did cause the networks to cast more widely for novel material or approaches.[61] Reduced overall expenditures on program development left the networks handing over smaller rents to talent, both writers and actors.[62]

Programs' Ratings and Turnover

The more the audience exogenously shifts away from the broadcast networks, the smaller should be the minimum rating (share of TV households tuned in to that program) that would keep a show alive on their schedules. The opportunity cost of a given program's survival is governed by the most promising alternative available to replace it. If the variance in perceived quality among replacement candidates stays unchanged, there is no expected gain from raising the ratings threshold for a show's survival.[63] Trade publications give the impression that the performance threshold for survival was raised in the 1980s and 1990s as oligopolistic rivalry intensified among the networks. But the large fixed cost of a new scripted program (pilot) and the eroding network audience imply a decline in the minimum rating needed for a show to survive. That effect seems recently to have grown more visible.[64] Networks hold fewer replacement candidates in reserve.

Broadcast Programs' Diversity

In at least one way, increased competition in broadcasting (stirred up by new broadcast networks, but cable networks as well) tends to retard the loss of audience to cable. The larger the broadcaster's profit from a given high rating, the greater the temptation to engage in head-to-head contests for the largest audiences, as with the Thursday night shootouts described in Chapter 1. As margins are squeezed and more broadcast networks offer programs, the lower the potential payout of pursuing such warfare relative to providing more differentiated programs (counter-programming). Differentiation here pertains not just to basic program types but also to a network's forgoing the placement of its most popular program of a given type opposite a rival's counterpart program. Halting that matching practice is welcome to viewers who do not use their VCRs for time-shifting.[65] Avoiding head-to-head contests should also tend to retard the movement of viewers to cable. Network executives' cognizance of counter-programming's charms demonstrates the dilemma that is involved.[66]

One glimmer of relaxed program rivalry is the dispersion of networks' chosen times for introducing new programs. While all debuts once occurred in one week in September, the autumn introduction period has become somewhat diffused, and some programs are introduced in the summer or later in the autumn.[67] The delayed introduction of some shows allows more time to refine them. It also permits more efficient promotion when viewers are not befuddled by a blizzard of new programs; viewers get more of a chance to sample any given new program. It removes the stigma of emergency replacement from random introductions. And it generally dampens the move-matching practices that used to govern the September introduction week.[68]

CHAPTER 5

Cable Networks and Upgraded Cable Programming

The audience diverted from broadcast programming is pulled by the spread of cable and satellite service and their enriched program offerings. Cable's expansion has two components. One is the spread of local cable systems, which reached 17.7 million households in 1980, 39.9 million in 1985, 54.9 million in 1990, 63.0 million in 1995, and 73.0 million in 2002. The other is the continually expanded channel capacity of cable systems, which increased from an average of nineteen per household in 1985 to sixty-two in 1999.[1] This growing capacity enlarged the number of cable networks within each household's reach and thus the typical household's willingness to pay for cable service. This process supplies an exogenously expanding market for each viable network. Those that entered early and claimed a place on most extant cable systems may have run out their growth opportunities, while later and more specialized entrants continue to enjoy such opportunities as cable systems' capacities grow.

This exogenous expansion of the market for cable programming ignited the mechanism of *endogenous fixed cost* and enlarged the investments in programming that cable networks could profitably incur. It also led many new networks to attempt to enter the market. The process thus involves an interplay of vertical and horizontal differentiation of cable's product. With cable programs being upgraded and broadcast programs downgraded (Chapter 4), the extent of vertical differentiation between them has shrunk. And with cable networks proliferating, their horizontal differentiation has filled out in the sense that more small niches of viewers' preferences get served, and more cable networks provide close substitutes in the larger niches. The TV programming market, in which separate suppliers formerly served broadcast and cable distributors, is now joining into one continuous market, *infinite variety.*

Ecology of Cable Networks

Requisites for Entry

As market entrants and participants, cable networks resemble their broadcast brethren. Each needs to assemble both a portfolio of programs and a far-reaching distribution network. The quantitative difference between cable and broadcasting is considerable, however, as shown by the sheer numbers of each class in operation. The seven English-language broadcast networks are dwarfed by 308 national cable networks (in 2003, an increase from 87 in 1992 and 145 in 1996).[2] The proportional rate of growth of the number of networks has held roughly constant since the early 1980s, and is likely to continue, owing to the expanded channel capacity of digital cable systems.[3] The process of establishing a network starts with a format or business plan, to identify the audience sought and the types and sources of programming to be offered. The format is shopped to the multi-system cable operators (MSOs) as a candidate for carriage on their local systems. Devising the format is not particularly costly, but the nascent network usually faces considerable uncertainty as to whether it can get carriage on enough cable systems (or get it quickly enough) to make its operation viable. The operating losses suffered while the new entrant attracts sufficient cable systems and viewers can be much larger than the cost of developing the format. For example, Fox News Channel invested $100 million by the time of its launch but was expected to lose up to $400 million in the next five years.[4] One consequence is to make the population of cable networks an imprecise concept. At any time, numerous entrepreneurial toes are dipped into the cable-system waters that will never result in viable entries.[5] According to one count, in 1995 more than thirty networks were slated to launch, but "postponed" because of inability to access channel capacity, inadequate finance, or other impediments.[6]

How Entrants Mobilize Their Assets

Since an entrant cable network needs to acquire both content and commitments to carriage on cable systems, entrants (like their incumbent predecessors) tend to be affiliated with or joint ventures of content producers, cable systems, or both. The CBS network started its (unsuccessful) Eye on People channel expecting to draw heavily on CBS News and *Sixty Minutes* for program material. Toon Disney was planned as an outlet for old Disney cartoons and a complement to the established Disney Channel. An earlier entrant of this type, Cartoon Network, became profitable quickly, thanks to its access to cartoons in the Warner Bros. library.[7] NBC's CNBC network (consumer and business news) drew on a joint venture between NBC and Dow Jones, providing it with world TV rights to Dow Jones business-related editorial material and resources.[8] Similarly, the sports news channel CNN/SI rested on an agreement between news network CNN, with its news-gathering capability, and the magazine *Sports Illustrated,* with its storytelling ability.[9] The women-oriented Oxygen channel was a project of veteran TV executive Geraldine Laybourne, talk-show star Oprah Winfrey, and the Carsey–Werner independent program studio. It also had strong financial backing.[10] The Odyssey channel, seeking to provide sophisticated family entertainment, involved an alliance of content producer Hallmark Entertainment, the puppeteer and producer Jim Henson, and Liberty Media (an affiliate of TCI, then a large MSO).[11] Rainbow Media, owned by Cablevision Systems (a major MSO) and NBC, has launched a diverse group of networks over the years.[12] By 1997 NBC had acquired equity in about twenty cable networks, in the spirit of options on any opportunities that they might uncover as well as to make use of NBC's intangible assets.[13] These examples correctly convey the impression that entrant cable networks depend heavily on cheap sources of programming that could be recycled from vaults or adapted from the resources of broadcast-program suppliers. Other input suppliers may also help to bankroll new networks. Advertisers sometimes commit to future ad-spot purchases at very heavily discounted prices.[14]

MSOs hold minority blocks of shares in many cable networks. This pattern is studied in Chapter 9, where the reasons for the minority status are considered.

The fact that entrant networks can collect the necessary assets—discrete, heterogeneous, and not available on competitive markets—is the good news. The bad news is that joint ventures, a natural vehicle for assembling them, suffer from organizational and governance problems that can lead to disputes, underperformance, and even dissolution. These are prevalent among the cable network coalitions. The E! Entertainment network once belonged to a media firm with a majority share and a group of cable operators holding minority stakes. It received nobody's close attention and survived on crusts of syndicated broadcast programming. A transfer of ownership to Disney and the MSO Comcast led to a much-elevated programming budget and a coherent strategy.[15] Another problem is that the interests and situations of joint-venture partners can shift over time, owing to changes in their other business assets and conditions in other markets where they operate. They can come to prefer mutually inconsistent policies for their shared venture. An example is the Court TV channel, which was owned by NBC, Time Warner, and Liberty Media and run by its founder, Steven Brill. Time Warner had acquired Turner Broadcasting, making its owner, Ted Turner, a power within Time Warner. Turner was the founder and still proud parent of CNN (Cable News Network), and was fearful that Court TV would compete with CNN. He sought to merge Court TV with CNNfn, one of CNN's channels that had attained very limited carriage (relative to Court TV) on cable systems. This proposal displeased Brill, who left the company when his offer to buy out Turner was declined. It also displeased NBC, which saw the merged networks as a close competitor to its own CNBC. Court TV was left in the hands of Time Warner and Liberty Media, which had been withholding its capital contributions on account of the bickering.[16] Such shifting interests and incentive problems in joint ventures have led to buyouts and reversion to single ownership.[17]

Entry Barriers and Niche Strategies

Cable entrants' practice of arriving with bundles of assets testifies to both the extent and character of barriers to entry into this market. Incumbents do enjoy an advantage of position, in that contracts for carriage and goodwill with viewers provide a substantial first-mover advantage, and the entrant facing an incumbent competitor can expect a disproportionately smaller profit.[18] This advantage is demonstrated by the mean difference in the number of households reached (penetration rates) by early entrants and by recently founded cable networks. We selected the fifty basic cable networks with launch dates early enough to have celebrated their fifth birthdays by 2001 and observed their penetration rates in that year (Table 5.1). The networks were arrayed by founding date and grouped by deciles. Note that almost half of them were launched re-

TABLE 5.1 Percentage of U.S. cable homes receiving cable networks five years after their launch date, by networks' order of entry

Entry cohort	Time of launch	Mean penetration rate	Standard deviation
1–10	1976–1982	61.7%	18.6%
11–20	1982–1987	54.9	26.1
21–30	1988–1994	52.3	24.1
31–40	1994–1995	36.0	21.5
41–50	1995–1996	36.1	28.9

Source: Calculated from Kagan World Media, *Economics of Basic Cable Networks 2002* (Carmel, Calif.: Kagan World Media, 2001), pp. 42–43.

cently, 1994 through 1996. The table shows that their mean penetration rates drop substantially from the earliest entrants to the most recent two years, and their standard deviations tend to increase as if penetration were growing more risky. A particularly striking case is the rivalry around 1995 between AMC (American Movie Classics, entered 1984) and the newer Turner Classic Movies. Ted Turner made foresighted investments in film libraries of the MGM, RKO, and Warner Bros. movie studios and accessed 4,500 to 5,000 films, compared to AMC's 1,000. Yet AMC reached 54 million households, Turner only 3 million, and Turner had no effective way to erase AMC's lead.[19] Bundles of assets can be mobilized to achieve parity with incumbents, as the coalition-based entrants show, but the available bundles are few and must be assembled by contract—not just bought on some open market.[20] Symmetrically, bundles of assets held by their incumbent direct competitors shrink the cash flows that entrants can expect to capture. A crucial point is that many of the relevant assets—film libraries are an excellent example—have fixed and sunk costs and no incremental cost when put to competitive uses. This is the *ars longa* property of creative industries.

Incumbents' first-mover advantages tend to divert the entrant toward occupying an empty niche rather than pushing into a larger but already occupied turf. The historical pattern of entry confirms this. The opportunities for new cable networks showing a broad range of programs, such as USA and TBS, apparently closed in the 1990s, and subsequent entrants have concentrated increasingly on finding niches that are unoccupied or not fully served by incumbents.[21] The Outdoor Channel appealed successfully to men who hunt, fish, and/or prospect.[22] Black Entertainment Television (BET) entered successfully, charging a low price to cable operators and relying heavily on advertising revenues. Some specialized cable networks can often obtain high prices (CPMs) for their ad spots by providing in concentrated form an audience that an advertiser cannot effectively reach otherwise.[23] In 2002 Viacom's incumbent networks MTV and Showtime began exploring a premium-tier (pay) channel aimed at gay viewers.[24]

First-mover advantages also imply a readily confirmed fact: the incumbent cable networks have themselves been prominent organizers of new networks. These usually provide close-in extensions of the programming already offered by the network, so that their cost of development is modest. The cost associated with gaining access to cable systems remains substantial, although some bundling with the parent network may smooth the way. Many such extension networks have been developed recently to occupy the much-enlarged channel capacity that will accompany digital cable.[25] Instances of strategic expansion to stave off or preempt entrants or incumbent rivals are discussed subsequently.

As the population of cable networks expands and niches become occupied, new entrants trying their luck can squeeze into still narrower niches, expected to provide smaller audiences. Or they can seek to claim segments of large niches that contain one or more fairly close competitors—rivals who may react by modifying their own programming.

Rivalry among Incumbent Networks

Entry and Aftermath

The continual expansion of cable systems' channel capacities aids the entrant by sparing it the need to displace incumbent networks, even as it competes with other novices. When systems have no idle channels, however, the entrant must make an offer sufficiently attractive to induce the operator to dump an incumbent. The contract between cable system and basic cable network involves a payment per subscriber per month as small as ten cents for a low-profile niche channel, or as much as $1.50 for a network such as ESPN that supplies costly program content. An entrant might hope to offer a format novel or attractive enough to displace an incumbent on merit. Commonly, though, it must knuckle down and compete on price. Systems and MSOs that sign early with new networks enjoy heavily discounted prices and front-end concessions (e.g., no charges in the first year).[26] Nowadays, entrant networks must usually offer cable operators substantial up-front payments to gain carriage. News Corp. spent heavily to establish Fox News Channel, its politically conservative competitor to CNN, apparently offering launch fees that averaged $10 per subscriber and may have reached $14.[27] As an alternative Fox considered offering TCI, then a giant MSO, a 20 percent equity stake in Fox News.[28] Refurbished and upgraded channels also may offer per-subscriber payments in order to expand their coverage.[29]

The consequences of these offers obviously should depend on the reaction of incumbent networks to would-be entries. The business press contains no reports of payments by marginal incumbents to keep their places, although suspended networks have sometimes mounted extensive campaigns to rouse loyal viewers to protest.[30] The entrants' offers, though, interact with the pricing practices of incumbent networks, which commonly raise their monthly subscriber charge by a few cents each year, and more when contracts come up for renewal. While these increases are consistent with the upgrading of cable networks' programming (discussed subsequently), to some degree they also extract rents accessible to successful incumbents, owing to their advantages of position over entrants. These increases meet vigorous resistance from cable operators, who add them onto subscribers' monthly cable bills but then face the wrath of viewers who are unaware that the cable networks are the culprits. The cable operators then lose out in the ensuing public-relations battle, getting the blame when the cable network pulls its signal in order to enforce its demand for higher subscriber fees. In 2004 disputes of this type spread to the Dish Satellite distributor.[31] With only two satellite distributors in the market, they might be thought to enjoy more monopsony (buying) power, and some evidence suggests that they do. At the time of their start-up, however, they had to pay generously to get into the market, and this premium has not vanished.[32] Some interaction can be detected between the rate of increase of the incumbents' charges and the supply of entrants. Between 1991 and 1996, carriage fees to incumbent basic networks rose on average 18.8 percent annually; in the wake of News Corp.'s bribes for carriage of Fox News, this inflation rate was projected to drop to 7.6 percent in 1997.[33]

Relevant to the rivalry between entrants and incumbents is the possibility of an incumbent's substantially changing its programming and repositioning itself. Indeed, if repositioning is inexpensive, an entrant gains the leverage of potentially being able to expel an incumbent from a niche (by forcing losses if it remains in its current domicile). The evidence from a few cases, however, suggests that repositioning is hazardous and costly. Loyal viewers are forsaken, new audiences are untested *(nobody knows),* and cable operators may seize the opportunity to reopen the carriage agreement, with adverse consequences.[34] Incremental changes of position can result, though, from competition with entrants or simply the process of upgrading a network's programs (discussed subsequently). In sum, *infinite variety* clearly applied to the universe of potential cable network formats; diversity is limited but still extensive among actual networks.

Retransmission

Entrants' purchases of tickets of admission took another form associated with a Federal Communications Commission (FCC) policy. The FCC has long been concerned lest local broadcasting stations should be starved out by their cable competitors through refusal to carry the broadcast signal, and so it has required each cable system to carry the signals of all broadcasters deemed to operate in its market. This policy was overturned by the courts in 1985 but restored by Congress in 1992.[35] It leaves open the question whether one party should pay the other for what is (in effect) a joint venture: the cable operator can offer broadcast programs desired by its local subscribers, while the broadcaster can collect revenue from advertisers for the additional viewers reached through cable. Under the 1992 legislation, broadcasters held a right to retransmission and could simply demand it from the local cable operator without compensation. Or the broadcaster could forgo this option and take its chances—negotiating for payment for carriage from the cable operator but facing the chance of losing carriage if a stalemate was reached. The cable operators successfully stonewalled demands for cash payments to carry the broadcasters' signals. The station groups and broadcast networks, however (negotiating on behalf of their owned stations), were able to extract value in kind by obtaining carriage for cable networks (often of modest pretensions) created just for this purpose. A number of cable networks unlikely otherwise to enter a cable box obtained carriage this way.[36] Indeed, most broadcast networks and station groups launched or acquired cable networks solely to reap the rents created by the FCC's retransmission policy.[37]

Normative Issues

The turnover of cable networks raises two questions about the economic efficiency of the process. Suppose that incumbent networks' annual price increases are not always regarded by cable operators as justified by improved program quality.[38] Suppose also that incumbents get no chance to bribe cable operators bent on ejecting them for replacement by bribe-paying entrants. In that case networks carried on cable systems will turn over excessively, with some incumbents that create more value (enjoy viewers' greater willingness to pay) getting dropped for entrants that will create less. Events matching this scenario are reported in the trade press.[39] Clearly, this will not happen if incumbents can open their wallets and bid to retain their channels. How and why they should avoid such auctions is not evident.

The second question concerns the rent extracted in some cable networks' monthly per-subscriber charges. The prime example is ESPN, at the mercy of professional sports leagues' demands for the cash that viewers will surrender in order to watch their heroes on the playing field. ESPN can only pass the bill along to cable operators, who in turn roll it into the subscriber's charges.[40] This increment to the monthly cable bill will drive away some sports-phobic cable customers who gain insufficient pleasure from the other channels that they watch. Is a market failure involved? Consider this example. In a cable system's basic tier ESPN is bundled with ten miscellaneous, competitively supplied networks. The cable system's customers consist of one hundred sports fanatics each valuing ESPN at $2 a month, and one hundred ordinary viewers who value each of the ten miscellaneous channels at ten cents a month. The competitive channels charge a fee of zero per subscriber (covering their fixed costs with ad revenue). The sports fanatics get no utility from the miscellaneous channels, the ordinary viewers none from ESPN. If ESPN charges $1 a month per subscriber, and the cable operator simply passes this charge along to customers, both ordi-

nary viewers and sports fanatics will subscribe (the ordinary viewers buy the bundle to receive the miscellaneous channels), and
ESPN will earn $200 a month. If ESPN charges $2 a month, only
the sports fanatics will subscribe, and ESPN again earns $200 a
month. Suppose that goodwill considerations cause ESPN to prefer
the $1 charge. Now let the sports fanatics' valuation double to $4
per month each. ESPN will prefer to charge $4 per subscriber, driv-
ing away the ordinary viewers and absorbing all the rents from the
sports fanatics to earn $400. This outcome of bundled pricing
shows that the sports fanatics in the first case benefit from being
pooled with the ordinary viewers (who get served, but enjoy no net
surplus after paying their $1); in the second case ESPN extracts the
maximum rent from the sports fanatics while leaving the ordinary
viewers unserved (though no worse off). The example could easily
be modified so that the ordinary viewers enjoy some consumers'
surplus when cable is priced to serve them, none when it is priced to
extract maximum surplus from the sports fanatics. On the one
hand, the ordinary viewers would be no worse off, and generally
better off, not being bundled with the sports fanatics, who themselves generally gain from being bundled. On the other hand, ESPN
does not benefit from being bundled.[41] In practice, sports leagues
have acted as if their interest lay in being bundled with other networks on the cable system's basic channel, capturing some surplus
from the sports-indifferent viewers. The cable systems have aggressively sought to segregate the high-price sports leagues in separate
bundles, implying that some of their own profits are being captured.[42]

If the cable systems' technology allowed them to transmit to each
household its preferred bundle of networks, households would gain
immunity from rent extractors in such bundled transactions. But
the cable operator itself might want to employ bundled offers as a
price-discrimination device. Policymakers have shown some interest in requiring cable systems to offer unbundled channels to view-

ers, protecting them from rent extraction through price discrimination by both cable network and cable system.[43] Cable operators have objected vigorously, asserting that a limit on bundling would shrink the number of viable channels. The welfare economics of the issue prove complex. Offering only a bundle, or offering it at a large discount to single channels bought à la carte, amounts to an "all or nothing offer," which should indeed increase the number of viable channels. Its attraction lies in the bundle purchaser's ability to view another channel at no additional charge, in line with the operator's zero marginal cost.[44] Furthermore, most viewers probably value the option of access to channels that they do not normally watch, because the continual turnover of programs can always turn up something interesting on an unexpected channel. Ideally, cable operators would charge a bundled price that would exclude only those costly programs–the ESPNs and HBOs–appealing to a select but eager audience. That is close to the pricing system actually in force.

Patterns of Rivalry

How incumbent networks compete with one another matters for the roster of programs they present to the public. Generalizations come hard, but a few illustrations can suggest what is at issue. Subscription price and related terms do affect cable networks' competitive positions, but they tend not to compete actively on price. For example, CMT (Country Music Television) in 1998 found itself facing an entrant rival, Great American Country, little differentiated from CMT but offering up-front payments to cable operators, lower subscription fees, and twice as many ad spots for local sale by the operator. CMT had lost a million subscribers (out of 41 million) to the entrant, but Great American's terms were so generous that CMT elected to rely on its superior video library and exclusive deals with some popular artists, stick to its price, and accept the (slow) erosion of its subscriber base.[45]

Competition in the quality and style of programs seems more common, as illustrated by the rivalry among women's channels. In 2000 Lifetime (reaching 31 million homes) faced the well-endowed entrant Oxygen Media (described previously) as well as an incumbent, WE (Women's Entertainment, formerly Romance Classics), offering escapist fare. Lifetime once was noted for saccharine scripts and themes of women in peril. Through both its basic style and its quality programming, Oxygen sought to differentiate itself from Lifetime by appealing to a more discerning and self-aware audience.[46] Also, Oxygen, which had raised $450 million, planned to make heavy use of its Web site, regarded as a major route of appeal to its viewers. Lifetime responded, however, considerably elevating the seriousness of its programming, tripling its programming budget (with a focus on new movies and shows), and doubling its advertising outlays. It managed to become the highest-rated cable network in prime time. Oxygen met with cool responses from critics. Its Web strategy failed in the manner of its kind, and its distribution expanded only slowly. Oxygen, however, was infused with additional cash and got itself on New York City's main cable system. That gain coincided with a successful new push for original programming, and its backers brought it high-profile off-network syndication commitments—*Roseanne* in 2003.[47]

Other cases illustrate the opportunities for incumbents to deter entry, notably MTV in the pop music segment. In 1981 MTV pioneered a music channel aimed at teenage and young adult viewers and focused on broadcasting the promotional music videos that major record labels had been producing since the mid-1970s. Because airplay of videos led to palpably increased sales of recordings, MTV was for a time able to obtain rights to broadcast them without charge. In 1983, now reaching 22 percent of U.S. TV households, MTV began charging cable operators.[48] Competition arrived in 1984 when Ted Turner denounced MTV as a corrupter of the young and started Cable Music Channel as a sanitized rival. He picked a moment when a number of MTV's affiliation contracts were expiring and offered CMC free to cable operators for five years. Although Turner's initiative was not fully credible to the cable operators, it did bestir MTV to start VH1, a network aimed at the same, somewhat older CMC viewers. VH1, which cost MTV little to develop, was distributed free to cable systems carrying MTV. Turner's channel survived for only five weeks, and two later entrants achieved no more long-run success.[49] VH1, paradoxically, staggered along for years without establishing an effective identity, but eventually settled into the pop-music-for-adults niche to which it was originally consigned.[50] Other instances of strategic introductions of new channels can be found, such as CNN's creation of CNN/SI to counter ESPN's invasion of the sports news market with ESPNNEWS.[51] MTV also defended its position by means of agreements with record labels that gave MTV a period of exclusive use of some fraction of a label's video releases. The agreements also stipulated that no other channel should be allowed to broadcast a video before MTV. MTV's payments of cash and advertising spots made it profitable for the record labels to abet this restraint on competition. The labels kept the desirability of these restraints under review, but most continued to accept them.[52] Exclusivity agreements with content providers who are few in number provide an entry deterrent in other cable segments as well, notably the premium movie channels. A competitor or entrant can bid away such assets, but first-mover advantages tend to make that unprofitable.[53]

Improvement of Program Quality

Basic Cable's Two Income Streams

Basic cable networks enjoy a fundamental advantage over their broadcast cousins for covering their fixed costs: they receive income from both the sale of ads and the monthly per-subscriber fees paid by cable operators. To observe how this advantage is used, we obtained data for sixty-nine basic cable networks and calculated the ratio of license fee revenue in the year 2000 to the sum of that and net advertising revenue (net of advertising agency commissions).[54] We simply ranked the networks from the lowest to the highest values of this ratio and looked for common characteristics of networks clustered in particular parts of the distribution. A heavy concentration of ratios occurs between 20 and 50 percent (the median is 42 percent). The most popular and longest-established networks are heavily concentrated between 30 and 50 percent. Thus, the typical network relies more on ad revenue than on subscriber fees, but the fees make a substantial contribution—to fixed costs generally, and to the networks' ability to fund upgraded programming.

Several clusters of similar channels appear in the distribution. A distinctive group of channels rely heavily on license fees (75 to 100 percent)—old-movie channels and channels that seem to appeal to high-income households (Golf, Ovation, Trio). The Disney Channel is also ad free. Willingness to pay for programs rather than endure ads may be a "normal good," its consumption increasing with income. Networks relying little on license fees (0 to 20 percent) include those reaching audiences otherwise difficult for advertisers to access (Lifetime, Tech TV) and hence probably getting high ad prices. They also include networks with young audiences who might be relatively receptive to advertising (MTV, VH1, A&E, Comedy Central, CMT, Great American Country). The sports networks draw relatively high shares of their revenue from license fees: ESPN just under 50 percent and ESPN2, ESPN Classic, Speedvision, and Fox Sports all in the 50 to 70 percent range. While advertisers welcome their audiences, the viewers' own high willingness to pay translates into rents for the sports leagues that get collected in high subscriber fees.

Thus, the cable networks seem to optimize their mix of revenue sources as an aspect of setting each type of fee at its profit-maximizing level. We now consider whether the recent substantial increases in both subscriber fees and ad revenue are consistent with this impression. Are these increases proceeding toward an imminent limit of market equilibrium? Is it relevant that the U.S. government has twice intervened to cap cable operators' charges to households, including the basic cable networks' per-subscriber charges?

Conditions for Increased Program Outlays

The upgrade of cable networks' programming can be documented in various ways. One is the plethora of large boosts in annual programming budgets reported in the trade press. These frequently follow increases in the number of cable systems carrying a network and the associated increase in total subscribership and/or in Nielsen ratings.[55] They also occur during bouts of active rivalry between networks. They follow increases in advertisers' "interest" in a cable network; interest may or may not mean actually increased ad revenue, since the networks seem confident that original programming (versus reruns) will support higher ad prices (CPMs).[56] Upgraded quality induced by growth in subscribers is an important mechanism, reflecting as it does the phenomenon of *endogenous fixed costs* that drives so many processes of change in broadcasting. An initial impression is provided by the annual percentage increases in combined programming expenses of the basic cable networks estimated by Kagan World Media.[57] Keep in mind that these reflect both increased spending by incumbent networks and new networks entering the market. These annual increases rose from an average of 21 percent in 1985–1987 to 36 percent in 1988–1990. They then plunged to 15 percent in 1991–1993, likely owing to the regulatory cap (rollback) imposed by the FCC on cable systems' subscriber charges, following legislation passed in 1992. This regulation was removed in 1996, however, and growth rates revived to 18 percent during 1996–1999. Thus, although lower than the growth rates in the 1980s when cable networks were first establishing themselves, aggregate growth rates in the latter 1990s are consistent with the large discrete jumps reported in the trade press for some cable networks.[58]

Were these booming investments in programming a leap of faith in cable's future, or did they follow on tangible successes that the networks were enjoying? A close statistical tie between a cable network's increasing outlays on programming and its swelling revenues would confirm the importance of the mechanism of *endogenous fixed costs* and tend to put aside other influences. We related data from Kagan World Media on individual basic cable networks' annual outlays on programming (rights and program production) from 1989 through 2000 to assorted measures of their current and prospective cash inflow—net advertising revenue (net of advertising agencies' commission), license fee revenue, the monthly license fee per subscriber, and the total number of households subscribing. We dropped networks that underwent a major change in format and/or ownership and networks started after 1994 (hence yielding no more than four full-year observations after a one-year lag is incorporated in the relationship). The Disney network was dropped owing to its shift from the premium to the basic tier. We were left with thirty cable networks and 291 network-year observations.

We employed a simple fixed-effects regression model of programming expenditures in year t as a function of license fee revenue and of net advertising revenue in year $t - 1$. The model was estimated in both natural units and logarithms, although we expected that the networks' decision rules would alight on fractions of revenue dollars plowed back into programming rather than proportional changes in revenue and outlays (thus favoring natural units). The results appear in Table 5.2, in which the models differ only in the fixed effects included. As expected, models (1) through (4) estimated in dollar units show substantially higher explanatory power than models (5) through (8) estimated in logarithms. (Firms make

TABLE 5.2 Summary of coefficients, regression of networks' programming expenses on lagged license fee revenue and net advertising revenue

	License fee revenue	Net ad revenue	Year dummies?	Network dummies?	$\overline{R}^2$
Estimated in dollar units					
1.	0.59	0.41	N	N	0.86
	(20.0)	(16.3)			
2.	0.76	0.38	Y	N	0.89
	(23.0)	(11.7)			
3.	0.34	0.40	N	Y	0.98
	(10.2)	(19.6)			
4.	0.31	0.39	Y	Y	0.98
	(8.9)	(16.9)			
Estimated in logarithms					
5.	0.22	0.18	N	N	0.57
	(13.7)	(11.4)			
6.	0.18	0.26	Y	N	0.63
	(10.4)	(13.9)			
7.	0.05	0.44	N	Y	0.94
	(3.6)	(16.3)			
8.	0.01	0.20	Y	Y	0.96
	(0.9)	(7.3)			

Notes: t-statistics appear in parentheses beneath coefficients; each equation is estimated on 291 observations.

decisions about dollar amounts, not growth rates.) The coefficients of both exogenous variables are highly significant except for the coefficient of license fee revenue when all fixed effects are included. In the dollar-unit models the coefficient of net advertising revenue consistently implies that each extra dollar of revenue is associated with about forty cents' increase in programming outlays. The marginal advertising dollars of course respond to previous increases in carriage and subscribers as well as the basic seismic process that lures advertisers to cable from other outlets (including broadcast

TV). The coefficient of license fee revenue is highly sensitive to the inclusion of fixed effects but does alight on a figure slightly over thirty cents when network fixed effects are included. Since much of the variation in the data is between networks, our faith should be placed chiefly in models that include network fixed effects. Models (5) through (8), estimated in logarithms, show more instability in the coefficients as well as less explanatory power, but they do not contradict the conclusion that programming outlays depend strongly on preceding revenue flows.

Upgraded programming should increase viewers' willingness to pay for a cable channel, so we expect that the forces encouraging enlarged programming outlays would also increase the networks' profit-maximizing monthly charges per subscriber. Monthly subscriber charges were regressed on combinations of the lagged revenue inflows already mentioned. The models show considerable instability depending on which fixed effects are included. The lagged number of subscribers is generally not a significant determinant of monthly charges. It may be that new networks give the upgrade of their programming low priority while they are striving to achieve a high level of national coverage.[59] License fees are positively and significantly related to lagged advertising revenues, but the coefficient varies greatly with the fixed effects included. Most variance in license fees is between networks. Little variance appears over time within networks, since the individual network commonly boosts its monthly charges by a penny or two every year. It seems clear that cable networks collect revenue that reflects their subscribers' willingness to pay for better programs, but no robust relationship to the networks' revenue growth can be pinned down.

Upgrading, Differentiation, and Rivalry

Except for news and sports channels, cable networks in earlier years relied heavily on the syndication market for reruns. Original programming was confined to talk shows and similar inexpensive fare. The common denominator of most networks' efforts to upgrade was to provide "quality" original programming to replace reruns, or to raise the quality of originals already supplied. The percentage of original programming is a commonly mentioned indicator of the network's vertical differentiation. Yet upgrading also embraces higher-value off-network syndication (programs less stale or more popular originally).

Original and Licensed Films

The process of upgrading a cable network's programming often accompanies a shift in the mix of programs. Shifts in quality of the network's programming can potentially widen or reposition its audience, increase audience loyalty, or improve the network's strategic position vis-à-vis its close rivals. An attractive practice for many cable networks has been to offer original movies or miniseries. Documentaries serve the same role.[60] In contrast to broadcasters' prime-time series, these can be promoted as special, distinctive products without the network incurring the downside risk of a series program—a season's worth of episodes of a palpable turkey. Movies can be recycled—licensed abroad or packaged for licensing to other networks. They can be focused on subject matter suited to the network's niche. They can be repeated numerous times and perhaps swapped with other networks (especially corporate siblings).[61] Furthermore, movies can, within limits, be ordered to suit the network's budget, so that one form of upgrading takes the network from $2–$4 million budgets to $15 million budgets for each film (plus substantial promotion outlays).[62] Original films were once confined to cable networks offering broad and diversified programs (TNT, USA Network, plus premium networks such as HBO), but they have spread to the more specialized networks—Fox (now ABC) Family, E! Entertainment, FX, VH1, A&E—as the exogenous enlargement of demand has come to justify the fixed costs. The intensified concentration of the Hollywood studios on blockbusters for teenage audiences has widened the potential audience for original films on the cable networks. Another positive factor is the international market for TV movies and documentary programs, making it worthwhile for a cable network to obtain international rights to its upgraded programs.[63] The networks regard movies and other specials as generating a "brand" identity for them—presumably meaning that viewers adopt more favorable expectations about the quality and character of the entertainment that a cable network offers.[64] Syndicated reruns, by contrast, project no coherent image for the network showing them.

Another way for a cable network to upgrade its movie offerings is simply to bid for licenses to show recent, popular cinema films. Cable networks have made many deals with broadcast networks to license prominent films, sometimes with the cable network getting the first TV showing. The collaborative deals have tended to occur, though not exclusively, within corporate families.[65] In the exhibition queue for cinema films, cable networks are ensconced ahead of independent TV stations, partly because the entry of new broadcast networks has depleted the independent stations and shrunk the duration of their film license contracts.[66]

Series Programs

Traditional dramatic series programs have also played their part in upgrading cable networks. By virtue of their specialized audiences and freedom to pursue mature subject matter, they can readily differentiate themselves from over-the-air network series. They can enlarge the core audience for a specialized cable network, and increasingly they have a shot at rents obtained from off-cable syndication.[67] The FX Network developed *The Shield,* an unusual series about a rogue police detective, intended to provide quality programs while differentiating the network from Fox, on the one hand, and HBO *(The Sopranos),* on the other.[68] The more specialized cable networks especially have developed series programs cautiously for their particular audiences rather than relying on the broadcast networks' traditional barrage of pilots.[69] An exception, though, is MTV, which carries *nobody knows* to its ultimate, trying large numbers of quickly produced series, in response to the changing fads among its youthful audience. These are generated by both in-house teams and independent producers, each allowed to run freely with any green-lighted proposal.[70] An alternative to ordering original series is to pick up series that were cancelled after they began life on broadcast networks. Because programs can be profitably shown to much smaller audiences on cable than on broadcast networks, failed network programs can sometimes thrive after transplant. An aborted broadcast series may fit well with a cable network's niche position, where it can gain enough audience to warrant the continued production of new episodes.[71] For the purchase of new episodes to continue, though, it is sometimes necessary to devise ways to cut production costs. For example, Fox's program *Sliders,* cancelled in 1997, went to the Sci-Fi Channel, with producer Universal Television cooperating to get production costs down from the $1.5 million for Fox episodes to something approaching $750,000 (studio set, reduced compensation to actors in exchange for the show's guaranteed continuation).[72] Cable buyers may simply license the stock of episodes of a cancelled series made for broadcast as an off-network syndication, paying perhaps one-tenth of their production cost.[73]

The other way to upgrade series programs is by bidding for superior material in the off-network syndication market—more popular programs, earlier in their rerun cycles. A favored investment of this type has been the one-hour adventure drama, not popular in the broadcast syndication market but sometimes a good fit for a cable network. Thus, the newly refurbished National Network (formerly

The Nashville Network) spent $500,000 per episode for the off-syndication action-adventure program *VIP*.[74] Among popular sit-coms *Ellen* was the first to debut in syndication on cable—Lifetime Channel, with its obvious affinity for the program.[75] Cable networks have won some expensive auctions for off-network syndications of popular programs. These include the acquisition of *Seinfeld* by TBS and of *Ally McBeal* and *The Practice* by the FX network. Each of these transactions took place between units of the same media conglomerate, suggesting that an internal hedge encourages more risk-taking behavior.[76] An encouraging factor is that syndicators seem able to sell bartered ad spots on cable as readily as on broadcast outlets.[77]

A common feature of much upgraded cable programming is that it combines serious and mature subject matter with a certain amount of spicy ("cutting edge") content. The broadcast networks in their primordial social contract accepted a substantial amount of self-censorship that excludes both seriousness and spice from their programming. While they have pushed this envelope with increasing vigor, the constraint remains important: witness NBC's public outcry about its hands-tied position.[78] The cable networks, free to respond to their viewers' tastes, have had the opportunity to work both dimensions, often simultaneously—not surprisingly, given that many substantial works of literature manage to combine seriousness with erotic content.[79] *South Park,* a popular cartoon program featuring foul-mouthed grade-schoolers, was shopped widely by its creators to both broadcast and cable networks before being picked up by the (then) low-rated Comedy Central network.[80] In 2004, however, the FCC was pressing the cable networks to intensify their self-policing.[81] An interesting sidelight on this issue is the ambiguity felt by cable network programmers about the medium's reliance on professional wrestling. As of 1998, five of the ten most popular programs on cable were wrestling shows. Ad spots, once sold cheaply to advertisers of motor oil and do-it-yourself products, came to fetch good prices (CPMs). Yet several networks found wrestling's lower-income and less-educated viewers meshing poorly with their desires to upgrade programming.[82]

As mentioned previously, investments in upgraded programming often seek to shift and thereby enlarge the network's audience. Sports network ESPN, with four twenty-four-hour channels to fill, commissioned made-for-TV movies aimed to broaden its audience beyond the core sports fans and, incidentally, establish a line of programming not vulnerable to the rent-siphoning skills of the professional sports leagues, the source of much ESPN programming. The Home & Garden Television network enlarged its program budget by 40 percent to acquire a lengthy series of special programs appealing to viewers with interests running more to lifestyles than pruning shears.[83] Male- and sports-oriented TNT much increased its outlay for original movies, prime-time specials, and miniseries designed to attract a broader, more female audience.[84] The Learning Channel, conceived as explicitly educational, leavened its "Great Books" series with more immediately appealing types of programs. One wonders whether these decisions to broaden the program mix of specialized channels might prove self-defeating by making them closer substitutes for other diversifying cable networks while diluting their appeal to hardcore buffs.

Networks' decisions to upgrade their programming of course often respond to upgrading and other competitive moves by their close rivals. Nickelodeon attributed its 25 percent increase in outlays on programs for the 1999 season to intensified competition with direct rival Disney Channel, The Cartoon Network, and Fox Family Channel.[85] The competitive escalation of program outlays among women's networks was described previously. That viewers continue on balance to shift away from the broadest cable nets suggests that this process has not run its course.[86]

Particularly interesting is the situation of premium channel HBO (and its sibling Cinemax), which faces competition from other premium channels relying heavily on cinema films (Showtime, Starz!) and from basic cable networks upgrading to movies. HBO enjoys a larger subscriber base than its premium competitors, so it can outbid them in rentals for showing recent box office hits while still spending much less per viewing household than would a smaller rival. Any network (basic or premium) can show cinema films, however, so HBO has also offered expensive miniseries *(Band of Brothers)* and high-profile series programs adroitly combining sex, violence, and serious themes *(The Sopranos)*.[87]

Convergence in Programming Market

The reduced vertical differentiation between broadcast and cable networks' programming implies that their once-separate markets are likely to converge into a largely continuous market for new and recycled programs. This outcome implies an increased flow of off-cable syndicated programs to over-the-air broadcast, countering the stream of hand-me-downs that has long passed from broadcasting to cable. Isolated examples of such flows go back years, but the volume does seem to have stepped up.[88] For example, *Politically Incorrect* was moved from Comedy Central to the ABC network's late evening time period, a slot for which ABC had unsuccessfully sought to develop its own program.[89] Several similar examples exist of shows styled to cable networks' distinctive needs and constraints that travel well to broadcast outlets—*nobody knows*.[90] In this vein Buena Vista Television (Disney's syndication unit) launched two game shows on cable networks with the expectation that they would go into syndication after a year, with the cable networks holding an equity share.[91] Programs successful on cable have come to be serious candidates for syndication to broadcast stations, with *Tales from the Crypt* and *The Hitchhiker* providing two examples of programs with successful runs in off-cable syndication.[92] Another transborder flow of programming is short-term rebroadcast on a different outlet; *It's Garry Shandling's Show* was rebroadcast thirty days after cable broadcast on Fox, a deal similar to the broadcast networks' recent heavy use of rebroadcast on cable.[93] Nickelodeon, the top-rated TV network for children's programming, found itself able to produce more quality programming than its own network required and started a syndication branch to market both new and off-cable shows.[94] The main limit on this flow of programming from cable may be not its general quality level but its targeting to particular demographic or interest groups of viewers and the cutting-edge character of many successful cable programs.[95]

Another form of trade in programs is implied by the increasing occupancy rate of the audience niches available for cable networks and the closeness of competition among them: *infinite variety* approached in practice. That is the exchange of program series among the cable networks. Examples are not abundant, but one involved *Breaking News,* a dramatic program developed by New Line Television for the TNT cable network (both are units of Time Warner). After paying for a pilot and twelve epiodes, TNT nonetheless decided not to run it. The Bravo network was pleased to take it over, however, apparently for a price that left most of TNT's sunk cost unrecouped.[96]

A recent convergence of broadcast and cable lies in the broadcast networks' burgeoning interest in cable networks as vehicles for early repeats of first-run broadcast programs. As Chapter 4 indicated, the most profitable number of repeats of a new episode may be greater than the broadcast networks' traditional single repeat on the original channel. Repeating on a different channel and time slot may attract more viewers and create more value. The broadcast networks have been aggressively increasing their equity holdings in cable networks to support this process. Disney (ABC) bought the Fox Family Channel, while NBC acquired full control of the Bravo network. CBS changed its Nashville Network into The National Network for this purpose, while Fox relied increasingly on its own FX cable network for short-run repeats.[97]

The contrary motion of quality levels of broadcast and cable programming implies that they should increasingly draw on a common pool of suppliers. Reflecting their own audience specialization, cable networks have tended to rely on specialized and "boutique" producers, the lack of syndication potential averting the financing problem that these firms face in producing prime-time network programming (Chapters 1, 7).[98] Cable's demand for original program series is met by a "cottage industry" of many small producers. Some of these specialize in particular types of programs, but most of them exert constant effort to devise new series to serve whatever needs they detect. They are in effect pure competitors unlikely to enjoy more than normal profits. They can supply *infinite variety,* including enhanced quality when cable networks demand it.[99] Cable networks' increased willingness to spend has led them to deal with producers who usually work with broadcast or premium cable networks.[100] When poor commercial results caused Columbia Tri-Star (the studio owned by Sony Corp.) to exit from producing prime-time broadcast programs, it successfully shifted into producing for cable, and later returned to the broadcast program market.[101] By 2001 all the major studios were producing some programs for cable networks and obtaining license fees comparable to what broadcast networks pay. Greater creative freedom on cable has also been a drawing card for top producers.[102] Premium channels (especially HBO) offer creative freedom and a high-quality ambience that gives them easy access to the most creative producers.[103] Parity in quality also implies more opportunities for collaboration between broadcast and cable networks. NBC's cooperation with CNBC and MSNBC is in place, and in 2002 ABC and CNN were discussing (though unsuccessfully) a similar arrangement.[104]

CHAPTER 6

Broadcast Networks, Stations, and Rents

Broadcast and cable networks alike need access to local distributors of their signals. In most local markets potential distributors number only a few (broadcast stations) or only one (cable operators). The network itself generates a differentiated stream of content *(infinite variety)* and usually has few competitors (broadcasting) or few in its niche of content (cable networks). In general we expect bilateral monopolies or oligopolies to reap some excess profit (rent) to be split between them. These vertically related content assemblers and distributors fit the pattern. And when viewers of TV broadcasts exogenously switch to cable (or satellite, or Internet), the rents for the broadcasters shrink, and those for the cable networks expand.

This redistribution of profits *by itself* might not affect the flow of programming beyond the fallout of the *endogenous fixed cost* mechanism (Chapters 4, 5). The economic theory of bilateral monopoly declares that the best outcome for network and distributor together is to select the mix of programming that maximizes their joint profits and then (independently) hold a "melon-cutting party" to divide the rents between them. Without this two-step process, individual decisions by each party that affect the rents landing in its own pocket are bent to serve that objective rather than maximizing the joint profit. If the broadcast network decides on the division of ad spots, while the station decides on the hours of network programming it will show each day, the two parties' combined rents are reduced, and viewers receive a different though not necessarily preferable bundle of programs. When some disturbance shrinks the bundle of rents to broadcast network and station, the deal between the two parties (however perfect or imperfect it may have been) is upset. We expect to see the parties grope toward some new set of terms.

This chapter focuses on the contractual relationship between broadcast networks and stations. It shows how the bilateral near-monopoly relationship arose from public policy decisions that left the stations in a favored position. The shift of viewership away from the networks, however, disproportionately shriveled the networks' slice of the rents, forcing them to wrestle some of the flow away from the stations.

Background: Organization of Broadcasting

This bilaterally concentrated market for broadcast programming emerged from a long history of U.S. public policies, but it needs only a brief summary here. The stations gain their rent-yielding advantage from the scarcity of the broadcast spectrum resource which, as doled out by the Federal Communications Commission (FCC), restricted all but small and isolated broadcasting markets to fewer stations than would have resulted with an unlimited spectrum resource. The original station owners paid nothing (except lobbying costs) for this scarce asset. With the FCC's allocation initially allowing three commercial channels in major metropolitan areas, fewer in small cities, and with a successful network needing nearly complete national coverage, there was evidently room for just three networks. ABC, CBS, and NBC thus prevailed without further competition until the latter 1980s, when the FCC's authorization of many new stations made room for additional networks—Fox, then UPN and The WB (see Chapter 7).

Once the three networks were paired with a market's three stations, no party had any outside option that it could readily invoke in order to improve its bargain. The contracts that linked networks with their affiliated stations governed a long period of tranquil relationships between networks and stations until the 1990s, although the networks did seek to own as many of their major-city affiliates ("owned-and-operated stations," or O&Os) as FCC rules would allow. Each Big 3 network has long paid a steady flow of compensation ("comp") to its affiliated stations for carrying ("clearing") its programs. Comp is related to the network's benefit from this distribution service, in particular for carrying the commercial messages sold by the networks to nationwide advertisers. Comp was calculated so as to induce the affiliate to carry all or most of the network's programs, limiting the alternatives of locally originated programs and syndicated programs purchased à la carte from other suppliers. Nonetheless, it functioned as a tax on the networks' profits and thus exerted a negative effect on their profit-maximizing choices of program quality. The bounteous flow of rents supported a life of comfort for each party, free from the tensions of hard bargaining.[1]

Several snakes invaded this Garden of Eden. The appearance since the 1980s of competition from cable, satellite, and the Internet has steadily compressed these rents. The parties' adjustment to this adversity differs considerably from the renegotiation one would expect under a complete contract or even a reasonably efficient incentive contract. Over time some of the original station owners sold out, capitalizing their rents and leaving the new owners to earn only a normal return on their investments. An unanticipated squeeze on such capitalized rents could threaten bankruptcy. In the 1980s the entry of new stations changed a small-numbers game of network-affiliate bargaining into one with more players. Eventually (in the mid-1990s) they undermined the long-stable dancing-partner relationships between Big 3 networks and their affiliates and made affiliation shifts by the stations common enough to upset the previously placid contractual relationship.

In this chapter we report on the changing terms of broadcast network–affiliate contracts, revealed in a large sample of those signed during the 1990s. This sample provides some evidence about the efficiency of both the underlying deal and the parties' adjustments to their much-altered circumstances. Appendix A reports a statistical investigation of the determinants of comp payments to individual stations.

Logic of Network-Affiliate Contracts

As background to recent changes in these contracts, we compare the principles of an efficient contract to the deals actually observed before the disturbances of the 1990s. The network functions as a packager of programming, presumably selecting as best it can a preferred amount (hours per week) and mixture of programs and national advertising. One might expect the network to offer its package to the affiliate on an all-or-nothing basis, supplemented by an optimal amount of locally produced (local news) and syndicated programs acquired or inserted by the station. Ad spots in these program streams should be divided between those sold nationally by the network and those sold locally by the affiliate so as to maximize their combined net revenue. Their respective receipts of net revenue—ad revenue collected by each partner minus costs incurred—would be implicitly pooled and redistributed by comp based on their relative bargaining power. In a complete contract with these properties, the various contingencies ("states of nature") for which the parties should plan would include varying levels of advertisers' demands for ad spots and consumers' interest in the programs offered. The direction in which comp flows between the parties is theoretically indeterminate and depends on both bargaining power and the distribution (national versus local) of demand for ad spots.

A complete contract is only a conceptual reference point, because negotiators can specify and plan for possible contingencies in only the roughest way. In broadcasting, two factors in particular conspire to deny the comforts of a contractual completeness. The first is the fundamental uncertainty in any creative industry about consumers' reservation prices for goods (here, programs) new to them. *Nobody knows* the audience ratings that any program series will generate. Consequently *nobody knows* the cost to network and station together of providing programs that will apprise a given number of viewers of an advertiser's message. The second factor is the FCC's policy of forbidding the network to impose its program package on the station as an all-or-nothing offer. In particular, the FCC asserts a station's right to reject network programs or episodes deemed unsuitable in taste or content for its local audience. A network must then try to adjust incentives so as to induce the station to clear programs that maximize the profit flowing back to the network. These incentive provisions must be reconciled with the flow of comp as determined by bargaining power. The Big 3 networks have long used the same formula to set these incentives and determine comp. According to the formula, the flow of payments to the station increases with the hours of network programming carried, adjusted for the time of day, the number of ad spots per hour of programming, and the ratings achieved in the local market. This weighted sum is multiplied by a station-specific factor, the network rate. The formula thus takes the form $y = a + bp$, where p is adjusted program hours and a and b are parameters. It is important that a can be negative, so that any given flow of comp dollars y can be consistent with a strong incentive (high b) for the station to carry the network's marginal program. Decisions about the program package thus become independent of decisions about the division of spoils—a fundamental property for a contract's efficiency.[2] Although failure to clear a network program imposes a financial penalty on the station, that penalty seems often to fall short of the next-best programming opportunity for the network, because the contracts contain other provisions (described subsequently) limiting and penalizing the preemption of network programs. Furthermore, a good deal of post-contract haggling occurs over preemption, even given these contractual incentives.[3]

The network-affiliate relationship is a long-term one in the sense that each party makes durable investments specific to the relationship and forecloses alternatives that can be retrieved (if at all) only upon payment of substantial switching costs. That locked-in relationship highlights the importance of the contract's duration and the terms under which it can be reopened or cancelled by either party. Here again the hand of public policy has been heavy: until 1989 the FCC limited the duration of affiliation contracts to two years, intending to weaken the bargaining power of the entrenched networks and pry the door open for entry by new ones. Whatever the merits of that objective, the policy clearly tended to increase the riskiness of relationship-specific investments for both network and station. At the same time, the parties found it less worthwhile to negotiate terms under which soured contracts might be terminated, since the ticking clock would bring termination and relief within twenty-four months. We could regard these as hypotheses to be tested. Since economic analysis offers no general models of incomplete contracts, however, we take an inductive approach, teasing theoretical interpretations from observed patterns of dealing. This treatment is applied first to the contracts between networks and affiliates during the 1990s, then to the negotiations between these groups over major disturbances that arose during that period.

Sample of Network-Affiliate Contracts

Affiliation contracts must be filed with the FCC. From that organization we sought copies of all contracts on file that were signed between 1985 and 1999 by the Big 3 and Fox networks. We obtained

172 contracts that were usable in some degree, although only 85 contained all information needed for the statistical analysis that is described subsequently. The contracts we received represent less than the whole population. The FCC has apparently not enforced the filing requirement vigorously. Furthermore, some of the contracts are missing pages or have important parameters concealed with correction fluid. While the missing contracts and data certainly might follow a non-random pattern of strategic concealment, we cannot identify any specific motives for concealment that would bias the sample. An individual contract may pertain either to a single station or to a group of jointly owned stations. Notice that the sample includes contracts between networks and their O&Os. Intra-firm contracts might be deemed irrelevant to a study conceptually based on arm's-length bargaining; the networks, however, elect to treat their O&Os in the same framework as their independent affiliates, and so provisionally we keep them in the sample, which includes 31 ABC contracts, 51 CBS, 44 NBC, and 46 Fox. The distribution over time of the 144 that reported starting dates was: 1985, 2; 1989, 6; 1990, 13; 1991, 8; 1992, 25; 1993, 21; 1994, 27; 1995, 18; 1996, 16; 1997, 5; 1998, 1; and 1999, 2.

The distribution over time reflects the major changes that occurred in the 1990s. Short-term (two years) but routinely renewed contracts prevailed in the 1980s. When the FCC removed its curb on the maximum duration of contracts, networks and stations evidently concurred on lengthening them—to ten years, or sometimes five years renewable. That increase in duration occurred just at the time (1994) when the Fox network acquired the New World station group and shifted its stations' affiliations from the Big 3 (mostly CBS) to Fox. This disturbance spread as the displaced networks sought new affiliates. Our database indicates the affiliation switches to and from the Big 3 networks and Fox between 1994 and 2001. The sample covers 464 stations active in 2000. The (gross) number switching affiliations away from these four networks is 110, while

82 switched affiliation to these four. For comparison, during 1968–1977 only 46 switches occurred, mostly owing to the ABC network's rise to parity with CBS and NBC, and mostly in small markets with only one or two active stations.[4] The New World shock clearly prompted the networks to seek contracts of longer duration. This was not just the natural reaction of decision makers to an unfamiliar shock. In addition, the networks' programs on average suffered small but statistically significant losses of ratings when they were moved from one station (channel) to another.[5] Although the FCC removed its two-year cap on durations in 1989, longer durations were elected only after the shock; 13 CBS contracts in our sample signed before April 1993 had an average duration of 2.2 years, 36 contracts signed afterward a duration of 8.3 years. Thus, the mid-1990s contracts should reflect both a rebalancing of terms in the lengthened contracts and a shift of bargaining power toward stations whose affiliations were now credibly open to change. Also, these contracts were drawn at a time when the long-run erosion of the Big 3 networks' rents was growing evident. While this threat to the flow of comp exerted little overt impact on contract terms until recent years, it did limit the networks' maximum generosity to the stations.

Clearance and Preemption

With the networks forbidden to require the clearance of their programs on an all-or-nothing basis, and with the comp formula generating imperfect incentives, we expect the lengthened duration of contracts to make the networks seek tighter restraints on preemption by the stations. The networks' problem may also have been worsened by the evolving market for syndicated programs (see Chapter 2), creating closer competition for the marginal programs in the networks' packages. First-run syndicators live with the same interaction between program costs and market size as the networks.

The costs of off-network syndicators' products are largely sunk, however, so their rental fees are set solely to extract the stations' willingness to pay. Also, syndicators can offer programs to stations for cash or for "barter" (the syndicator keeps control of some of the program's ad spots and sells them directly to advertisers).

Besides financial incentives to clear their programs, the networks employ contract terms to limit preemption directly. The station might be restricted to a certain number of preemptions per week.[6] It might be precluded from preempting a particular program or programs, reflecting the network's short-run concern to protect the ratings of marginal shows.[7] NBC contracts since 1994 have required the station to notify it of acceptance or rejection of network program series as soon as possible, and most contracts require three weeks' notice of preemptions.[8] They also specify that network programs be run at their designated times except for preemption by local news. NBC contracts after 1993 (with some exceptions) required affiliates to report their actual program transmissions promptly, in order to facilitate policing preemption rules.[9] Furthermore, NBC may terminate a contract after ninety days upon finding a violation of preemption provisions. ABC has always allowed stations to refuse, reject, or substitute for ABC programming with fourteen days' notice, but in the 1990s ABC affiliates' compensation became increasingly tied to their commitment to refrain from preempting. After 1993 the comp formula was guaranteed against unilateral revision only for stations that keep preemption below a stated threshold. Preemption has been a particularly difficult negotiating point, with some affiliates claiming it as an inalienable right by virtue of their FCC licenses.[10]

Fox, paying no comp and unable to threaten its withdrawal, introduced constraints on preemption slowly. After 1992 a station had to give seventy-two hours' notice if it rejected a network program (on the basis of stated criteria). If a station made three unauthorized preemptions within twelve months, its contract could be terminated with thirty days' notice. A preemption could be excused, however, if the station "made good" by airing a preempted program at another time yielding similar ratings. The constraints on what constitutes making good were tightened over the 1990s, with Nielsen ratings specified as a metric for scheduling makegoods and seventy-two hours' notice and Fox's prior agreement required.[11] Prohibitions were expanded beyond preemption to embrace interruption, deletions and insertions, squeezing, alteration, and the like.[12] At the same time, Fox made some contractual changes to give more discretion to the stations. Paid political programs became valid preemptions (subject to make-good). Fox became more lenient about stations' determinations of the suitability of program content, which was stipulated as the sole responsibility of the station after KDFW (1995). In some contracts the station was relieved of the obligation to broadcast those Fox programs intended for transmission outside of the normal hours of national programming. The efforts to refine and settle preemption rules occurred against a background of the stations' lobbying the FCC to permit open-ended preemption rights.[13]

Joint Development and Promotion

Both network and station make many decisions that incidentally spill benefits or costs onto the other. The station's investment to upgrade its local programming affects its viewership and local ad revenues but also increases viewing of its network's programs and commercials. As contracts' durations lengthened and more economic value was at stake, we would expect contract provisions to address these spillovers. A principal differentiating factor under the station's control is local news. It gets attention in contracts because of its potential for "branding" the local station but also for enhancing collaboration on major stories between local and network newscasters. The collaboration matters particularly with those affiliates of the network, including the O&Os, located in large markets. The networks' focus on news collaboration was also sharpened by their escalating competition with cable news channels—CNN and its rivals MSNBC and Fox News. CBS contracts exemplify the shifting concerns. Contracts drawn before 1993 did not require local affiliates to share news stories with the network, while all subsequent contracts impose that obligation. Pre-1993 contracts did not even include network news programs in the components entering the comp formula.[14] WTSP (1994) first included a section about affiliates' news service and regional news cooperation. Similarly, NBC's agreements with KCRA (1995) and KTAL (1996) referred to the station's obligation to provide local news adjacent to the network news shows. WTVG (1994) elaborately addressed the sharing of news stories between the station's local and network's regional staffs. ABC lacks a cable news network to collaborate with ABC broadcast outlets, but WGNO (1996) and KGTV (2000) made specific reference to news ratings. In 1996 Fox began a major campaign to establish a local news presence in every market, a fixed cost that its plebeian UHF affiliates had generally not incurred on their own.[15] Fox was spending $30 million annually to upgrade News Edge, its news service to affiliates, and pressed stations to add local news. It relied when necessary on cooperative deals in which profits and expenses were shared between itself and its affiliates.[16]

Other contracts contain terms that commit some of the station's ad spots to promoting network programs. This policy can be efficient, because households choosing to view a channel at one time are obvious candidates for viewing it at another time. Also, some ad spots go unsold as the time for broadcast approaches, so their use for in-house promotion incurs little or no opportunity cost. ABC contracts have always asserted the station's obligation to promote, but only KGTV (2000) specified a cash transfer to the station to fund it. Fox as a recent entrant probably had more to gain from promoting its programs, and some of its contracts contain specific obligations as to the number of spots in prime time (WPGH, 1996) or the percentage of network promotional spots broadcast during periods not programmed by the network. Some contracts specify both a minimum number of station spots promoting the network and cash transfers to compensate for them; these became increasingly common in the late 1990s.[17] Other agreements such as KHMT (1995) specified bonuses in compensation tied to the growth of the station's audience share.

Transfers and Terminations

The market value of a TV station depends on its network affiliation, and a network's profits depend strongly on its possession of affiliates in large markets. One would therefore expect that conditions for terminating an affiliate to appear prominently in affiliation contracts. That role is modest, however, and confined to specifying possible causes for termination. One of these is preemption or failure to clear a network's programs. NBC contracts signed after 1993 make an affiliate's violation of the contract's preemption rules a basis for termination of the agreement after thirty days. Another is a change of the station's ownership. Contracts have long allowed the network to reject sale of an affiliate to an unqualified buyer.[18] Under most CBS contracts the network must offer a justification for refusing a transfer. Furthermore, unilateral termination is precluded, so the network cannot employ an ownership transfer as a pretext for termination.[19] When Fox deprived CBS of a dozen big-city VHF affiliates in 1994, CBS posthaste added to its contracts a provision granting it equitable relief from costs (e.g., of locating a new affiliate) incurred as a consequence of termination by the station. A quest for higher comp was an invalid reason for a station to terminate a contract. A number of 1994 and 1995 CBS contracts referred specifically to ownership transfers involving minority ownership by another network.[20] The longer a contract's duration, the more the parties are prone to specify conditions for termination. This is evident in NBC contracts, which before 1994 let the network enjoin an impending transfer that would purportedly have entailed irreparable damage to the network.[21] ABC (like NBC) required prompt notice once an intended transfer of ownership was negotiated. There is at least some evidence of networks' strategic use of provisions for approval of ownership changes, such as demanding a reduction in compensation.[22]

Long-term contracts signed in the 1990s (especially in the wake of the New World transaction) preclude unconditional termination. Up until 1994, ABC contracts had allowed either party to terminate with six months' notice. Some ABC contracts (WKRN, 1994) allowed the network to terminate an affiliate with two months' notice when it bought another station in the same market. Only Fox with its mostly UHF affiliates retained the blanket right to terminate a station (after thirty days), if termination was elected within ninety days of a change in the station's ownership. Fox has used the provision strategically to threaten stations that resisted the network's unilateral reallocation of ad spots to itself from the stations.[23]

Conclusions: Effects of Disturbances

Two major disturbances—the New World shock and removal of the FCC's two-year limit on contract length—coincided and had overlapping effects. Lengthened contracts increased the parties' payout from negotiating several terms explicitly, but major unexpected events also induced efforts to specify parameters or outcomes whose values had previously been subject to general understandings. Specifically, negative shocks to a party's benefit from a deal seem to stir reflexive efforts to truncate or limit the harm done if the unexpected event recurs.

Patterns of Network-Affiliate Relations

In this section we turn to the collective bargaining aspect of the networks' dealings with their affiliates. While the terms of stations' individual contracts determine the relative size of their comp packages, the total amount of rent distributed also depends on market-wide forces and collective interaction. Their effects appear in the variation of total comp over time.

Flow and Ebb of Comp

By the late 1980s it was widely recognized that comp would ultimately become unsustainable. Cable, with subscribers' monthly payments as a source of income, had an unstoppable competitive advantage. Each of the Big 3 networks had undergone a recent change in control that increased the heat on network managers to produce value for shareholders.[24] CBS head Laurence Tisch was particularly vocal in seeking an end to comp, and in 1990 obtained an across-the-board 20 percent reduction, partly offset by a transfer of some ad spots to the affiliates.[25] ABC, then in a ratings slump and losing around $70 million annually, asserted that it could not both pay prevailing comp and fund outlays for high-quality programs. Its affiliates stonewalled its attempt to lower comp by 15 to 50 percent, however, and ABC settled for reorganizing comp with an incentive component.[26] In 1987 comp payments totaled $120 million by ABC, $174 million by CBS, and $130 million by NBC.[27] These levels stayed largely unchanged until the New World shock of 1994, when they increased by $60 million (ABC, CBS) and $100 million (NBC). The increases were directly tied to the bribes needed to lure the stations into long-term contracts. In the latter 1990s they stood in the neighborhood of $170 million (ABC) and $200 million (CBS, NBC).[28] Data are lacking on individual stations' comp levels around 1994, but these increases apparently did not just go to stations enjoying a bidding war for affiliation, but provided blandishments for all affiliates to sign long-term contracts.[29] Certainly the networks gave up some control over comp; after 1993 ABC contracts dropped a clause allowing the network to change the comp formula at any time. Instead, ABC stipulated that if it were to alter a station's compensation, the station could terminate the agreement, though only if the reduction were at least 25 percent.[30]

The networks, however, soon resumed their efforts to curb comp. NBC contracts in 1996 and 1997 sought to cap the increase in comp by limiting its growth in relation to each year's defined total compensation pool.[31] By the end of the 1990s, the New World disturbance had run its course, so that stations with expiring contracts had only their own structural bargaining power. Individual networks floated diverse proposals to get comp under control by reorganizing its terms across the board. Conversion to a profit-sharing arrangement was proposed, or a linkage to the station's ratings (positive) or the network's programming costs (negative).[32] Another strategy used several times was to convert comp payments into investments in a joint venture between the network and its affiliates, with the venture's profits divided between them.[33] Although such a proposal could potentially leave both network and affiliates better off, the stations apparently saw too many opportunities for the network to intercept an affiliate's net benefits (moral hazard); they took a stonewall position. Distrust focused on the network's control of the joint venture's operation and the distribution of its net revenue. It derailed sophisticated consideration of the joint venture's allocation of risk and its effect on the parties' incentives in related transactions.[34] What is striking about the many meetings and negotiations between each network and its affiliates is the latter's unwillingness to acknowledge the problem for the exogenous squeeze that it was. The stations apparently saw no downside in a stonewall policy.[35]

The ABC network began making opportunistic use of its right to disapprove changes in affiliated stations' ownership, which had traditionally been rubber-stamped. When the Cosmos station chain purchased ABC's Wilmington, North Carolina, affiliate, ABC sought a 50 percent cut in compensation, but settled for undisclosed "other considerations" instead. A merger between two

Texas ABC affiliates similarly triggered a demand for a cut of nearly 60 percent in comp plus certain commitments on clearances.[36] Such moves probably gained ABC little, as they promised only to chip away at the flow of comp at the expense of considerable loss of goodwill.

With across-the-board recontracting unsuccessful, the networks shifted to negotiating reductions of stations' comp when their contracts came up for renewal. Whereas the collective stonewall strategy imposed only a small downside risk on the individual affiliate (e.g., decreased quality of the network's future program stream), the downside—loss of franchise—became large and palpable during negotiations over renewing its contract. Possibly as a warning to other affiliates, NBC staged an assault on its San Francisco affiliate, KRON. Seeking to purchase the station, which was on the market, NBC threatened it (and thus any competing purchaser) with a loss of the $8 million comp that KRON had been receiving annually. Moreover, NBC demanded $10 million in reverse comp, along with several other changes in terms favorable to NBC. KRON's vulnerable position frightened off all buyers except Young Broadcasting, an eleven-station chain, which indeed outbid NBC for the station. Young's winning bid was at the upper end of bankers' and station brokers' estimates of KRON's value, and Young shareholders' dismay occasioned a 19 percent drop in Young's market value.[37] Indeed, a large drop occurred in TV station stocks generally, implying that NBC's move was read to portend a general toughening of networks' policies.[38] After Young refused to pay the reverse comp demanded by NBC, the network announced that KRON's affiliation would be dropped when it expired in two years. In its place NBC negotiated an affiliation with Granite Broadcasting's KNTV in San Jose, a weaker-powered station whose signal could not reach all of the Bay Area. Granite was willing to pay a total of $362 million reverse comp over a ten-year period, which NBC presumably believed would offset the expected ratings loss when it switched from KRON to KNTV.[39]

During the KRON episode, renewal negotiations were under way with several important station groups. In early 2000 NBC concluded an agreement with Gannett Broadcasting for a seven- or eight-year renewal of Gannett's NBC affiliates that was estimated to reduce Gannett's comp by 75 percent over the contract's life. CBS was said to have eliminated comp in its agreement with station group Lee Enterprises and made a large cut in payments to Cosmos Broadcasting. The Hearst–Argyle group took a 25 percent cut from ABC for renewing one of its affiliates. Hearst–Argyle also accepted a cumulative 75 percent cut over ten years in comp for its NBC affiliates, getting in return a guaranteed minimum level of ad spots available for local sale.[40] These markedly reduced levels of comp negotiated with major station chains, which might be supposed to wield substantial bargaining power, suggest that the stations recognized reduced quality of future network programming as the consequence of clinging to high levels of comp. A secondary factor that depressed the expected payout of intransigence for the station chains was the increasing possibility that the Big 3 networks would distribute their signals to parts of the market via cable rather than over-the-air broadcasts. The WB had pioneered this practice for serving small markets, and industry observers estimated that the sums cable operators pay for the network signals they distribute could plausibly turn a leading network's $200 million outflow on comp into a $200 million inflow from cable subscribers.[41]

Sports Programming

If the networks long made little progress at directly reducing comp, they could exploit the many forms of incompleteness in the affiliates' contracts for routes of access to the affiliates' cash flows. These include laying claim to their additional revenues from ad spots sold locally in and around major sports broadcasts. Another initiative is to seize ad spots that the affiliates have traditionally held for local sale, or to create new ad spots that could be sold (discounted) to the affiliates for local resale. Recall that allocations of ad spots are unspecified in network-affiliate contracts—a fundamental incompleteness.

The rights to broadcast major professional sports (Major League Baseball, National Football League, National Basketball Association) and the Olympic Games are periodically auctioned to the networks. The public's demand for viewing such programs is large and fairly predictable, as is the ad revenue that a network can capture. Hence, the bidding process serves efficiently to extract for the sports enterprises the rents due to the networks' sports broadcasts. Indeed, regular reports of financial losses subsequently suffered on major sports contracts suggest that these rents are overextracted. Sometimes a major sports franchise is seen as establishing the parity standing of an entrant (Fox) or brightening the image of a stodgy incumbent (CBS), spillover benefits that inflate a network's willingness to pay without promising directly attributable cash flows. The subsequent sports broadcasts displace other network programming, so the comp formula itself does not automatically channel back into the network any of the rents going to affiliates (ad spots that they can sell in and around the broadcasts). The network hence has a strong equity case for demanding that the affiliates contribute to covering its costs of major sports broadcasts.

The late 1990s provide a vivid case of bargaining over the costs of professional sports programming. In 1998 the networks completed negotiations with the National Football League committing them to pay $17.6 billion over eight years for rights to various components of the NFL schedule—a doubling of the annual license fee, since in the preceding four years the total cost had been only $4.4 billion. ABC, CBS, and Fox all obtained components of the NFL rights (NBC, with rights to the Olympic Games into the 2000s, stayed out). Naysayer NBC and various financial analysts predicted that the winning bidders would incur substantial losses, and the networks themselves counted heavily on spillovers and reputation

benefits.[42] Each network's board of affiliate representatives conceded that broadcasts of the games generated considerable cash for
the stations, so some contribution was clearly in order. As ABC,
CBS, and Fox sought to recoup from the affiliates, though, their incomplete contracts had important implications. First, no contracts
defined explicitly any obligation of the affiliates to fund the networks' costs of special programming. Second, each network's
group of affiliates had one or another unresolved dispute simmering
over some policy of its network, ready to submit for reciprocal
compromise by the network in exchange for an NFL contribution.
Each network eventually settled for a contribution by the affiliates
on the order of 10 percent of its NFL license fees, but with various
concessions on other issues that rankled the affiliates.

ABC and CBS both ultimately settled with their affiliates on
terms involving a complex exchange of ad spots, the affiliates either
receiving less valuable spots in exchange for more valuable ones or
buying spots from the network to sell as best the affiliate could.
Reaching the settlement took much longer for ABC, because the
affiliates' quest for guarantees of exclusive access to the network's
programs continued to fester. ABC had more extensive cable assets
at that time (ESPN, Disney) and was aggressively developing cable
outlets (SoapNet) that could reuse ABC programs (Chapter 4).
Compensation would not be paid to ABC affiliates in top 100 markets for clearing *Monday Night Football*.[43] Eventually (June 1999)
ABC and its affiliates reached a pact that would transfer $50 mil-
lion a year to the network, mostly in cash, partly through a give-
back of ad spots in Saturday morning children's programming in
exchange for eight new spots scattered among prime-time programs.[44] The give-back was limited to the three-year duration of the
agreement. ABC's affiliates also obtained a slice of equity in the
SoapNet and guarantees about the minimum time elapsed between
original broadcasts of network programs and their rebroadcast
elsewhere.[45] A similarly broad agreement centered on ABC's *Mon-*

day Night Football was reached in October 2002, covering (inter alia) the stations' pledge of no preemption and caps on rebroadcast and cross-promotion between broadcast and cable signals.[46] In June 1998 CBS reached a similar agreement with its affiliates involving a 10 percent contribution to NFL license fees, an exchange of ad spots, and confirmation of previous commitments by the network on exclusivity.[47] The obvious source of difference between the situations of ABC and CBS lay in CBS's (then) lack of affiliated cable networks and the rebroadcast opportunities that they offer.

Fox's agreement with its affiliates on the 1998 NFL fees was conditioned by the deal in place from Fox's first major NFL agreement four years earlier, when the affiliates had signed over revenues due them from retransmission consent with cable operators (see Chapter 5). It was also affected by the affiliates' preference for payments in kind over outright cash payments. Ultimately Fox obtained its NFL funds partly from the rebate of revenue from local sale of three prime-time ad spots plus two newly created spots in the games themselves. The affiliates also surrendered their interest in a previously organized joint venture, Fox Children's Network. Like ABC, Fox was actively seeking increased net revenues from recycled programming. The affiliates sought exclusivity guarantees, but Fox declined to submit to constraints on repeated programming, and the issue was left under consideration.[48]

Unilateral Reallocation of Ad Spots

The lack of contractual commitments on ad spots not only complicated the negotiations over sports programming but also directly raised issues about discretionary changes made by the network. The highest-profile dispute over the distribution of ad spots involved the Fox network, paradoxically in that Fox ceased to pay comp early in its life. Fox announced in 1999 that twenty (22 percent) of its affiliates' ninety local ad spots per week in prime time would be retrieved by the network. This edict was grounded in the network's ratings success with key demographic groups (young adults). In return for accepting this transfer, the affiliates could buy back the purloined spots at a discount, and also receive a dividend of fifteen newly created ad spots that they could sell locally, but with the network taking 25 percent of the proceeds from their sale.[49] In general this plan promoted efficient distribution of ad spots between network and affiliates, because it held more attraction for stations getting higher prices for local ads (and facing local advertisers with elastic demands). But only accidentally would it achieve the best allocation of ad spots for any given affiliate.[50] The board representing Fox's affiliates turned the proposal down, offering instead to pay $40 million annually in reverse comp. Fox, which could have imposed the original plan unilaterally, instead declared that it needed $80 million in additional revenue but chose to negotiate further. In the ensuing compromise, the affiliates agree to pay $60 or $70 million (sources disagree) but could keep their current allocation of prime-time spots. In addition, they received the fifteen new spots and could keep all the revenue that those spots generated. The agreement was to run for three years.[51] In 2000 the reallocation deal caused more prime-time ad spots to be placed with the affiliates than they could readily sell, and some adjustments were necessary for stations in small markets.[52] Other networks (ABC and NBC) also sought to retrieve some ad spots from their affiliates.[53]

Rebroadcasting Network Programs

A source of contractual slippage previously mentioned is the short-term rebroadcast of original network programs on another outlet—a cable channel or a different broadcast network. As was explained in Chapter 4, given a program's fixed production cost, the near-zero direct cost of repeating it, and the dispersion of individuals' preferred times of viewing, the optimal frequency for showing a new program may be twice or more (cable channels repeat costly programs numerous times). Repeating on a different outlet likely offers the advantage of reaching an audience less overlapping that for the first showing. The practice riles network-affiliate relations, however, because the station that first broadcasts a new program (episode) will generally lose some viewers who prefer other times or channels. If rebroadcast is profitable for the parties overall, some compensation scheme could make it acceptable to each of them, but negotiators may have trouble reaching it, with no agreement in place on the station's property right in exclusivity of network programming. Contracts have generally been devoid of provisions governing rebroadcast.

In the mid-1990s those content providers newly integrated vertically with distributors started to explore new ways to extract value from their program investments. ABC, already linked to the cable sports network ESPN and now to Disney, started showing *Second Noah* on the Disney Channel. In cooperation with cable operator Comcast, it began planning the SoapNet, which would rebroadcast ABC soap operas later on the same day.[54] Contractually, ABC did not need its affiliates' consent, but their complaint about the diversion of audience and ad revenue clearly needed to be addressed. NBC faced similar resistance when it broadcast post-game shows for some National Basketball Association games only on its cable channel CNBC.[55] In each case the affiliates saw not only a direct diversion of revenue but also a long-run strengthening of their direct competitor, the cable operator. Affiliates' primary demand was that rebroadcasts should stop; barring that, the affiliates should be "made whole." Rather than working out a compensatory payment, the networks stuck to their rights under existing contracts or reached out for purely procedural solutions, such as promising to consult the affiliates on future rebroadcast plans or setting a minimum delay between the initial and the repeated broadcast.

The problem worsened as most networks continued to expand

their rebroadcast practice. Fox desired a short interval between network broadcast for its first-run programs and reuse on the FX and
Fox Family Channels, and ABC integrated its sports programming
with ESPN.[56] Attempts were made to assuage the affiliates' objections by creating new ad spots that they could sell. This action was
potentially an efficient response to the elevated sports license fees,
if those increases indeed reflected greater revenue productivity of
ad spots in the major sports broadcasts. Without such a change,
though, increasing an already optimal number of spots would reduce the combined revenues of network and affiliates. NBC at one
time did offer its affiliates a buyout on exclusivity: specific exclusivity guarantees in exchange for 15 percent of the affiliates' comp.
The affiliates declined the offer.[57] Only ABC appeared to reach a
general resolution of rebroadcast rights with its affiliates, permitting it to rebroadcast up to one-fourth of its prime-time programs,
for compensation to its affiliates of cash and an exchange of ad
spots (new prime-time spots to the affiliates in exchange for Saturday A.M. spots).[58] Other networks reached more or less comprehensive settlements with their affiliates over the reuse of programs.
NBC in the short run backed off its plan to rebroadcast certain
programs on the Pax network but reasserted its intention to be a
major program supplier to Pax.[59] It was widely remarked that Pax
gave NBC a supply of alternative local affiliates. This cogent plan
foundered, however, on the incompatible audiences pursued by
programmers for NBC (urban sophistication) and Pax (hinterland
piety).[60]

Stations' concerns about revenue lost owing to repeats have
spilled over into the negotiation of affiliation contracts. After 1994
NBC began to offer affiliates the right of first negotiation on any future ventures that would involve rebroadcast.[61] The contract with
the Gannett chain (2000) refers to the use of the Pax network as a
vehicle for rebroadcast, but promises only that NBC will in good
faith seek to inform affiliates of any rebroadcast agreements.

Threats of Unraveling

The strained relationship between networks and stations is subject to at least two threats of unraveling. One—vivid to the stations—is that the networks would buy them out and eliminate the festering arm's-length relationship between the parties. The stations have vigorously opposed the networks' efforts to relax or repeal an FCC rule that caps the maximum share of U.S. households reached by any given station group (including networks' O&Os), which would legalize additional purchases of stations.[62] In 2003 the FCC decided in the networks' favor, allowing a single owner to control stations reaching 45 percent of U.S. households rather than the previous 35 percent. A vigorous political campaign against this relaxation led Congress to order a rollback of the maximum coverage to 39 percent. This coverage is understated, however, because the reach of UHF stations' signals is discounted 50 percent in recognition of their technological inferiority to VHF transmission. It seems perverse for business units to demand exclusion from the market of potential eager buyers of their assets. The likely reason: the stations fear that the networks could rewrite the incomplete terms of their contracts so as to shrivel their prospective cash flows, allowing their assets to be bought at bargain-basement prices.

The erosion of the rents shared by network and affiliate and the frequent stalemates and standoffs in their negotiations raise a second threat of unraveling. The networks could distribute their signals directly on cable without a duplicating local over-the-air signal and thus achieve the second stream of revenue that they now lack.[63] In a few instances (NBC in San Francisco, CBS in Jacksonville), stations pressed by networks for major reductions in comp have given up their affiliations and gone independent.[64] The affiliates have lodged complaints with the FCC about the networks' conduct, seeking to make political trouble for them.[65] Meanwhile, the networks have made opportunistic use of their power to reject transfers of station ownership. Nonetheless, the evidence from stations' ratings and stock-market values continues to affirm the benefits of affiliation with a Big 3 network.[66]

Conclusions: Incomplete Contracts and Haggling

An efficient bargain between two parties separates the distribution of the surplus from the allocative decisions made by the individual parties. A corollary holds that an exogenous disturbance to this distribution should not beget inefficient reallocations of inputs and outputs. The major short- and long-run disturbances to comp raise just this issue. While the stations markedly resisted making direct cash payments, they were receptive to potentially efficient reallocations, such as the exchanges of ad spots. Large haggling costs have been incurred, however, owing to lack of agreed-upon property rights in exclusivity of programs and the national versus local allocation of slots. These haggling costs are that much greater because the need to adjust some parameters regularly evokes a dispute about whether some compensation is required. Also, disputes over unsettled parameters tend to arise and get tied to independent issues needing resolution: because you are gaining a net benefit from the current adjustment of A, we should reopen issue B on which I maintain I have shared less than fairly.

Determinants of a Station's Comp

The previous section addressed the efficiency of the deal between network and station, the transaction costs involved, and the outcomes of disturbances. Comp played a central role. In Appendix A we report a statistical analysis of the determinants of comp flowing to a sample of individual stations in 2000. The model treats comp as a bargained outcome that increases with the value of the station's services to the network, decreases as the minimum (break-even) reservation price of the station declines, and responds appropriately to any bargaining chip that one party possesses. In the results, VHF stations receive significantly more comp (they are more effective distributors). Comp increases with the extent of cable systems' penetration into the local market. Two conflicting interpretations can explain this result: the complementarity between local broadcasters and cable's retransmission services raises the value of a station to its network; or the competition between cable systems and local stations cuts the station's profitability where use of cable is heavy, requiring comp to make the station profitable. Comp is lower where more stations serve the local market (their density is measured by the actual number of stations normalized by the market's household population), indicating that more local outlets weaken a station's bargaining power with its network.

We expected that comp would be larger for small-market stations pressed to cover their fixed costs, but the data reject this hypothesis; apparently a station's fixed costs are so thoroughly endogenous that any irreducible minimum is very small indeed. Comp does drop off, however, for large-market stations that on average earn high rates of gross profit, relegating comp to the status of "small change." We expected that comp might be larger for group-owned stations (more bargaining power) and for stations that had undergone a shift of network affiliation, but neither hypothesis was confirmed.

This statistical analysis turns out not to possess much explanatory power, consistent with the role of comp as a historical legacy. It does not appear to play much of a part in preserving small-market stations that otherwise could not cover their fixed costs. Comp does respond to bargaining power, however: the density of stations in the local market, and also the swings in aggregate comp following the New World shock.

PART THREE

BARGAINING TABLES
AND MEDIA CONGLOMERATES

CHAPTER 7

Program Supply, Integration, and the Fin-Syn Rules

In this part of the book we explore how the structural traits of creative industries condition the dealings that take place between providers (producers, assemblers) of program content and its distributors when the parties on both sides are few in number.

Bilaterally Concentrated Markets in Creative Industries

A standard piece of economic analysis is the theory of bilateral monopoly: a single seller facing a single buyer. It remains a useful framework when more than one but only a few agents sit on each side of the table (bilateral oligopoly). The theory of bilateral monopoly has two distinct branches—both useful for application to the creative industries, but the second especially so.

Price and Quantity

The first branch of the theory pertains to what is central to any market's performance: the price that is set and the quantity of output that flows through the market. The best outcome—for the parties, and for society as a whole—occurs when the parties agree on the output that maximizes their joint profits and then independently divide that profit between them. This output is the same as what we expect when there is a single monopolist at some stage in a chain of production stages. While it falls short of a competitive output, it exceeds the output that emerges if one of the bilateral monopolists sets its own best output and its opponent then reacts as best it can.[1]

Complex Products and Contracts

Different considerations arise when the product passing through the bilaterally concentrated market is not homogeneous (a ton of steel). In particular, the parties face a deal-making problem when the value of the product passing through them depends on the contribution each party makes to its fabrication. Ideally, each should be compensated for the extra value of the throughput that results from its input (effort, or value of inputs). The parties, however, may be unable to measure these input and output values, or to measure them objectively in the eyes of the deal partner, who naturally suspects opportunism. Each party might seize investment opportunities that are specific to their mutual relationship and increase its value but incur hazards that can infect an ongoing relationship. The seller specializes its services to this particular buyer, incurring a sunk cost, risking that the buyer will execute a holdup, demanding a low price that (at worst) covers only the seller's variable cost. This is a problem of ex post bilateral monopoly, one that can arise even if ex ante many parties are present in the market. Fewness ex ante, however, shrinks the opportunities for fleeing a bad marriage. Vertical integration (vertical merger) is a natural defense against holdups in a contractual relationship, if managers of the buyer and seller components of a vertically integrated firm can be instructed by top management to do the right thing.

Traits of Creative Industries

The special features of creative industries, layered atop these general traits of bilaterally concentrated markets, lie behind the behavior described in the next three chapters. First, the prevalence of fixed (sunk) costs tends to widen the bargaining range between seller and buyer. The seller whose costs are wholly fixed would settle for receiving a penny rather than no deal at all, and that can embolden a buyer to risk a stalemate or inflict costs of haggling on both parties. The property *nobody knows* makes the value of individual product units unpredictable; contractual specifications cannot be completely detailed, and/or haggling arises over their fulfillment and enforcement. *Infinite variety* refers to individual product units that have many complex traits and dimensions but nonetheless may be close substitutes for one another. Price haggling over them individually tends to be unproductive, so that sticky and conventionalized prices tend to prevail. Finally, the physical and economic longevity of some program types *(ars longa)* means that many transactions in bilaterally concentrated markets for programming indeed pertain to licensing products with wholly sunk costs, again widening the bargaining range.

These frictions and transaction costs of bilateral concentration provoke the parties to seek smoother-working and less uncertain relationships. One of these is the full vertical integration mentioned earlier: buyer and seller come under common ownership and administrative supervision. Short of full vertical integration, however, are devices such as joint ventures and partner relationships organized for particular purposes. Decision rights over the project (or its separable phases) can be allocated and incentives tuned (by the allocation of ownership shares in the profits) so as to maximize the project's expected value and divide the rewards amicably, or at least predictably.

Other reorganizations that can occur in bilateral oligopoly include "horizontal" mergers between parties on one side of the market. These can prove strategically attractive for increasing that side's bargaining power even if they bring no gain in real productivity of the resources deployed by the combining firms, or even if they inflict some loss. Purely strategic combinations in bilateral oligopolies can also take the form of vertical mergers. Suppose that one buyer and one seller in a bilateral oligopoly undertake a vertical merger, dealing only with each other and "dropping out" of the market. This defection leaves each remaining independent with one fewer potential transaction partner on the other side of the market. That tends in turn to increase the value of further vertical mergers in order to avoid strategic vulnerability and uncertainty. In this chapter we see that this "foreclosure" motive for vertical merger takes on considerable importance in the broadcasting industry.

Context: Fin-Syn Rules and Their Repeal

The selection of prime-time network programs described in Chapter 1 has long occurred in a largely arm's-length market where program producers meet networks. Vertical integration stands as an alternative—the networks integrating backward to produce their own programs, the studios integrating forward to distribute their productions, or network and studio merging. In fact, a good deal of integration has occurred during the past decade or so. The proximate reason for this reorganization is clear: the repeal in 1995 of the financial interest and syndication rules adopted by the Federal Communications Commission (FCC) in 1970 made vertical integration a legal option. But why was it a preferred business policy? In this chapter we review the demise of "fin-syn" and the adjustment that ensued.

The fin-syn rules limited the property rights that the (then) three broadcast networks, ABC, CBS, and NBC, could acquire in the prime-time programs they broadcast. The financial interest rule prohibited their owning rights to the earnings of programs in off-network syndication, either in the United States or abroad.[2] The syndication rule prevented the networks from engaging in the business of offering programs in syndication in the United States. These rules sprang from a concern, then widespread, that the networks enjoyed substantial monopoly and monopsony power and insulation from the threat of entry. The rules were intended to reduce the networks' monopsony power over program suppliers, encourage new entrants into program production, and promote diversity in the sources (and perhaps the content) of programs.[3] Encouraging entry into a market by excluding some incumbents is hardly a procompetitive policy, of course. The suppliers who remained enjoyed fewer competitors with their programs and increased bargaining advantage against the networks, denied access to self-supply. Fin-syn's beneficiaries included two groups of producers described in Chapter 1, the major motion picture studios and a fringe of small firms organized around individual writer-producers.[4] Other beneficiaries from fin-syn were the TV stations affiliated with the broadcast networks but independently owned. They stood to gain bargaining power against the networks from access to more programs from non-network sources ("first-run syndication") that could substitute for programs in a network's package. The fin-syn rules were accompanied by a related constraint imposed by the FCC: the prime-time access rule. It restricted the networks to providing programs to their affiliates for no more than three of the four hours of prime time (7 to 11 P.M.). This rule also aimed at diversifying the sources of broadcast programming. It had the additional effect of strengthening independent broadcasting stations (i.e., without network affiliations), which could schedule off-network syndicated programs between 7 and 8 P.M. that were often more popular than the game and entertainment news shows available to network affiliates. The prime-time access rule was removed at about the same time as the fin-syn rules.

These rules were hardly in place when their premise of network monopoly began a slow and continuing erosion owing to cable and satellite television (described in Part Two). Also, fin-syn produced no evident enrichment and diversification of networks' prime-time programming. By 1983 the FCC had soured on the rules, and their repeal was narrowly averted by a blitz of lobbying by fin-syn's beneficiaries. The rules came under renewed scrutiny in 1991, precipitated by newcomer Fox network's argument that entrant broadcast networks were disadvantaged by them, quite contrary to the FCC's intention.[5] In a complex series of legal actions during the early 1990s, the FCC first proposed relaxing the fin-syn rules to allow the networks to hold equity in up to 40 percent of their prime-time programs. When the revised rules failed to survive a court challenge, the FCC acquiesced in their outright repeal in 1995.[6]

The end of fin-syn was accompanied by a considerable reorganization of the program supply market, with a majority of the networks' prime-time programs now produced in-house or owned jointly (co-produced) by network and studio. Obviously, the networks decided that ownership stakes in programs were often in their interest. What were the reasons for this preference? Did they derive from the structural elements of creative industries, or from other (of the numerous) theoretical explanations for vertical integration? Descriptive evidence helps us to screen theoretical reasons why networks should want whole or partial ownership of the programs they broadcast. This process uncovers two lines of plausible theoretical models that are then put to some tests.

Inducements to Integration

We consider first the main features of arm's-length dealings between producer and network, then explanations why the parties choose to allocate ownership between them as they do. This question shades into another: Why should networks integrate vertically into self-supply of programming, or the producers into self-distribution?

Contracting to Supply Program Series

We saw in Chapter 1 that arm's-length deals on prime-time programs between producer and network raise important questions of decision rights, because each party makes choices important for series' cash flows in both first-run network showings and off-network syndication. Contracting on these various policy choices, complex enough on its own, becomes especially problematic because of the viewers' unpredictable reception and the difficulty of specifying in advance how the parties will respond to unexpected events. The contract takes the form of an option agreement whereby the network buys the right to order, on pre-specified terms, additional episodes of the show over a period of years (traditionally four). The network agrees to pay a sum that is closely related to the studio's cost of producing an episode and covers a large proportion of it (commonly 80 to 85 percent).[7] The proportions seem to vary in the ways we would expect if program supply is competitive, so that networks' license fees are set to yield the program suppliers normal profits on their outlays. Ratios are high for programs either unlikely to hold much syndication value or promising enough to compel a high competitive bid by the network. If a dramatic program succeeds on the network, it will likely generate large immediate cash flows from advertising and a prolonged influx of syndication rentals, and thus a high internal rate of return for its equity holders.

Allocation of Decision Rights

This contract framework allocates decision rights between program supplier and network, clearly indicating that both the studio producing the program and the network exhibiting it make decisions that can vitally affect its future cash flows. The producer, in consultation with the network, selects the inputs into the program—actors, writers, episode directors, along with the contributors associated with set design, photography, musical score, and other creative and technical factors. While the primary task is to combine heterogeneous inputs into a package that "clicks," there is also a dimension of quality or vertical differentiation in both the initial (choice of key actors) and continuing decisions about the production of a show (the *A-list/B-list* property). Decisions made at the outset are to some degree contractible between producer and network, but even that limited contractibility falters for continuing decisions that the producer must make about the writers, episode directors, and other inputs that may be varied as successive episodes of the program are filmed. A strong case emerges for an incentive contract that motivates the producer with a substantial profit share in the program's future cash flows.

The network broadcasting the program also makes decisions with important effects not only on its own advertising revenues from first-run exhibition but also on cash flows expected from domestic syndication and other subsequent uses. The number and demographic mix of viewers seeking TV entertainment vary exogenously with the time of day and week, so that a program broadcast at a popular hour accesses a larger potential audience and has more opportunity to build goodwill. The network may schedule a program opposite weaker or stiffer competition from programs aired in the same slot on other networks, affecting its share of the potential audience. Its placement in a network's schedule also involves granting (or denying) it benefits from being shown adjacent to the network's most popular programs and being provided with a transition designed to keep the audience in place.[8] Viewers who do not change channels when a popular program ends find themselves sampling the one that follows, and they may like it. A parallel spillover occurs when viewers tune in to a channel before the start of the popular program, thereby sampling its predecessor.

The network makes many other decisions that affect syndication value. The program may be advertised both by network broadcast spots and in other media such as newspapers. Network advertising time is sold partly on season-long contracts, partly on a short-term market. Advertising spots occasionally remain unsold as their broadcast time approaches, so that their use to advertise its own programs incurs little or no opportunity cost for the network.[9] A very important decision is whether to renew a series for another season. A program that dies young has limited value in syndication. Specifically, the per-episode value of a series in syndication tends to increase (up to a point) with the number of episodes accumulated during its initial run on a network. A common generalization holds that a half-hour program needs to accumulate ninety to one hundred episodes to be attractive in the syndication market—sold to outlets likely to broadcast it five days a week over a number of months ("strip" it). Although shorter series with attractive qualities increasingly command a price in syndication to cable networks, this threshold remains influential.[10] The network thus makes a crucial decision about renewing a program for another season, in particular for the season that will boost the number of episodes in the library over this threshold.

Programs compete with one another for favorable treatment in a network's decisions about scheduling and renewal. In each given part of the broadcasting day, the network fills a customary amount of time with programming transmitted to its affiliates. Adding one program requires cancelling another. Giving a more favorable place in the schedule to one denies it to another. Renewing one series implicitly excludes renewing another or picking up a newcomer. Any difference in the network's participation in programs' profits from subsequent exhibition therefore might lead to decisions that substantially redistribute their syndication values.[11]

With both producer and network making decisions that are important for a program's expected syndication value, an optimal incentive contract needs to award either of them one dollar for each extra dollar of syndication value due to that party's effort. While contracts can be written that award the whole marginal dollar to each of several collaborating parties,[12] the deals observed in the market for TV programs do not exhibit incentive elements more sophisticated than simple profit shares. The parties thus choose between a joint-venture type of contract with substantial though suboptimal incentive provisions and a sole-ownership arrangement with one party acting as principal dealing with whatever agents (input suppliers) it will.[13] The choice that maximizes joint profits should depend on the parties' respective chances to augment expected first-run and syndication value and their opportunity costs of these actions.

Allocation of Risk

While making the best assignment of decision rights provides a compelling criterion for allocating the ownership of TV programs, the objective of sharing risk efficiently between networks and producers has also been advanced. Great uncertainty surrounds any new TV program's appeal to viewers, and empirical evidence shows that a program's cash flow cannot be predicted even by experienced market participants fully informed about its basic elements.[14] For efficient risk-bearing to matter for allocating programs' ownership, studios or producers and networks should differ substantially in their ability to diversify the considerable risks associated with individual TV programs. A broadcast network assembles a package of programs, advertisers, and local stations to provide unpriced entertainment and information for TV viewers. Risks associated with the uncertain appeal of individual programs (new or continuing) are directly pooled in the package, making the network a good candidate for bearing ownership risks. The situation with the program suppliers is more complicated, because this group encompasses both the major cinema film distributors and small entrepreneurial firms built around individual producers or teams (Chapter 1). The studios can evidently diversify their TV program investments by pooling cash flows with their cinema films, first-run syndication, and other entertainment products. The independents, however, produce few programs each and carry on few if any other business activities. They would seem poor risk-bearers, which helps explain their prevalent partnership arrangements with the studios and other larger enterprises. Nevertheless, with capable risk-bearers on both sides of the market for TV program material, the efficient allocation of risk does not seem a compelling influence on how to distribute programs' ownership rights. Furthermore, the implication that fin-syn denied independent producers the opportunity to shift risks onto the networks runs squarely counter to the fact that independent producers did not object to preserving fin-syn.[15] We thus set aside the hypothesis that fin-syn's removal mainly permitted more efficient allocation of risk.

Role of Vertical Integration

Another important business arrangement raises these same theoretical issues of allocating decision rights: vertical integration between content producers (such as movie studios) and distributors (networks). Rather than allocate decision rights on each deal, the whole set of allocative decisions can be thrown into the integrated firm, which (economists usually assume) resolves everything by means of astute managerial decisions. This "black box" treatment of internalized decisions is a cheat to the empiricist, who wants to know why particular decisions get made as they do. In the last section of this chapter we approach vertical consolidations in the aftermath of fin-syn in a pragmatic way. Who resorted to vertical integration? In what circumstances, and to what end?

Transformation after Fin-Syn

In the late 1980s the networks could foresee the end of fin-syn and began speculating publicly on their responses and the profits they could reap. They had, after all, routinely taken 50 percent interest in programs before 1970.[16] The resulting reorganizations appeared on two fronts: the development of producing units within the network enterprises and the expansion of deal terms negotiated between networks and producers to embrace the sharing of ownership. The networks undertook some production in-house under fin-syn. They were permitted to prepare their own news and sports programming, which held no syndication value. Also, the Justice Department consent decrees (which effectively duplicated the fin-syn rules) allowed three and one-half hours of in-house programming a week. Nonetheless, these loopholes were too small to support substantial production shops, which effectively had to be started from scratch. Likewise, the window opened in the early 1990s for networks to negotiate ownership shares in at least some programs supplied by independent producers. We present some data on changing patterns of program ownership, then look beneath the data at the reorganizations and shifts in bargaining that occurred.

Shift toward Network Ownership

We collected data to show the evolution of whole and partial network ownership during the adjustment period of 1995–1999. For the four networks that were well established by 1995 (ABC, CBS, Fox, NBC; UPN and The WB entered that year), we obtained information on programs shown during prime time. The Fox network had never been constrained by the fin-syn rules (it initially broadcast too few hours per week to fall within the FCC's definition of a network and later obtained a waiver). It thus provides a control for the other three networks, which had been constrained by fin-syn since 1972. All programs broadcast in prime time were included except for news broadcasts (including newsmagazines such as *60 Minutes*) and sports programs.[17] We collected data on each program in the year it was introduced and each year for which it was renewed. Observations were included for programs that had been introduced before 1995 and renewed into this period, because the

TABLE 7.1 Ownership status of programs broadcast by four networks
between 1995–96 and 1998–99, by year

Ownership share held by network	1995	1996	1997	1998
Zero	72%	76%	66%	57%
Partial	20	12	21	23
Full	8	12	13	20

Source: International Television & Video Almanac (New York: Quigley
Publishing Co., various years).
Note: Columns may not add to 100 percent owing to rounding errors.

TABLE 7.2 Ownership status of programs broadcast between 1995–96 and
1998–99, by network

Ownership share held by network	ABC	CBS	NBC	Fox	Total
Zero	93%	68%	76%	56%	75%
Partial	4	30	18	40	21
Full	2	3	6	4	4

Source: International Television & Video Almanac (New York: Quigley
Publishing Co., various years).
Note: Columns may not add to 100 percent owing to rounding errors.

networks were then expecting fin-syn's demise.[18] The resulting database contains 445 program/year observations.[19] The database indicates whether each program was subject to full, partial, or zero
ownership by the network broadcasting it. A fully owned program
usually was developed and produced by the network itself. One
partly owned by the network generally was developed by an outside
producer or studio (or, in a few instances, another network). Information is not available on how shares in partially owned programs
were divided; occasional references in the trade press commonly
place networks' shares in the range of 10 to 50 percent.

Tables 7.1 and 7.2 show the distribution of ownership status by year and by network (averaged over the years). One-fifth of all programs had come under partial ownership by 1995, while full ownership (dependent on the networks building up their production units) rose gradually to account for another one-fifth. The Fox network, with its head start, took equity interests in 44 percent of its programs over 1995–1999. CBS aggressively sought to obtain partial equity interests, while ABC was passive until its acquisition by Disney in 1995. NBC approached in-house production cautiously. The trend continued past the period covered by our data, as shown in a tabulation of pilots prepared for the 2001–2 season. ABC held an interest (part or whole) in twenty-four of thirty-one pilots, CBS ten of twenty-four, Fox seventeen of twenty-five, and NBC seventeen of twenty-four.[20] The pattern is consistent with the fin-syn rules' having imposed a binding constraint, and their relaxation setting off an adjustment process that (likely) is now complete.

More light is shed on these changing ownership patterns by measuring changes in the shares of programs owned by various functional classes of producers and networks. Since the early 1990s, the larger independent TV program producers have undergone considerable turnover, often through acquisition by or long-term alliance with either a network or a studio. Using data from the *International Television & Video Almanac,* we calculated the shares of various types of suppliers of prime-time programs in 1991 and 2001. The bulk of programs in both years were produced jointly by two (occasionally three) parties, one a network or studio, the other an independent that might be nothing more than a profit-share front for a writer-producer or featured actor. We gave each party full credit for any show in which it held equity, whether full or partial ownership. A sixty-minute program was counted as equivalent to two thirty-minute programs. The four older networks had equity in 7.4 percent of all programs in 1991, 35.0 percent in 2001. The studios that started the UPN and WB networks or the integrated firms that owned these networks had equity in 9.8 percent of programs in 1991, 10.8 percent in 2001. Other movie studios accounted for 13.7 percent in 1991, only 4.7 percent in 2001. Large independents (involved in more than sixty minutes of programs) accounted for 24.0 and 20.5 percent, while small independents (sixty minutes or less) faded sharply from 45.1 to 29.0 percent. Thus, production overall shifted toward the vertically integrated and the large-scale organizations.[21]

Did in-house programs outperform those from independent suppliers and certify the vertical-integration model? A careful answer would require a statistical comparison of cost and profitability, including revenues ultimately reaped from off-network syndication. Such a project is only now becoming feasible. The evidence does suggest that the performance of the newly internalized shops was mixed at best. Despite the mobility of top writer-producer talent among organizations, at any one time some studios are regarded as hot, some not, and while the hottest eventually cools, the process is sometimes slow. Although the randomness of success impairs measuring a studio's true temperature accurately, there was some consensus that during the transition NBC's in-house productions were arriving chilled. Some programs were pressed upon reluctant schedulers by network managements. ABC's attempt to rely on programs developed in-house (including its owner Disney) appears quite unsuccessful.[22]

New Deals and Holdups

The network buying a license to exhibit a program should expect to pay more if it also acquires a share of any syndication revenue, a view commonly expressed early in the fin-syn adjustment.[23] For example, one independent producer reported a network willing to finance the producer's gap between production cost and the network's license fee in exchange for 30 to 40 percent of future syndication revenues.[24] The trade press in the 1990s, however, reported numerous complaints from producers about demands for ownership shares arriving as holdups. The network's license fee for a new program is said to be a sticky price in the sense that the ratio of rental to production cost appears not verysensitive to expectations about the program's success.[25] The insensitivity is plausible, for two reasons. First, because *nobody knows,* the deal participants' expectations about the success of any given program are likely both diverse and held with little confidence. Especially since the bargaining parties deal repeatedly with one another, conventional focal points in the bargaining between them likely hold considerable attraction.[26] Second, because a studio negotiates a program sale with one network at a time, it is offered to another only when the first passes, so that no auction takes place.[27] Consider the producer offering a pilot that is probably marginal for adoption, but in which significant resources have been sunk. If the producer declines the network's demand for a gratis share of syndication revenues, it has little chance to place the program with another network (at least, not immediately), because program scheduling operates (though decreasingly) on a regular seasonal cycle. And the marginality of the program shrinks the expected value of the syndication revenue. The producer's concession could well be prudent.

This scenario yields the important prediction that the networks could wind up partially owning weak rather than strong programs.[28] As corroborating evidence that such deals occurred, two studios with the best track records (Twentieth Century Fox Television and Warner Bros.) were also the ones that retained full ownership in the largest fraction of their new shows.[29] Another confirming pattern appears in differences between NBC and CBS, neither (at that time) affiliated with a studio, and their competitors who were so equipped. Without that filial source of programs and the corresponding element of bargaining power, NBC and CBS were particularly active first about demanding ownership stakes, then about developing their own program production units.[30] ABC and Fox, with studio affiliations, could credibly invoke the self-supply alternative in bilateral bargaining sessions.[31] Finally, in the race to exploit bilateral bargaining power, NBC could indulge in brinkmanship because of the superior ratings earned on average by its current stock of programs. Stalemates left some studios temporarily not on speaking terms with NBC.[32]

We expect an entity that possesses bargaining power to use it where it commands the most value. Claims on syndication revenues might compete with other benefits that a network could extract from a supplier. One of these is a longer duration for the network's option contract. The traditional four years can leave the network with a popular show, a cornerstone of its prime-time schedule, for which bountiful rents attributable to the supplier (and actors) face sudden appropriation by them when the initial agreement expires. The networks took diverse views of this hazard, not unnaturally reflecting whose rents had recently been snatched in the renewed contract for a successful show. In several instances networks and studios completed or at least considered renewal of contracts ahead of their expiration date, giving the network a choice between a known bloodletting today and an unknown exsanguination a year hence. The simplest of all uses of networks' bargaining power is to hold out for a last-minute cut in the producer's license fee.[33]

These uses of bargaining power shade into another group that is important for the slot and promotion assistance given a program by the network. For the 1999 season ABC in effect auctioned its choice slot on Wednesday at 9:30 P.M. to three competing program suppliers. ABC dumped the incumbent *The Norm Show* in favor of *Oh Grow Up,* for which Greenblatt–Janollari Productions accepted a six-year license contract and granted a 10 percent equity share to ABC. Likewise NBC provided a choice slot (Thursday, 9:30 P.M.) in exchange for an extended six-year license term.[34] Renewal decisions also could occasion holdups; *NewsRadio,* "on the bubble" for renewal on NBC, gained a reprieve conditional on an ownership share for the network.[35]

Ownership and Scheduling Decisions

When a network has acquired a portfolio of programs, some with and some without ownership interests, we expect it to treat them differently in decisions that will affect future syndication values. We describe some incidents that illustrate these choices and their consequences. One such decision is to give the favored program a particularly choice time slot (when the potential audience is especially large and/or advertisers' willingness to pay is especially high). NBC complicated its negotiations to renew the popular comedy *Frasier,* owned by producer Paramount Domestic Television, by moving the show to Tuesday from its prize Thursday evening slot, which was then conferred on the promising *Will and Grace,* owned solely by NBC.[36] The possibility of choices colored by ownership interests arises continually, because ultimately successful programs that yield rich syndication revenues often start out with weak ratings and might respond to being nursed along by the network.[37]

Networks increasing their ownership interests in their programs have run into significant drawbacks. The whole enterprise prospers if in-house programs succeed, but that engine also runs in reverse. In 1999 CBS's major-market owned-and-operated stations were losing heavily in daytime ratings from the poor performance of CBS's syndicated programs, and ratings for CBS newscasts were depressed as well.[38] Another problem that bedevils the entertainment conglomerates arises when the time comes for off-network syndication and the network's own affiliates are among the licensee candidates—for example, Fox licensing both *The X-Files* and *NYPD Blue* to its FX cable network. Talent (producers, actors) entitled to a share of syndication revenues naturally suspect that the Fox syndication arm will give a sweet deal to the Fox cable network, diverting rents from the profit participants to Fox.[39] Suspicion breeds litigation. The same problem arises in negotiations to renew a first-run license when producer and network broadcaster are corporate siblings. Producer Wind Dancer Productions sued Disney on these grounds over the renewal of *Home Improvement*.[40]

Evaluating Integrated Program Production

Many factors could explain why networks elect to produce programs in-house. Since the explanations hold diverse implications for economic efficiency, we want to know which possible determinants actually have statistical explanatory power. The qualitative evidence already reviewed leaves the field open. Favorable models—efficient allocation of decision rights, efficient use of information within the integrated firm—win some support. But so do models hostile to welfare: foreclosure, transitional holdups. Two recent studies make a start at the task. Karen Guo selected a sample of prime-time dramatic programs broadcast by the Big 3 or Fox during the years 1995–1999.[41] The programs scheduled in any given broadcast season might be newcomers or shows renewed from the preceding year. (Some network-owned programs debuted before fin-syn's formal termination in 1995.) She tested implications of efficient allocation of decision rights—that a program in which a network holds an ownership stake is likely to receive more favorable treatment than a program licensed at arm's length. "Favorable treatment" refers to the various ways a network can promote a program and generate both a large current audience and bidders eager to license the show in off-network syndication. These include scheduling it at an hour and day of the week when the potential audience is large, placing it just after or just before an established popular show, and scheduling it when competing networks offer only relatively unpopular programs.[42] For new programs introduced during 1995–1999, these treatment decisions were compared statistically for programs with no ownership, partial ownership, and full ownership by the network. Account was taken of differences in the network's identity, year, and type of program, and whether the program was introduced in the spring.

For the full sample of new programs, none of these decisions was associated with either full or partial ownership. Perhaps the effect of an ownership stake on promotion decisions holds only for new programs with distinctive competitive prospects—"hot properties" that with help might achieve large successes. Or perhaps it applies only to those with "middling" prospects, for which promotion might tip the chances toward success. There are no objective data on how hot a program was considered at the time of its introduction, but one can thrust *nobody knows* aside and conjecture that these ex ante guesses were correlated with the programs' actual subsequent performance. On that assumption, owned programs destined for "middling" success in fact did get significantly more favorable treatment of several types; owned high-flyers and duds did not.

Guo also studied the determinants of a network's decision whether or not to renew a program for another season. This was expected to depend strongly on the share it currently commands of the audience viewing TV at its day and hour. Controls were also employed for the number of years the show has already aired. Once again, the full sample of programs (and years) showed no indication that owned programs overall win more favorable treatment in the decision to renew. Some significant differences did appear between networks, with Fox more likely to renew either fully or partially owned programs, NBC disinclined to renew its own programs.

David Barth undertook a technically sophisticated and empirically rich investigation of renewal decisions' relationship to networks' vertical integration.[43] It was based on annual data on the cancellation or renewal of all prime-time network dramas and sitcoms broadcast between the 1991–92 and 2000–2001 seasons. The starting date picks up the beginning of the transition from fin-syn. In the research design, renewal is regarded as an investment decision that stacks a renewal's benefit in additional future syndication revenue against any opportunity loss associated with continuing a given program for another year. The analysis takes into account the network's license fee for the program and the price that its ad spots command.

Barth found that some though not all types of integration exert significant positive effects on renewal decisions. His model allows an estimate of the value that vertical integration adds to a program: one with middling ratings that give it a shot at renewal exhibits an increase in expected value of 11 percent for a new sitcom and 20 percent for a new drama. Vertical integration does not matter for high-rated programs that will be renewed in any case or low-rated ones that will not (a finding parallel to Guo's about the selection of slots). The type of integration that Barth found least supportive of renewal (indeed, hostile to it) is network co-production. That agrees with the circumstantial evidence we noted of holdups of the co-producer in the bargaining over license terms.

Overall, the statistical analyses of vertical integration and co-production generally agree that some forms of integration induce the network to treat a program favorably. The evidence is not so sweeping, however, that it disposes of the doubts raised previously about holdups in arm's-length bargaining and foreclosure as a motive for vertical integration.

Vertical Mergers and Entry

The decision rights just discussed can be assigned one project—even one step—at a time, or they can be shifted *en bloc* through the reorganization of enterprises (vertical integration). This section explores such deals, screening empirical patterns for clues to relevant theoretical models of vertical integration.

Integrating Program Producers

In the aftermath of fin-syn's repeal, the networks moved to establish in-house production units in the manner described in Chapter 1, recruiting writer-producers under various contractual arrangements that gave the network exclusive access to or first refusal of a producer's new projects. Portfolio strategies were commonly used. Fox Broadcasting collected a group of boutique shops, all independent of the Fox studio's Twentieth Century Fox Television. ABC in 1994 (before its acquisition by Disney) established an in-house unit (ABC Productions) and alliances with several independent producers. ABC also reached a seven-year agreement with the new studio DreamWorks SKG to produce and distribute programs for various day parts.[44] Some of the statements accompanying these moves mentioned information benefits, such as uninhibited flows of sensitive information within the network enterprise and sensitivity to the network schedulers' needs. Specific examples include Twentieth Century Fox Television's preparation of syndicated programs designed in style and quality for Fox's owned stations, freshly augmented by Fox's purchase of the New World stations.[45] The networks clearly believed that covering the full production cost of series programs (rather than the customary 85 percent or so) was commonly a good deal in exchange for expected syndication revenues.[46]

While fin-syn's removal prompted "backward" vertical integration by the Big 3 networks, it also stirred "forward" vertical integration by means of program producers' entry into network operation. The Fox network was launched in 1986 by News Corporation, which also owned Twentieth Century Fox, a producer of TV as well as cinema films. While the entry decision long preceded the end of fin-syn, it clearly rested on an expectation that repeal would occur before the rules became binding on the Fox network. Paramount and Warner Bros. started the UPN and The WB networks, respectively, in 1995. These entries set in motion the slow reshaping of the old network oligopoly by bringing new rivals into the market (as vertical mergers did not). The newcomers scaled entry barriers that had been commonly thought impregnable, so their strategies warrant some attention.

New Networks' Experience

An entrant broadcast network needs a set of affiliated stations that can reach a large share of U.S. households. (With program costs fixed, starting with a few cities and gradually expanding incurs large costs for small revenues.) Affiliates can be plucked from the ranks of independent stations or pried loose from incumbent networks. The former strategy is clearly the more attractive. Fox entered at a time when 177 new stations had started up in the preceding five years, and so it found many potential affiliates eager for programming. When UPN and The WB entered, the stock of stations was growing more slowly (14 percent in 1990–2000, versus 48 percent in 1980–1990). TV advertising revenues were abundant, however (1994 saw a 15 percent increase over 1993), so the entrants sought ways to capture stations affiliated with existing networks. Those owned by the networks (O&Os) were clearly out of reach. Bribing Big 3 affiliates to switch was unpromising, because their market values contained the capitalized values of the rents that the networks had long paid over to them. Still, nothing prevented deep-pocketed new networks from buying control of stations or station groups and switching their affiliations. Such a transaction in 1994 (see Chapter 6) much enlarged Fox's affiliate group at the expense of Big 3 affiliates. Each entrant network relied at the outset on a deal to ally it with a station group covering a number of the nation's largest metropolitan areas. Fox's entry rode on the 1985 purchase by its parent, News Corp., of the Metromedia Stations group.[47] UPN was founded by a partnership of Paramount and the United Television station group, which had about 18 percent national coverage. Also, Paramount fell heir to a station group that belonged to its acquirer, Viacom.[48] Finally, The WB's principal affiliates belonged to the Tribune station group, which covered numerous major markets. Tribune took a 12.5 percent equity position in The WB.[49] After start-up the entrants made some purchases of individual stations in order to fill important holes in their coverage, and UPN and The WB got into some bidding wars.[50] A crucial fact about the entrant networks' access to affiliates is that they were able to avoid systematic payment of compensation ("comp"), and indeed The WB obtained some reverse comp, a share of a new affiliate's gain in profits.[51] The Big 3's comp burden amounted to a "gateway to entry," reducing the relative costs for the new networks.

At various times the multi-system cable operators (MSOs) proved useful allies to the entrant broadcast networks. In 1990 Fox made a deal that TCI, then the largest MSO, would receive Fox's network feed by satellite and broadcast it in areas where Fox lacked a broadcast affiliate.[52] The WB and UPN also used cable systems to supplement their broadcast affiliates' coverage.

The entrant network's other major need is to mobilize a schedule of successful programs, a task with no sure or cheap options *(nobody knows)*. All three sponsoring studios were successful producers of TV program series. The parents of UPN and The WB were flourishing as program suppliers, with Warner Television producing thirteen and Paramount twelve hours of prime-time programming for the networks in 1995.[53] Warner also owned a large library of cartoons that it could exploit more fully through a controlled network.[54] At any time, however, an incumbent network has a stock of more or less successful programs, whereas the entrant must either grow its own or bid licenses away from competing networks. All three entrants attempted the same strategy for competing with the closely parallel programming strategies used by the Big 3 to fill the prime-time hours. In economic terms, each entrant sought to occupy a niche that could divert substantial numbers of viewers from the Big 3 but not provoke overt competitive reactions from them. Fox chose to concentrate on edgy shows that would attract the young viewers for whom advertisers will pay dearly. Reality programs were an early source of success, but they were later overworked when Fox's attempt to edge into closer competition for the Big 3's mass audience increased the mortality rate for its programs. UPN and The WB picked strategies similar to Fox's, concentrating on young viewers (especially female, for The WB) and urban minorities. Each strategy's success or failure overall depended on the fate of its key programs; in this, the entrants ceded no obvious advantage to the incumbents.

The entrants did make relatively heavy use of programs supplied by affiliates. Fox drew on both its successful producing affiliate Twentieth Century Fox Television and an umbrella organization for independent producers recruited to devise new shows suitable for the Fox network.[55] The success rate of these talents was not particularly high *(nobody knows)*, but eventually the writers and producers recruited by Fox delivered such successes as *Ally McBeal* and *The X-Files*.[56] The Fox network early found itself addressing a problem linked to the foreclosure motive: it sought to convince the program supply industry that it was not just an outlet for Twentieth Century Fox Television, but welcomed dealings with all program suppliers. The studios naturally discounted Fox as a licensee, because of its assumed propensity for self-supply but also its smaller audience, which would add less value to a program's expected syndication revenues than would a show on a Big 3 network. This caused independent producers to demand license fees that fully cover production costs.

The entrants have found viable though not clearly profitable niches in the broadcast market. A network needs to cross a threshold coverage of U.S. TV households (80 percent is commonly mentioned) to be deemed national. Fox, UPN, and The WB all succeeded. Fox had 86 percent coverage by 1988 and 96 percent by 1994.[57] In 1997, after WB snatched Sinclair Broadcasting stations from UPN affiliation, both entrants had 72 percent coverage through primary affiliations, over 85 percent if secondary station affiliations are counted. By 2001 UPN was at over 80 percent from primary affiliations.[58] Another dimension of successful entry is the ad prices that the entrant can command, depending on coverage, program quality, and demographic mix. Discounts in outlays per thousand viewers (CPM) from what the Big 3 obtain are prevalent. Fox, when it began in 1986, suffered a 20 to 25 percent discount. By 1990 this was down to 10 to 15 percent, and Fox also received a 20 percent premium over the ad rates that successful syndicated programs achieve.[59] In 2001 UPN was incurring a 20 to 25 percent discount in CPM rates.[60] The profitability of these entry investments is not easily assessed, but the verdict seems clearly negative for both UPN and The WB. By the end of the 1996–97 broadcast season, UPN and The WB had each cumulatively lost about $600 million; UPN's cumulative loss was cited at $800 million in 2000 and $1 billion in 2001.[61]

Concerns about Foreclosure

Economists generally welcome the arrival of new competitors in markets that contain only a few. Indeed, the new networks offered expanded choices to viewers and an increased supply of advertising spots to ad buyers. Structural changes that result from vertical mergers do not offer these benefits, although they may increase economic efficiency in ways analogous to improving the allocation of decision rights (explained previously). They may carry the virus of foreclosure, however—a vertically unintegrated enterprise's concern with being rationed out of a market. Because of pervasive fixed costs, this is a serious threat to broadcasting enterprises. Consider the acquisition of the ABC network by Disney in 1995. Disney held a large library of films that could be licensed to ABC (and other networks) for exhibition. Before the acquisition ABC presumably chose between Disney and (say) Paramount films on the basis of which was likely to attract the largest audience and add most to its profits. After acquisition, Disney held a strong incentive to press Disney films on ABC. These might generate less profit *directly* for ABC than their Paramount counterparts. But the substantial payment that ABC would otherwise have made to Paramount is now avoided (it becomes an internal transfer within the Disney empire). Deals can thus be motivated by fear of being on the losing end of foreclosure. Vertical mergers can reduce the efficiency with which the market's array of products is chosen. It could happen that foreclosure-driven mergers leave all firms in the market vertically integrated and less profitable than before, yet each vertical merger decision looks more profitable than the alternative at the time when it is made.[62] These mergers could exact organizational costs, such as creating complex enterprises whose parts require different management and coordination arrangements. They give rise to "strange bedfellow" costs; the organization of creative industries seems to reflect an effort to keep artists and corporate bureaucrats out of each other's hair.[63]

The presence (or dominance) of a foreclosure motive cannot be proved rigorously. Two factors, however, can sustain a strong suspicion: public statements to that effect by the enterprises involved, and the occurrence of waves of vertical hookup or races to complete vertical combinations. The transactions in broadcasting since 1995 seem to display these properties. The entries by UPN and The WB clearly sought to ensure against foreclosure. Warner's chief executive officer identified the end of fin-syn and the need to ensure an outlet for the studio's programs as necessary conditions.[64] The Disney studio acquired the ABC network in 1996 for various reasons that clearly included guaranteeing an outlet for Disney's TV programs and cinema film library.[65] In 1999 CBS was acquired by Viacom, the owner of the Paramount studio and also of several cable networks including MTV.[66] Even the holdouts confirm the underlying process. NBC (owned by General Electric) caught everyone's eye as the only unintegrated broadcast network, leading to widespread speculation that it would combine with one of the few remaining studios.[67] NBC's long-standing position atop the prime-time ratings heap no doubt lessened its concern with ensuring a program supply: getting a series into NBC's prime-time lineup would attract even the program units of rival networks.[68] NBC first extended its network assets, buying a 32 percent interest in the Pax Network, a chain of stations originally programming only home shopping and infomercials, and the Spanish-language network Telemundo and its stations. In 2004 NBC finally did acquire Universal Studios, which had been caught up in the series of control changes. Among the studios Columbia Tri-Star at first voiced confidence that it could operate successfully without formal ties to distribution channels. It later exited temporarily from program production for broadcast TV.[69]

Direct evidence of foreclosing transactions, desirable to confirm this hypothesis, is difficult to assemble. One suggestive example is found in the popular entertainment news programs such as *Entertainment Tonight*. An entertainment conglomerate has an equity interest in each of these, and they are observed to slant their news fluff toward movies distributed by their owners.[70]

This game of vertical linkages showed a prisoner's-dilemma character, in that no network voiced an unqualified desire to produce all of its own prime-time programs. All parties recognize the value of a "deep" set of participants on the other side of the market. Fox's chief operating officer opined that the main reason for in-house production of programs was the defensive one of sustaining bargaining power and averting holdups.[71] The head of programming at CBS spoke of needing to ration the ownership shares the network took in its programs in order to pledge openness to the industry's creative community.[72] Disney's Touchstone Television, while dominating affiliate ABC's program supply, made much of placing programs with three other networks as well.[73] This loss of an open market was amplified by direct drawbacks that surfaced in integrated production. The networks recognized that me-too programs tailored to the sibling network's needs of the moment seldom rise above mediocrity, and that the big hits come from idiosyncratic combinations of an original idea with effective casting and implementation.[74] Production-studio executives heavily involved in supplying affiliated networks may declare their readiness to deal with all comers, but they are well aware of the "lemons" problem they will encounter selling programs to unaffiliated buyers, who will assume that they were passed internally.[75] A studio may be heavily preoccupied with internal supply because its sibling network has fallen on hard times, and other suppliers downgrade it as a preferred destination for the week's hot programming idea.

An implication of corporate combinations to avoid foreclosure is that the profit and/or the operating efficiency of combined firms may deteriorate. Notably, in early 2005 the idea was circulating through Hollywood that operating effectiveness had in fact suffered. Starting from Viacom, where dismantlement was receiving consideration, the concern was spreading to other entertainment conglomerates.

CHAPTER 8

Broadcast Stations:
Lengthening the Chains

A question not yet addressed about the TV sector's economic organization concerns the extent of common ownership of groups of stations and its effect on the selection and distribution of programs. When the VHF licenses were originally distributed gratis, the Federal Communications Commission (FCC) generally dropped them into the outstretched hands of local business interests. In the FCC's worldview, they were the parties most likely to use this gift of public property—the spectrum frequency assignment—in the best interest of their fellow townsfolk. This attitude implies a hostility to multi-station ownership. The FCC's goal of maximizing independent "voices" in the telecommunications sector set it firmly against common ownership of stations within a local market. And the preference for local ownership meant a distaste for common ownership of stations in different markets. Groups were long restricted to a maximum of seven stations nationwide, then (in 1985) to twelve; the numerical limit was dropped in 1996. Besides lowering a barrier to group ownership of stations, public policy also gave it an inadvertent push. In 1975 the FCC restricted cross-media ownership (TV stations and newspapers) in a local market, forcing many divestitures. A media company denied a TV station in its home city commonly chose to acquire one (or more) elsewhere,

212

triggering the development of groups. During the 1980s a number of family-owned station enterprises chose to "cash out" and sell to larger groups. Thus, in 1986, 90 percent of VHF stations were group-owned, whereas thirty years earlier only 50 percent had been.[1]

Parallel to Chapter 7, we get to observe an experiment triggered by public policy that once restricted the horizontal integration of TV stations but then greatly relaxed the constraint. The key features of creative industries turn out to explain the occurrence of this horizontal integration, just as they explained the vertical integration and joint ventures prompted by fin-syn's repeal. A TV station's costs largely boil down to the acquisition of programming and its physical operation. Each is fixed, so they have the potential to be reduced through pooling that would be impossible if all costs varied with the number of households served. The programming costs are endogenous, depending on the station's (and network's) desired quality level as well as the pricing strategies of syndicators (Chapter 2). The operating costs include technical expenses and fairly routine managerial functions. *Infinite variety* applies to the station's own programming choices: its options are numerous, but the choices made among close substitutes likely do not matter much. These administrative tasks (both programming choices and technical operations) appear to vary little among markets except for the differences associated with higher quality of programs supplied by a profit-maximizing station when the audience is enlarged. Thus station chains apparently have opportunities to reduce duplicating costs. Chain integration might also provide some bargaining power, but against whom?

The first section of this chapter explores the reasons why TV stations might join into groups and the casual evidence bearing on them. We then review the changes in ownership patterns that have followed relaxations of government rules. The last section of the chapter summarizes a statistical test of several explanations for group ownership in a similar sector—radio broadcasting.

Motives for Horizontal Integration

Operating Economies

The participants in acquisitions of stations or groups have identified a number of gains that they anticipated. The normative implications of these gains range from the promotion of efficiency to the pursuit of increased bargaining power. Outright efficiency motives turn up commonly in transactions that involve groups of small-market stations. Indeed, the fact that a group's members tend to be concentrated either in the largest markets or in mid-size and small ones itself suggests something about the economies involved. Mergers among small-market stations are frequently touted as leading to more efficient operations. TVX Broadcast Group applied a highly specific managerial blueprint for operating the independent UHF stations that it acquired (e.g., each had exactly thirty-seven employees). Specific sources of efficiency gains included both the local operation of the acquired stations (many of them in the hands of inexperienced owners who had only recently started up) and the acquisition of syndicated programming. National advertising sales could be efficiently concentrated on one national representative.[2] The Sinclair Broadcast Group, an active acquirer, reported substantial economies in stations' operations and engineering, though not in advertising sales (purely local markets).[3] Numerous press reports indicate that station chains centralize some operations in order to reduce fixed administrative costs.[4] The NBC network confirmed this source of economies by centralizing broadcast sales, traffic, and master control operations in regional hubs that could serve several of its owned-and-operated stations (O&Os).[5]

The small-market stations linked in these efficiency-oriented agglomerations commonly exhibit substantial geographic concentration. Sinclair's acquisition of River City Broadcasting left the combined firm concentrated in the central United States and in medium-sized markets.[6] Other acquisitions pooled stations concentrated in the South, or with clusters in Texas and in the Midwest and Great Lakes states.[7] Large-city station groups almost inevitably show little geographic concentration. Indeed, they might be seeking national coverage of the largest markets in order to facilitate the sale of advertising in a national marketplace.[8]

Relationships with Networks

Another motive commonly affects groups operating in diverse-sized markets. It is to pool and represent the interests of stations sharing affiliation with the same network. Commonly most stations in a group are affiliated with the same network, but with a few "strays" linked to other networks. Mergers and acquisitions often increase this concentration. For example, Sinclair Broadcast Group's acquisition of Sullivan Broadcast Holdings brought Sinclair's holdings to fifty-five stations, and Sullivan's ten Fox affiliates raised Sinclair's total to twenty-four.[9] The Hearst–Argyle chain's acquisition of the nine-station Pulitzer group fortified Hearst–Argyle's status as the largest group affiliated with ABC and the second largest affiliated with NBC.[10] Purchases of individual stations also commonly raise the concentration of a group's network affiliations; Tribune's acquisition of a San Diego station affiliated with The WB network raised Tribune's WB concentration to eight of nine.[11] The Belo group's acquisition of a San Antonio station affiliated with CBS enhanced Belo's position as the largest chain of CBS affiliates.

What motives lie behind this pattern? Does an owner seek to amass affiliates of a network in order to increase its bargaining power? Or do network and station group internalize their shared interests, approximating the pooled interests of networks and their vertically integrated O&Os? If so, merger and acquisition deals contribute to the parties' joint surplus rather than entailing a grab for bargaining power to affect its division. Casual evidence supports the hypothesis of cooperation. So do the coalitions formed by entrant networks. New networks either are organized as joint ventures involving a station chain, or depend on agreements with a large group (Chapter 7). A station chain attached to a network as a bloc, though, can also be detached as a bloc, as Fox's acquisition of the New World chain (mostly CBS affiliates) vividly showed.[12] Also, evidence in Chapter 6 on the renegotiation of compensation paid to affiliates indicates that chains of affiliates tend to internalize the system-wide effects of decisions about comp while individual stations do not. The difference amounts to less aggressive use of bargaining power by the groups. A larger-size station group seems to reap not so much favored pecuniary treatment as a slant of the network's major commercial decisions toward its interests.[13] Some acquisitions made by station groups have the air of favors done for the network, as in Tribune's acquisition of a San Diego station at an auction-determined price considerably higher than the station's cash flows would justify. Allbritton Communications, entirely affiliated with ABC, bought two CBS stations that would be switched to ABC. At least two instances are reported of reciprocal investments or investment options designed to align the interests of network and group. And it was noted that Sinclair's acquisition of Sullivan occurred when the Sullivan stations' Fox affiliation agreements had seven or eight years to run, so they gave Sinclair no leverage for bonus compensation.[14]

Acquiring Programs

The acquisition of programming and other inputs are candidate sources of economies to station groups. Groups can pursue operating economies in the centralization of programming decisions and purchases, quashing a tradition of leaving substantial autonomy in programming with the individual station managers.[15] Although standardized formats apparently generate lesser economies for TV station groups than they do for radio chains (evidence is presented subsequently), they do exert some influence. Advantages also arise in both the production of programs and their purchase from syndicators. The larger station groups sometimes find it profitable to produce some programs (other than local news) styled to their particular needs. They can also offer their programs for license to other buyers in the syndication market.[16] The Tribune station group's acquisition of Renaissance Communications gave it extensive (35.4 percent) coverage of the U.S. national market and a concentration of its stations' affiliations with Fox and The WB. Affiliates of these two networks have similar needs for (non-network) programming, and this offers economies in programming costs; also, affiliates of the new networks simply need more syndicated programming, because their networks supply fewer hours per week than do the Big 3.[17] Tribune indeed proceeded to expand its development slate for programs in various day parts and to arrange with syndicators for cooperative development of programs.[18] Such collaborative deals to develop programs not only spread fixed costs over wider in-house use but supply a launching pad as well for licensing programs to other distributors (stations, cable networks).[19]

Large groups also gain an advantage of bargaining power against suppliers of syndicated programs (Chapter 2). The fixed and sunk character of costs for the syndicator, the large minimum national coverage of households needed to make a first-run syndicated program viable, and the increasing bilateral concentration of the market all contribute to generating rents for the larger station group as buyers. Dealings between syndicators and station chains encounter the same issue of allocating decision rights that arose for producers and networks after fin-syn's expiration (Chapter 7). A station group's choice of slot for a syndicated program can strongly affect its ratings and its future value to the syndicator. Major syndicators have been acquired by entertainment conglomerates or developed within them, propelled by the same forces that promoted integration between studios and networks.[20] The chains in addition are said to exercise bargaining power against the suppliers of technical equipment. Those vendors seem to be both concentrated and specialized, thus able to charge monopoly prices from station buyers lacking the bargaining power of a large station group.[21]

Policy Changes and Station-Group Concentration

While economic logic and participants' comments confirm numerous reasons for the amalgamation of stations into groups, they do not explain why mergers and concentration followed the trajectory that they did during the 1990s.[22] For this, changes in public policy play a major part. The Telecommunications Act of 1996 eliminated previously binding limits on the number of stations that could operate under common control and loosened the other constraint on stations' concentration—a limit on the maximum share of U.S. TV households that could be reached by a group's stations. This was raised from 25 to 35 percent.[23] The relaxation of this constraint was widely anticipated by the industry (in 2004 it was further relaxed to 39 percent). Thus, when in 1995 station chain Group W was combined with the O&O stations of CBS, the fifteen stations could reach 33 percent of households. Gannett acquired the Multimedia group, with fifteen stations now reaching 14 percent of households.[24] With the 1996 legislation in place, a wave of horizontal consolidation took place as independent stations and small groups decided whether to sell or make a run at establishing their own chain.[25] Time-series data on the value of TV stations changing ownership indicate a total of $28.7 billion over the years 1995–1998, while the preceding four years saw only $4.3 billion—15 percent as much.[26] The price/earnings ratios at which stations and groups were sold swelled greatly, as the top twenty-five station groups increased the share of all stations that they owned from 25 percent in 1996 to 33 percent in 1997 and 36 percent in 1998.[27]

The 1996 legislation also addressed control arrangements in individual city markets. Before 1996 a pair of stations in a market had been permitted to enter into a local marketing agreement (LMA), with one operator managing both stations and selling advertising for both. By 1995 at least three dozen existed, ten in the top thirty markets. By 1997 the count was seventy within market areas and another thirty uniting stations in different markets. Of the LMAs in effect in 1997, nearly two-thirds involved a new station, indicating the dominance of this choice when it is an available option.[28] LMAs effected considerable cost savings, though (according to advertisers' complaints) at the cost of reduced competition in pricing local ads.[29] LMAs run for limited periods of time up to ten years, so they presumably offer less potential for integrated operation than does full common ownership.

In the wake of the 1996 legislation, the FCC in 1999 for the first time permitted the common ownership of two stations located in the same market area, subject to various restrictions. Court decisions have been pressing the FCC to permit dual ownership more liberally. In the industry a pair of stations in a market under common ownership is referred to as a "duopoly."[30] Because local stations' costs are largely fixed, they offer considerable potential for cost reduction. Joint operation in one instance improved a station's operating margin by 65 percent, reduced its staff by 80 percent, and cut its program costs by 60 to 75 percent by means of combined news and marketing organizations.[31] In addition to these straightforward reductions of (largely) fixed costs, duopoly deals facilitated the networks' efforts to increase the short-run repeats of their costly programs (Chapters 4, 6).[32] The reduction of real cost is undoubtedly large, but so is the scope for duopolies to exercise market power. Syndicators, as well as local advertisers, are at hazard. They of course have their own market power, being able to set license terms for their programs independently from market to market and extract each station's willingness to pay. Syndicators avoid no costs when they fail to clear a program in a given city market, however. If the stations gain bargaining power as a duopoly, the syndicator might license its program almost for free, because the syndicator avoids no cost if no deal is struck.[33]

By April 2002, sixty-eight duopolies had emerged in forty-three markets, with four in two markets and three in three others.[34] This development resulted from a considerable flurry of transactions in TV station ownership, coinciding with much-increased values of stations and station chains in the top fifty markets that were duopoly candidates. Many of the duopolies resulted from swaps of stations between station groups, and major ownership changes in stations or groups intended either to produce duopolies or to provide trading stock that could be swapped to obtain them.[35] Substantial numbers of LMAs were converted to duopolies. Important mergers were encouraged by the duopolies that they would permit— Viacom's acquisition of CBS and News Corp.'s purchase of the Chris-Craft stations.[36]

The FCC has been under considerable pressure from the courts to review its rules on duopoly and other ownership issues and either provide better justifications or else eliminate them. For instance, in determining the permissible extent of duopolies, why should the FCC count only TV station "voices" and not radio, newspapers, the Internet, and so on?[37] In terms of economic benefits and costs, it was noted that the proportional cost savings to TV broadcasting operations from duopoly are greater in small than in large local markets, the opposite of the policy preference.[38]

Growth of Station Chains

Factors Affecting Station Chains

The hypotheses competing to explain the expansion of station groups clearly invite formal statistical tests. Alas, practical difficulties intrude at every turn: the period of adjustment since 1996 is short; the stations have few intrinsically fixed characteristics except for their license location and VHF/UHF mode; the number of large groups (say, reaching more than 15 percent of U.S. TV households) is fairly small, and the vertically integrated O&Os make up a generous share of these. We employ a very simple procedure that starts from a ranked list, developed by a trade publication in 1995 (the eve of the FCC's relaxation of its restrictions), of station groups in descending order of the estimated share of U.S. TV households reached by their signal.[39] Each group's number of stations is also given, letting one calculate the average size of the markets served by a group's stations. We created a parallel list of the largest twenty-five groups for 2002. The exercise involves some guesswork, since the 1995 list carries no description of how it was prepared, and significant choices must be made; our own choices are explained in a note.[40]

The resulting lists appear in Table 8.1, along with each group's accessible share of U.S. TV households, its number of stations, and the audience share with access to the group's average station. The data suggest several conclusions. In 1995 the groups' numbers of stations were clustered just under the FCC cap of twelve, suggesting that the policy constraint was binding, and that the larger groups would grow if permitted. Indeed, most groups that appear on the list in both years substantially increased their numbers of stations. This usually occurred through mergers between groups. Several entities new to the 2002 list own large numbers of stations in small markets, collected in numerous purchases of individual stations and small groups. The station group serving the smallest average market size shown on the 2002 list, Entravision Communication, reaches about 327,000 households; the twenty-seven stations of Benedek Broadcasting, which would rank twenty-seventh on an extended list, reach on average about 148,000. The variance among groups in number of stations and average market size (share) increased markedly, suggesting differences in their self-assessed abil-

TABLE 8.1 Largest 25 station groups ranked by share of U.S. TV households accessible, 1995 and 2002

Station group	Share of households accessible	Number of stations	Average households per station
1995			
1. Capital Cities/ABC	23.5%	8	2.94%
2. Fox Network	22.4	12	1.87
3. NBC Network	21.7	6	3.62
4. Tribune Broadcasting	20.4	8	2.55
5. CBS Network	19.0	7	2.71
6. Silver King	18.3	12	1.52
7. Chris–Craft	17.9	8	2.24
8. New World Group	13.9	12	1.16
9. Group W	12.9	8	1.61
10. Univision	10.4	9	1.16
11. Gannett Broadcasting	9.9	10	0.99
12. Telemundo Holdings	9.2	6	1.53
13. A. H. Belo Corp.	8.1	7	1.16
14. E. W. Scripps Co.	8.1	9	0.90
15. Cox Enterprises	7.6	6	1.27
16. Post–Newsweek	7.0	6	1.17
17. Hearst Television	6.7	6	1.12
18. LIN Television	6.4	9	0.71
19. Renaissance Broadcasting	6.3	9	0.70
20. Pulitzer Television	6.1	10	0.61
21. Hubbard	5.8	9	0.64
22. Paramount Studios	5.7	6	0.95
23. Walt Disney Corp.	5.2	1	5.20
24. Providence Journal	5.0	11	0.45
25. River City Broadcasting	4.8	7	0.69
2002			
1. Fox Network	47.2	34	1.89
2. Viacom International (CBS)	46.4	35	1.61
3. Univision Communication	39.2	26	1.85
4. Tribune Broadcasting	38.3	20	1.84
5. NBC Network	26.9	12	2.24
6. Walt Disney (ABC)	24.1	10	2.41

TABLE 8.1 *(continued)*

Station group	Share of households accessible	Number of stations	Average households per station
7. Telemundo Holdings	21.3	9	2.91
8. Sinclair Broadcasting	21.0	37	0.57
9. Gannett Broadcasting	18.5	22	0.84
10. Hearst-Argyle Television	17.4	30	0.58
11. Trinity Broadcasting	17.0	22	0.77
12. A. H. Belo Corp.	16.6	17	0.97
13. Cox Enterprises	13.7	14	1.06
14. Raycom Media	12.4	31	0.40
15. Young Broadcasting	11.3	16	0.71
16. E. W. Scripps Co.	10.6	10	1.06
17. Meredith Corp.	9.9	11	0.90
18. Media General	8.2	25	0.33
19. Clear Channel	7.7	20	0.45
20. Emmis Communications	7.3	24	0.32
21. Granite Broadcasting	6.1	9	0.94
22. Entravision Communications	5.9	13	0.31
23. LIN Television	5.5	11	0.50
24. Pappas Television	4.9	14	0.35
25. Allbritton Communications	4.9	8	0.61

Source: For 1995, *Broadcasting & Cable,* July 10, 1995, pp. 8–9; for 2002, see text.

ity to benefit from further enlargement. Some groups made a dash to claim advantages of larger scale, while others chose to cash out. Keep in mind, though, that in 2002 the largest groups still faced an FCC constraint on the maximum shares of U.S. TV households they could reach. These are the groups formally (the O&Os) or informally linked with broadcast networks (including two Spanish-language networks). The networks clearly regard these caps on shares as a binding constraint, although they apparently do not consider full vertical integration (owning all affiliates) to be ideal.[41] Group membership increased more rapidly among the smaller-market stations. Thus, the combined numbers of stations that are members of the top twenty-five groups increased from 202 to 480, while little increase occurred in the total number of stations. The median group's average share per station fell from 1.16 percent to 0.77 percent. Thus, what the FCC's twelve-station rule precluded (up to 1996) was apparently the realization of scale economies by groups owning numerous small- and medium-market stations.

These changing profiles of the leading groups seem consistent with several hypotheses about the economic relation between sources of scale advantage and group organization. First, the small-market groups (often geographically concentrated, as noted previously) evidently pursue scale economies in providing managerial and programming services to similar small firms. Second, the vertically integrated station groups apparently moved from being limited by the FCC's twelve-station constraint to being limited by its market-share constraint. The difficulties with network-affiliate relationships (Chapter 6) evidently disposed the networks to extend their vertical integration as much as permitted. Third, despite the attraction of vertical ownership links, the medium- and large-market station groups have also grown without diversifying their network affiliations (indeed, concentrating them further). Two models of viable organizational linkage between networks and their principal affiliates seem to co-exist: vertical integration and contractual quasi-integration with large station groups.

Findings from Radio Chains

Several hypotheses about the advantages of gathering stations into groups seem to hold explanatory power, and it would be attractive to test them statistically. We passed up this exercise for a number of reasons. They include the prevalence of large mergers, the apparent importance of unmeasurable strategic considerations, and the prevalence of vertically integrated O&O groups. It did, however, prove feasible to test appropriately modified versions of these hypotheses on the radio industry, which shows a number of structural similarities to the TV broadcasting sector. One similarity lies in the major disturbances that struck both markets in the 1990s—the relaxation (for TV; removal, for radio stations) of restrictions on the number of stations commonly owned. The group-size restriction had clearly been binding in both sectors, and so both underwent major consolidations, the profiles of which should expose the advantages sought in the consolidations that followed. The other similarity lies in the key structural properties of the two industries. In each case the business unit (station) is relatively small and simple, with very similar managerial tasks (acquiring programming, selling ads) confronting all units in each sector. Both sectors have negligible marginal costs of serving additional consumers, but their fixed costs are endogenous and variable to achieve a profit-maximizing quality of the output. For each sector the task of selling ads is pursued on both local and national markets. Means of acquiring programs show some similarity: most TV stations depend chiefly on a network's program bundle; for the radio station, a format plays a role somewhat similar to a network's in TV. Radio has the statistical advantage of many more entities (stations, groups) available for analysis.

In Appendix B we report tests of three hypotheses parallel to patterns noticed among the TV station groups. The first concerns whether the groups' member stations are more concentrated geographically than if each group's stations were drawn at random. This hypothesis is strongly confirmed, parallel to the evidence of geographic concentration in groups of small-market TV stations. The second hypothesis addresses scale economies in sharing common formats—somewhat similar to TV station groups sharing affiliation to a network. This hypothesis is confirmed for the larger station groups. One has reservations about rejecting this null hypothesis, however, because economies of a common format (a fixed cost) ought to matter more for small than large station groups. The confirmation is consistent, however, with the clustered network affiliations common among TV station groups. The third hypothesis, explicitly introduced for TV stations, holds that radio stations operating in the largest (top fifty) metropolitan areas compose their groups so as to pursue national coverage—the better to attract national advertisers. The null hypothesis holds that adding a station in a top fifty market where a group is not represented is no more (or less) attractive than adding it to another top fifty market where the group already has one or more stations. The data roundly reject the advantage of national coverage. The test may be inappropriate, however, because it covers groups of all sizes rather than the largest ones for which the hypothesis is most relevant. Here, radio and TV probably part company, because national coverage offers manifest advantages to the larger TV station groups for self-supply of syndicated programming and dealing with arm's-length suppliers.

Consolidation and Viewers' Welfare

Viewers' welfare is affected by these features of station organization and reorganization, though the subtle issues raised by differentiated goods *(infinite variety)* are hard to address. LMAs and duopolies offer the paradoxical prospect that less competition among local stations might yield more choice for viewers, because stations operated in common will not offer near-identical programs at the expense of unserved minority tastes. On the one hand, to the degree that station groups centralize their sourcing and scheduling of programs, cost-efficiency might gain at the expense of suitability to the local market (the FCC's traditional concern). On the other hand, station groups may be able to raise the quality of member stations' programming, either by producing their own or obtaining better-suited or more cost-effective programs from arm's-length suppliers (as suggested in Chapter 2).

CHAPTER 9

Cable Networks and Cable Operators: Ownership Links and Carriage Decisions

Cable system operators transmit to their subscribers bundles of program series provided by cable networks. The multiple cable system operators (MSOs) produce little or none of their own programs and rely on the cable networks (and local broadcast signals) for program supplies, just as the cable networks rely on MSOs and other distributors for access to household viewers. Each group's profitability depends heavily on the deals it can strike with the other. Vertical ownership linkages between them are prevalent—through either common ownership by media conglomerates such as Time Warner or equity in cable networks held by MSOs. In order to understand this ownership and its consequences, one must first identify the historical context and theoretical explanations for the prevalence of vertical integration. Then comes the main focus: determining the effect of ownership ties on the likelihood that a cable system will carry a given basic cable network.

A cable operator purchases, typically on a price-per-subscriber basis, the rights to air a basic network's programming, which it bundles with other networks and sells to consumers for a monthly service fee. While at the end of 2002 the average system offered sixty-five channels of cable networks and retransmitted broadcast stations, 308 national networks competed for carriage. This surplus allows the cable operator to make a selection and imposes a stiff

227

opportunity-cost test for any network newly seeking carriage (Chapter 5).[1] Networks "bid" a stream of programs and a monthly payment per subscriber, and the cable operator selects the mix of networks that (within the limit of its channel capacity) maximizes the willingness to pay of the households it reaches, net of the networks' charges. A contract between an operator and a network is usually negotiated at the MSO level; it deals principally with the duration of carriage, arrangements for sharing promotion expenses, and fees and payment procedures.[2]

This relationship between network and operator differs in several ways from the vertical interfaces between broadcast network and station. The cable operator is not cloaked in the identity of the network, as are broadcast stations. The operator prepares little or no programming of its own, simply transmitting the full daily schedule assembled by each network.[3] The broadcasters' problem of allocating decision rights arises only in a small way (for premium channels that are sold individually to households).[4] The relationship between cable network and operator, however, is subject to the hazards of small-numbers bargaining. The many local cable systems have coalesced into a small number of MSOs, for reasons that may include bargaining power against cable networks (this and other reasons are discussed subsequently). Cable networks (Chapter 5) provide differentiated services that honor *infinite variety*. Yet some face much closer substitutes than others. Some that lack close substitutes and that appeal to many viewers enjoy some market power. The extreme cases are the sports networks (ESPN and regional sports channels), which deal with monopolistic suppliers of professional sports entertainment (leagues and associations) that can use the franchised cable network as the cat's paw to collect rents from sports-loving viewers. The network-operator nexus also reflects other traits generally found in creative industries. Cable networks' costs are almost entirely fixed but are selected so as to yield a program stream of the most profitable quality. Cable operators do incur significant marginal costs to service more households or provide more channels, but they nonetheless have high fixed costs. The possibility of stalemates in small-numbers bargaining is clearly present.

Historical Background

The foundations for the cable industry were laid in the late 1950s and early 1960s, when cable emerged to distribute broadcast television signals to locations too remote to receive them. Cable operators were closely regulated by the local governments that granted them exclusive distribution franchises within their municipalities. The mid-1970s brought a shift in the industry, as entrepreneurs such as WTBS's Ted Turner and USA Network's Kay Koplovitz saw cable as a means to distribute national network programming and not just to improve the reception of local broadcast signals.[5] Stations such as WTBS transmitted their signals via satellite to be distributed over the local cable systems, becoming national "superstations." While these networks initially offered little more than syndicated reruns of broadcast programs, entrants soon began to feature original programming and cinema films.

Cable systems now make service available to nearly all households in the United States: the proportion of TV households with access to cable television climbed from one-third in 1975 to 96.6 percent in 2003. The once fragmented cable industry had consolidated to the point of dominance by a handful of MSOs such as Tele-Communications Inc. (TCI, now part of Comcast), Cablevision, Time Warner, and Cox Communications. They had expanded by purchasing many independent systems in smaller markets and had built most of those recently installed.[6] The horizontal concentration of MSOs has a number of possible explanations that are relevant to vertical integration. They gained bargaining power against the cable networks as program suppliers. They also may have enlarged the local system's bargaining power against the municipal franchising authority.[7] Finally, size probably carried an advantage for funding the expansion of their highly capital-intensive distribution systems. Investments in expanded infrastructure caused the operators' average capital cost to leap from $120 per subscriber in 1975 to $900 per subscriber in 1984 ($504 in 1975 prices).

Bargaining power against cable networks should theoretically accrue at an increasing rate as the MSOs grow more concentrated. Comcast's purchase in 2003 of TCI's assets from AT&T apparently boosted Comcast's bargaining strength a good deal. Comcast promised its investors a cut of nearly 7 percent in program costs, and examples of deals announced with major cable networks are consistent with this figure.[8]

If concentration might have increased MSOs' bargaining power against program suppliers, they also faced competition not only from traditional broadcasters but also from new distributors. Rival technologies of video distribution, including Direct Broadcast Satellite (DBS), Satellite Master Antenna Television (SMATV), and the VCR, placed limits on cable's potential status as a dominant programming distributor. Four out of five new subscribers to multichannel video services now select DBS over cable, and the non-cable share of the market in 2003 reached 24 percent. This competition was intensified by the Satellite Home Viewer Improvement Act (1999), which allowed DBS companies to retransmit local broadcast signals, thus matching cable's ability to provide local news and sports. By December 2000 this service was available to 51 million households.[9]

Cable systems have undergone a complex history of waxing and waning regulation by the Federal Communications Commission (FCC) and are now deregulated under 1996 legislation. Two features of their regulatory history bear on MSOs' integration with cable networks. First, the regulatory history involves two episodes of controls on the price of basic cable service to households, followed by periods of deregulation. Research on this experience shows that, while the local cable system clearly enjoys monopoly power over its household subscribers, this power was not effectively restrained by price regulation (nor unleashed when it was removed). The reason is (yet again) *endogenous fixed costs:* price-constrained cable operators could substitute cheaper cable networks for more costly ones or force the networks to reduce quality in response to the MSOs' reduced willingness to pay. They also transferred channels from the basic to the premium tier. As a result, regulation failed to constrain the quality-adjusted price of basic cable services, and the effect of price regulation was not to increase the number of households subscribing to cable (as one might expect) but to reduce it (because of the lowered quality of the programming offered).[10]

Second, vertical ownership links between MSOs and cable networks have encountered some challenges from antitrust authorities, notably the acquisition of Turner Broadcasting by Time Warner in 1996. Time Warner was one of the largest operators of cable systems, as well as supplying pay-TV networks (especially HBO). Turner was a major operator of basic cable networks—TBS, TNT, Cable News Network (CNN). Important for the antitrust issue, prior to acquiring full ownership of Turner, Time Warner had held a 23 percent interest in it, as had TCI, then the largest MSO; following the merger, TCI's stake in Turner was converted into a 9 percent stake in Time Warner. Also, TCI obtained an agreement with Turner that specified the terms under which TCI would carry various Turner channels for twenty years in return for a price 15 percent below the average paid by other cable operators. Prior to this case the FCC had adopted "channel occupancy rules" that prevented a cable operator from devoting more than 40 percent of its channels to networks in which it held 5 percent or more interest, or demanding a financial stake in a network as a condition for carriage. The Federal Trade Commission (FTC) was concerned with several aspects of Time Warner's acquisition—such as reduced competition between Time Warner and Turner as suppliers of premium cable networks and between Time Warner and TCI as buyers of programs. In particular, Time Warner as a cable operator might refuse carriage to networks competing with CNN, and TCI might favor Time Warner networks over their premium-channel competitors. The defendants pointed to the advantages of vertical linkages for supplying a base of carriage commitments that aided the launching of new networks. They also argued that TCI's 9 percent share in Time Warner, which was non-voting, offered too weak an incentive for favoritism for TCI to pass up superior competing networks preferred by TCI subscribers, or to deny these competitors carriage in order to weaken them. Furthermore, preserving Turner's monopoly power would likely force TCI to pay higher prices for Turner networks. The case was settled by a consent decree that let the new ownership arrangements stand and prevented Time Warner only from forcing cable operators to take a bundle that included both Time Warner premium and Turner basic channels.[11]

Vertical Integration

Prevalence

David Waterman and Andrew Weiss constructed a record of the extent of vertical integration in cable in late 1995, based on sixty-five cable networks.[12] This group includes all basic and pay-per-view networks reaching 10 percent or more of U.S. households and premium networks that reach at least 1 percent. Waterman and Weiss also examined the twelve largest MSOs, which include most cable systems having any integration with cable networks (only two smaller MSOs are known to have such links). Of forty-seven basic networks (not including home shopping), twenty-six are integrated with MSOs. A higher rate of integration prevails for premium channels (seven of eight), pay-per-view (four of six), and home shopping (four of four) networks. Ownership ties appear more prevalent among the larger networks. Vertical integration is also pervasive (all of the top twenty) in the regional sports networks, marketed as premium channels. The investments of individual MSOs tend strongly to be minority shareholdings, and ownership of a network is commonly shared between two or more MSOs (fourteen of thirty basic and home shopping networks with MSO ownership). The premium networks, however, all have majority owners. The basic networks' owners also include many content producers (twenty-two of the basic networks, when content-producing owners are defined to include broadcast networks but not print-media firms). Of the largest twelve MSOs in 1995, eight had affiliations with cable networks.

Vertical integration increased from the mid-1980s to the mid-1990s. Of the sixty-five cable networks in 1995, thirty-nine had been launched by 1985, and sixteen (41 percent) of these were vertically integrated at the outset. In 1995, forty-one of the sixty-five (63 percent) were vertically integrated. Since large MSOs more commonly undertake vertical integration, it is relevant that the horizontal concentration of MSOs was increasing at the same time: the largest four raised their share of basic cable subscribers from 24.9 percent in 1985 to 47.4 percent in 1995.[13]

Historical and Theoretical Explanations

Many theoretical models stand ready to explain a firm's choice of vertical integration, creating a daunting task for the researcher who hopes to pin down one explanation and reject all the others. Fortunately, a consensus does prevail about how to explain integration between MSOs and cable networks.[14] The major vertical links were forged early in the development of the cable industry, when cable operators and networks were far from assured that they could reach deals in the market for programming that would make them viable. Cable operators make large, sunk investments to install and subsequently upgrade their systems to expand the number of channels and (recently) provide two-way communication capability. Cable networks incur fixed and sunk costs to generate streams of programming, the payout to which depends closely on the number of cable systems willing to license and distribute them. A network may spend $25 to $75 million prior to launch, then continue to lose similar sums for several years (Chapter 5). Investments by the MSOs in cable networks mitigated each of these problems. The MSOs ensured themselves a supply of programming. The cable networks served some customers whose purchases were partly pre-committed; these commitments might function as positive signals for other customers. And the MSOs' extensive tangible assets had more collateral value with lenders than did the format plan that constituted the resource base of a nascent cable network.

This explanation based on avoiding a freeze-out from the market is consistent with the preceding facts. Restricting ownership to minority shareholdings would ensure the supply of programming for an MSO without forcing it to assume a managerial role in a business demanding very different managerial skills. Ownership could economically be shared among MSOs, thanks to two properties. First, the cable network's stream of programming is a proprietary public good that can serve one cable operator without impairing its value to another, and second, most local cable systems do not compete with others for customers. The holding's minority status weakens but does not destroy the MSO's incentive to promote or otherwise enhance the value of a basic cable network. In any case, the MSO does little of this. It merely bundles basic networks together and charges the subscriber a bundled price for them. Premium and pay-per-view channels in contrast require proficient marketing and administration by the cable operator; enlarging the MSO's stake motivates these efforts, and majority ownership does indeed prevail. The explanation is consistent with most vertical investments' having occurred early in the industry's development. It is also consistent with these investments' commonly being bought and sold by MSOs. Once a cable network is established, the ownership bond should be transferable without loss of value to another MSO. While turnover in vertical ownership links is not readily tabulated, examples suggest some patterns. A good deal of it occurs, either independently or incidental to mergers and other changes in control of business units.[15] This turnover of cable systems' minority investments contrasts with recently occurring switches of broadcast networks' investments in cable networks to majority or wholly owned status; the broadcasters need operating control to manage deals such as repeats of broadcast programming (Chapter 4).[16]

These same facts tend to rule out many competing explanations for vertical integration. An important class of them deals with contractual failures in arm's-length dealings between sellers and buyers. Those failures call for vertical integration in order to enhance the supply of transaction-specific assets (that is, investments that will lose substantial value if the party making them recontracts with a different partner). MSOs and cable networks, however, build no such shared assets beyond the goodwill of subscribers accustomed to receiving a particular network. The facts stated thus far are consistent with the pertinence of avoiding double marginalization—the distortion that results when a seller with market power charges a price exceeding its product's marginal cost, only to have the buyer impose another markup when it resells to final customers. The cable operator enjoys a local monopoly, and the cable network offers a product differentiated from its rivals', so double marginalization is indeed a hazard.[17] Scattered evidence suggests that cable networks give favorable license terms to MSOs with ownership stakes in them, and a statistical study by George S. Ford and John D. Jackson showed that prices received by cable networks vary greatly among their cable system customers; but that variation is not necessarily the result of ownership links. They investigated the relationship between a cable system's total cost of programming (per subscriber per month) and the existence of vertical links to one or more networks. They did find a significant negative relationship, but its magnitude is so large as not to be credible.[18] Double marginalization falters, however, as an explanation for these ownership links. It seems inconsistent with the minority and shared ownership of networks. To avert double marginalization, the cable network must cut its license fee to its marginal cost, which is approximately zero. A giveaway of programming to one MSO impairs the value of the ownership stakes in the network held by other investors (whether MSOs or not) and would hence be unacceptable without a comprehensive agreement and lump-sum transfers among all parties. No such contract form has surfaced.[19]

Some competing explanations for vertical ownership links identify important welfare problems that they may entail. Consider an entrant cable network that competes with an established network in which MSOs own equity stakes. The MSO that carries the new network suffers a decline in its expected profit from its investment in the incumbent (which loses revenue but avoids no costs). In order to offset this penalty, the newcomer must offer the prospect of lower cost and/or superior appeal to the MSO's subscribers. The equity link thus begets a barrier to the entry of an equally efficient competitor, unless it is sufficiently differentiated that it draws new subscribers or attracts viewers away from a wide variety of incumbent channels.[20] This is another aspect of the foreclosure mechanism discussed in Chapter 7. As an apparent example, this barrier has affected the entry of news networks, owing to the stakes held by major MSOs in incumbent CNN.[21] Paradoxically, the negative implication for welfare may not prevail, because successful and established cable networks can repel closely competing entrants without any help from MSOs.[22]

Previous Research

Most previous research on the effect of ownership links on carriage decisions was produced in the setting of regulatory proceedings and motivated by a concern for the possible foreclosure of unintegrated networks. Statistical methods have been applied to this question more fully than to other questions pursued in this book; Bruce Owen and Steven Wildman provided a convenient summary.[23] Benjamin Klein examined the percentage of four hundred cable systems that carried each of twenty basic and eight premium networks, comparing for each network the mean carriage percentages for systems without ownership links to systems belonging to the four most heavily linked MSOs. He found that the linked MSOs carried unaffiliated networks about 5 percent more frequently than did systems with no ownership links, indicating no discrimination against them.[24] Robert Crandall analyzed cable systems owned and/or operated by TCI, a large MSO, along with systems without vertical integration.[25] For each of twenty-four basic cable networks, he related carriage on TCI and other operators to the existence of an ownership link (with numerous controls for the system's size, age, channel capacity, price to subscribers, and community demographic variables). TCI systems proved significantly more likely to carry nearly all TCI-affiliated channels, but they were also significantly more likely to carry seven of fifteen unaffiliated networks, and significantly less likely to carry only three. Crandall concluded that favoritism of affiliated channels occurs but does not greatly disfavor independent networks.

Waterman and Weiss expanded the research design by examining the carriage percentages of four premium cable networks and eight basic cable networks in cable systems owned by the twenty-five largest MSOs.[26] They also found that integrated cable systems are more likely to carry a network in which they have an ownership interest. The effect is small among the more widely distributed networks, but large among those premium channels for which it is statistically significant. They took account of several decision variables deployed by cable system operators: the cable system's price to subscribers for premium channels and the proportion of households that subscribe to affiliated and unaffiliated premium channels. Only one case appears of an operator setting a significantly lower price for an affiliated premium channel, and none for subscribership rates. These results are not consistent with vertical linkages coming about in order to avoid double marginalization.

Another factor treated by Waterman and Weiss is the total number of networks offered, respectively, by integrated and unintegrated cable systems. Favoring an affiliated network necessarily denies carriage to some other network if channel capacity is given, but capacity is itself a decision variable, so the exclusionary effect of favoritism may appear in restricted capacity as well as carriage decisions. Indeed, Waterman and Weiss found a weakly significant negative effect of affiliation on the number of networks offered, but it is small, less than one network for large-capacity systems (fifty-five or more channels).

If vertical integration lowers the cable operator's cost of affiliated channels and increases (or does not substantially reduce) the number of channels provided overall, the subscriber might benefit from paying a lower price per channel. Hoekyun Ahn and Barry Littman analyzed cable systems belonging to MSOs with and without shareholdings in cable networks, finding that the vertically integrated systems received slightly but significantly smaller subscriber payments per channel per month.[27]

Tasneem Chipty's 2001 contribution pays attention to the interdependence of basic and premium services.[28] The data pertain to 1991, when cable-service prices to households were unregulated. In the core test, cable systems prove to carry significantly more basic networks of a given type if they are vertically integrated with a basic network in that category, once again rejecting foreclosure. For premium networks, however, the conclusion reverses: vertical integration reduces the number carried and presumably excludes competitors of the integrated network. A system that carries more networks (of a type) tends to charge more, but it also prices so as to steer subscribers toward the network in which it has an ownership interest. A system vertically integrated with a premium network tends to charge more for basic services. Thus, a diluted form of foreclosure seems to take place.

Recent Results

This group of studies yields a fairly clear set of conclusions. An ownership link between cable system and network increases the chances of the network's carriage. It apparently does not foreclose that network's competitors, however, or it impedes them to only a small extent. Some studies that take pricing into account suggest that ownership links are helpful against the distortion of double marginalization. These results usefully suggest that vertical links in cable do not pose a substantial problem for public policy. They do not really explain, however, why the MSOs acquired their ownership links in the first place. As background to this volume, we undertook a study generally resembling that of Waterman and Weiss, seeking to explain that investment decision and (thereby) shed light on its consequences.[29] We also employed some important control variables not used in previous studies. The data set includes 150 individual cable systems sampled at random, along with twenty basic networks selected by stratified random sampling.[30] The objective is to explain whether or not a given network will be carried by a particular cable system, given the presence or absence of an ownership link and many other features of the system, the network, and the two taken together. Variables specific to the cable system include its number of channels, its age, whether it was recently upgraded to accommodate two-way transfers of data, and the size (total subscribers) of the MSO to which it belongs. The cable system's economic environment is represented by the size and median household income of its urban area, demographic, and regional controls. Controls pertaining to the cable network notably include its popularity (national prime-time Nielsen rating), an important determinant of carriage not employed in previous studies; its age is also included. Finally, the nexus of the cable system and network is represented by the MSO's fractional ownership stake; variables indicating the system's carriage of competing networks will be described subsequently.

Our results confirm the finding of previous studies that ownership links encourage carriage of a network; a 10 percent increase in the ownership stake predicts a 2 percent increase in the probability that a network will be carried. For vertically integrated cable systems, a network's properties (its ratings and its age) continue to matter for carriage about as much as in cable systems that are not vertically integrated; an ownership link does not disconnect the key economic forces driving the carriage decision. We also tested whether a network loses out when the cable system owns a stake in one or more of its competitors (specifically, we measured the proportion of competing networks in which some share is held). Similarly, we tested whether a network's probability of carriage declines with the proportion of competing networks that are carried, a natural implication of how a profit-seeking cable system will compose its portfolio of networks. Neither of the two negative influences is confirmed; if anything, they lean in a positive direction, but the coefficients are not statistically significant. This pattern, which appeared in some earlier studies as well, probably results from the lack of a control for differences in the number of viewers interested in a given group (e.g., more households are interested in news channels than in hunting and fishing channels).

Even with a network's ratings controlled, its age is a significant positive predictor that it will be carried. This result supports the hypothesis that ownership links in cable reflect the parties' attempts to ensure their economic outcomes when the cable sector was young. A related finding is a significant positive influence on carriage of the age of the cable system, suggesting that it was in operation when these pioneering investments took place. Furthermore, the (present) size of the MSO does not affect carriage, which calls into question any explanation based on bargaining stalemates in bilaterally concentrated markets (although firm sizes might have mattered at an earlier time). This historical explanation for ownership links cuts against the competing hypothesis that those links provide a gateway for the entry of new cable networks. The data reject the latter hypothesis: an ownership link does not significantly influence carriage for the youngest one-third of networks in our sample, but it does for older networks.

Epilogue

An obligation of American intellectuals, eagerly accepted and enthusiastically performed, is to criticize the programming produced by the U.S. commercial television industry. This book has approached the small screen with a less emotive goal: to explain why the system produces the programming (quality, mix, target audience, etc.) that it does and why it is changing as it is. The answer requires an understanding of two very different sectors—the "creative industry" that produces programs and the commercial channels that bring them to viewers. The quality and character of the programs that the creative industry produces are what the distributors can most profitably present to the viewing public. Those profits depend on the numbers and types of viewers that various programs can attract and advertisers' willingness to pay for their attention. They also depend on the organization of the networks that package programs, the distributors (broadcast stations, cable systems, satellites) that transmit them, and the deals that they strike with one another.

This evidence will support a certain amount of crystal-ball service for the reader, though not very much. The erosion of the broadcast sector traced in Part Two has no natural stopping point. Whatever happens to the fad of reality programming, the logic of fixed cost gives the broadcasters no prospect (except lucky programming inspirations) for staving off the competing economic attractions of cable, satellite, and Internet-based program flows. Paradoxically, the erosion of broadcasting can be predicted with considerably more assurance than the long-term future role of services based on cable, satellite, and even telecommunication lines. That is because the future cost-effectiveness of each of these for high-speed broadband (two-way) communication is up for grabs.[1] What we have called "cable networks" throughout this book might wind up reaching your screen by any of these channels. In closing we briefly turn the focus to public policy, to illustrate how the features of TV as a creative industry interact with the making of policy.

Issues of Program Selection

An issue long central to economic policy on broadcasting was the inefficiency of program supply that arises when, with only a few channels available, they get filled with nearly interchangeable programs serving the majority's taste, while minority tastes go unserved. The problem arises from the fixity of broadcasters' costs; when a second broadcaster offers a close-substitute service to the majority taste, a new fixed cost is incurred, but no marginal cost is saved for the first provider, nor do any viewers get much benefit. In its primordial form the problem's importance is overstated, because viewers, within limits, can substitute between programs offered at different hours. The great increase in channel capacity brought by cable and satellites makes room both for many more programs at a given time and for the use of channels for rebroadcast. Besides, the viewer can draw upon steadily improving technologies for recording a broadcast at one time and playing it at some more convenient hour.

If there exists a present-day problem of market performance, parallel to that of oligopolistic imitation, it must involve the mixture of programs offered, even with their number being large *(infinite vari-*

ety). With many programs available, the normative problem results from many particular small distortions to the mix. Program suppliers respond not to viewers' willingness to pay but to their expected willingness to purchase the goods and services advertised on the program. Functionally specialized cable networks do much to serve all minority tastes backed by sufficient willingness to pay; public TV also contributes, though subject to its organizational infirmities. Some complex issues (not pursued intensively in this book) arise from the marketing of cable networks as bundles rather than à la carte.

The shift of viewing toward cable and satellites and the responsive changes in discretionary program quality display the pervasive importance of the mechanism of *endogenous fixed costs,* stressed throughout this volume. The capacity of cable systems and satellites for cable networks has expanded to the point where viewers with quite specialized tastes get served. They may be served programming of modest quality, but no obvious market failure is involved. Where subscriber charges per month can be freely selected, the program supplier can pick the quality level that elicits the greatest willingness to pay, net of program costs.

Placing TV broadcasting next to the other creative industries brings to mind an issue that has induced great concern in the performing arts, William Baumol's "cost disease."[2] Performances of plays, operas, concerts, and dance are all labor-intensive activities that offer little if any potential for productivity gains over time. As productivity increases for most other goods produced and consumed in the economy, real incomes and the value of labor rise. Without productivity gains, as labor grows more expensive, the performing arts' costs rise without limit, as do the prices that they must charge in order to cover costs. People do enjoy higher incomes from the rising value of their labor services, and they might therefore choose to spend more on performing arts despite these increases in relative ticket prices. But then, they might not. As Baumol pointed out, the making of cinema films and TV programs is subject to exactly the same logic of the cost disease, even though we do not perceive their backs pressed against the economic wall. While technology has greatly increased the capacity for delivering programs, it has not done much to raise the productivity of the process of preparing programs. Exceptions do come to mind: computer-based animation is certainly one; reality programming commonly finesses the problem by declining to pay its performing labor. These exceptions apart, the cost disease over the long run will promote what from this book's perspective are reductions in the quality of broadcasts. No obvious policy problem arises, but makers of predictions should take heed.

Structural Changes and Public Policy

Apart from the structural change wrought by the spread of cable and satellite-based distribution, other organizational changes have perturbed the dealings between networks and distributors. Most of them stem from changes in public policy that formerly limited both vertical and horizontal integration. The policies' restrictions were definitely binding, as shown by the substantial changes in organization that followed their relaxation or removal.

Vertical Integration

Vertical integration between the production and broadcast of prime-time programs was long limited by the financial interest and syndication rules, which prevented networks from producing much of their prime-time programming and from holding an equity interest in their programs' syndication revenues. Effectively the fin-syn rules also prevented vertical integration between the studios producing TV programs and the networks broadcasting them. The rules' demise thus had two layers of consequences. Network and producer could now bargain over the allocation of decision rights on individual program series—a desirable option, because each party's actions can substantially affect a program's economic value, and the balance could vary from program to program. Broadcast networks now hold some equity interest in the majority of their prime-time programming. The repeal also allowed vertical integration between the film studios and broadcast networks, which led to the creation of The WB and UPN networks, Viacom's ownership of both the Paramount studio and the CBS and (later) UPN networks, and more recently NBC's acquisition of the Universal studio. Networks do give more favorable slots to programs in which they hold equity when those programs' prospects for success are close to the margin. The evidence is mixed, however, on whether owned programs are favored for annual renewal. The mixed evidence is perhaps explained by transitional turbulence in the bargaining between studios and networks, whereby networks demanded equity interests in exchange for licensing programs with only marginal promise, in order to capture some of the up-side of a favorable surprise in a program's performance. The increasing prevalence of vertical integration between program suppliers and broadcast networks does raise a policy issue, because these transactions possess a defensive character. Integration ensures the firm against foreclosure (no outlet for its programming, or no programming to fill its distribution capacity). This private benefit lacks a social counterpart. Indeed, it imposes a cost in the creative industries, where the complete heterogeneity of the product *(infinite variety)* and the unpredictability of success *(nobody knows)* make it advantageous for sellers and buyers to have access to many potential partners. In a market for a thoroughly homogeneous product, there is no economic benefit— private or social—to a buyer from picking over the wares offered by numerous sellers. With *infinite variety* and idiosyncratic tastes, such shopping around conveys benefits (up to a point), net of shopping costs.

Vertical integration also played a role among the cable networks, owing to market forces rather than changes in public policy. The links between cable networks and both studios and broadcast networks increasingly reflect the broadcasters' efforts to extract more value from their programs through rebroadcast, reuse of material in news and sports programs, and the like *(ars longa)*. The different audiences attracted by the specialized cable networks contribute to the payout of these ownership linkages by reducing the transaction costs of arranging to repeat programs. One intervention by public policy does affect the process: the local broadcasting station's property right in transmission of its signal on cable systems within its market. The retransmission rules give the broadcaster two choices: to demand and get carriage but no payment from the cable operator, or to seek to negotiate payment, but with no guarantee of carriage (should the parties fail to agree). The cable operators have stonewalled demands for cash license fees for retransmission, but they have made payments in kind by carrying bargain-basement cable networks that the broadcasters created for just this purpose. This smacks of an inefficient bargaining outcome. It was illustrated again in 2004 by a controversy between Viacom and the satellite service EchoStar, which suspended broadcast of CBS and several of Viacom's cable networks when the parties reached an impasse on retransmission of CBS's owned-and-operated stations (O&O's). Viacom voiced an interest in buying a cable system that could provide leverage in such disputes.[3]

Vertical integration also occurs in the cable sector between cable networks and the multi-system operators (MSOs). It has at times been regarded suspiciously by policy makers though not formally limited.[4] A substantial body of research supports the hypothesis that MSOs' investments in cable networks have been undertaken to enhance the supply of programming available to fill the MSOs' channel capacities. Cable operators vertically integrated with cable networks are more likely than unintegrated cable operators to carry affiliated networks, but they also carry more networks overall, so no exclusion seems to be occurring.

Much of the vertical integration that has developed in TV was first confined to either the broadcasting segment (e.g., News Corp.) or the cable sector (TCI before its purchase by AT&T). Their shifting market shares and increasingly close interaction might be expected to expand foreclosure threats and opportunities across that dividing line. Prominent examples include Viacom (since it acquired CBS) and Time Warner (since it started The WB). The process continued with News Corp.'s acquiring control of satellite operator DirecTV in 2003 and NBC's acquisition of the Universal studio in 2004. The deal between News Corp. and DirecTV gained approval by the Federal Communications Commission (FCC) only with conditions that would deter News Corp. (Fox) from using DirecTV to strengthen its bargaining power with cable systems— especially that involving Fox's string of regional sports networks. The FCC considered the scenario of a temporary withdrawal of these (popular) networks by Fox in order to force an increase of subscriber fees. With the DirecTV acquisition completed, it could be profitable for Fox, the FCC concluded. That is because DirecTV could capture for Fox the revenue from bereft sports fans switching from cable to DirecTV in quest of their sports channels. Fox's broadcasting stations had the same sort of leverage potential, since EchoStar required Fox's retransmission consent to carry their signals.[5] Similarly, MSO Comcast's failed 2004 bid for Disney appeared aimed at bolstering its resources for bargaining with cable networks, once Comcast could threaten to rely on Disney's vaults and program studios.[6]

Horizontal Integration

Public policy has also addressed horizontal integration, in particular the common ownership of broadcast stations. Strict limits were imposed and then relaxed on the total number of stations under common ownership nationally, and no two stations could come under common ownership within a market area. Both limits were binding, and their relaxation led to a considerable increase in both forms of integration. The patterns of these transactions help us identify the principal motives for the integration. By conjoining in groups, broadcast stations seem to pursue several objectives. One is the efficient operation of stations serving small markets, by means of centralizing routine managerial tasks and reducing fixed costs per station. Common to groups of large-market stations is a different pair of goals: to develop programming for shared use by group members and for syndication to others; and to achieve and exert bargaining power—against networks, syndicators, and equipment suppliers. Yet the observed dealings between networks and large-city station chains suggest positive net benefits from collaboration in the development of programs and in resolving the problem of diminished rents and the inevitable adjustment of compensation. Both purposes are consistent with the fact that the network affiliations of large-market station groups are typically concentrated on a single network. Chains of small-market stations likely increase economic efficiency, but the case for large-market stations is not so clear.

Horizontal groups, especially of large-market stations, raise the same issue of strategic agglomeration as the vertically related media conglomerates. An increase in bargaining power on one side of a bilaterally concentrated market need not worsen economic welfare, and might in some cases improve it. But gaining size in order to enhance bargaining power need not be consistent with maximum operating efficiency. In the TV industry a factor of constant importance is the endogenous quality of programs, coupled with the impossibility of program distributors' contracting with producers on the quality of programs to be supplied. Consider, for example, large station groups' dealings with a first-run syndicator. An enlarged station group may be able to beat down the syndicator's price, but with the consequence that the stations receive a lower-quality program series while the syndicator's profits are nearly unchanged. This response limits the distortions that can emerge from the application of bargaining power. At the same time, it is a reason why the astute party does not use its bargaining power myopically.

The issue of real economies versus bargaining power also arises in cable MSOs. Early cable systems were typically independent local enterprises, but they have consolidated extensively into a handful of MSOs. Clearly these gain substantial economies of operation by centralizing large numbers of similar managerial decisions. Integration of neighboring systems in a region is strongly evident, consistent with these operating economies and also with the advantage of coordinated ad sales to advertisers who seek to reach customers throughout a large metropolitan area served by several cable systems. The consolidation of adjacent cable systems exacted the cost of eliminating competition at the borders of the two independent systems or where any "overbuild" existed. Nevertheless, the high capital cost per household of overbuild marks it as an expensive way to obtain the advantages of competition. Other factors appeared to promote horizontal consolidation. The task of recruiting and importing signals from cable networks required much-increased managerial sophistication.[7] It also generated the motive of exerting bargaining power against cable networks.[8] Combating the adroit rent-collection efforts of the sports leagues would be attractive to the MSOs and favorable to consumers' welfare. Exerting bargaining power against the typical cable network, however, invites the same distortion of reduced program quality associated with any squeeze of firms with *endogenous fixed costs* (Chapter 9). Again we find an important motive for consolidation with an uncertain but possibly negative welfare implication.

The remaining form of horizontal consolidation involves broadcast stations in local markets, which might combine with competing local stations or rival media—radio stations and central-city newspapers. The FCC long held that TV stations in a city market could not come under common ownership, nor could a TV station and a central-city newspaper. In 2003 the FCC voted to allow some common ownership of stations within sufficiently large markets, as well as common ownership of a TV station and a central-city newspaper. The substantial cost saving from joint operation of local TV stations is well documented for the "duopoly" local marketing agreements (Chapter 8); the case for station-newspaper mergers (not addressed in this book) presumably rests on shared news-gathering costs. The economic drawbacks of such mergers presumably include the use of market power by the co-owned units to raise the price of local advertising and perhaps reduce the quality of programs offered to the public. Syndicators licensing programs likely find themselves with fewer competing local customers. This liberalization was challenged in the courts, and in mid-2004 a U.S. court of appeals rejected the formula the FCC had devised to determine whether an increase in local ownership concentration should be allowed. In the absence of an appeal to the U.S. Supreme Court, the FCC would have had to go back to the drawing board (hearings, deliberations) and put off any implementation of new local ownership rules well into the future. The principle that the FCC could liberalize these rules, however, was accepted by the court. The previously authorized local marketing agreements (duopolies) were not affected.

Economics and First Amendment Concerns

While this book is not mainly normative, it relies on economists' conventional concept of economic welfare as the sum of surpluses accruing to consumers and producers. Much public policy applied to broadcasting in the United States has run on a different track, however. We close with a sketch of how the standard economic treatment can shed light on current policy questions with a major First Amendment content. This is important not only for putting to work our empirical conclusions about the industrial organization of broadcasting, but also for showing how normative economic analysis diverges from attitudes associated with the First Amendment that have dominated much of U.S. public policy toward broadcasting.[9] This sketch is particularly appropriate in light of the dispute that raged over one of the FCC's 2003 policy changes. Chains of TV stations under common ownership had long been limited—first to a maximum number of stations, later to a maximum combined proportion of U.S. households that could be reached by a group's members. In 2003 the FCC chose to raise this proportion from 35 to 45 percent.[10] This change might seem economically less consequential than the others that accompanied it (relaxed limits on commonly owned stations and on joint ownership of a TV station and central-city newspaper in a given city). Yet the national cap produced a firestorm of objections that led the U.S. Congress to vote by a large majority to reverse it (the cap was rolled back to 39 percent).[11]

Lying behind most public policies toward broadcasting are freedom-of-speech or First Amendment concerns that assert a substantial social value from giving one more "voice" access to the channels of public communication. The count of voices should be maximized, goes the implication, without regard to the cost of generating or disseminating that voice's message. This view, redolent of the town meeting and frontier democracy, prizes the voice of the individual citizen and correspondingly discounts that of the large, profit-seeking corporation.[12] Applied to a market setting, this preference for the maximum number of entities (voices) resembles a conclusion familiar from welfare economics—the preference of antitrust policy for a large number of competitors in the market. The economic analysis, however, runs on a different track. Almost every economic model of market competition implies that removing a firm from a market with few incumbent sellers causes market price to rise and the quantity sold to fall. Antitrust enforcement in the United States employs an established procedure to determine (say) whether a merger between two direct competitors might unduly raise price. The answer is expected to depend both on how closely the merging firms compete (are they really in the same market?) and how many competitors will remain after the merger. A substantial expected loss in consumers' surplus warrants blocking the merger. Yet the social saving from any cost reduction or efficiency gain due to the merger also matters. A sufficiently large gain in efficiency warrants putting up with some loss in consumers' surplus; in the best case, costs might even decline enough that prices fall, and consumers gain.

First Amendment policy differs greatly. It does not follow the approach of economic analysis: state a set of assumptions and derive theoretically grounded predictions or welfare judgments from them. The policymaking process would gain if the First Amendment worldview could be articulated in that form, because it would open the door to reasoned compromises with conflicting models of policymaking and the policy preferences that they yield. Using the FCC's ownership-cap change as a setting, this section probes the underpinnings of the First Amendment view.

In the ownership-cap debate, anyone acquainted with the economics of antitrust policy is struck by the First Amendment position's lack of concern with defining a marketplace in which "voices" can be heard and counted—the recipients' side of the communications. Adding stations in new locations to a chain's span leaves unchanged the count of voices audible in any given location. To infer a substantially increased concentration of voices, one must pool relevant outlets across the United States and rely on some measure of voices' concentration across the national population of auditors. If the First Amendment position on the concentration of voices appears unconcerned with the voice count reaching the individual auditor, it also appears unconcerned with the incremental value of another voice to the message stock reaching the individual auditor. It does not ask whether or not a given voice (that might be lost) does or does not have a flourishing close substitute. This differentiation (or its lack) seems particularly important in the context of network chains: when a network adds an existing affiliated station to its O&Os, most of its message—the network feed—remains unchanged. Regarding the differentiation of broadcasting voices, the First Amendment position is prone to contend that localism is good. The locally owned station is presumed to offer programming more suited to local tastes, more news (especially local),and so on. This is of course an empirical question.[13]

In economic analysis of a market's concentration, the reason for concern over the incremental value of a voice or message is that it incurs an incremental social cost. Let us put aside the auditor's cost of screening one more message. The voice reaching one more auditor incurs no marginal cost. When the number of voices is at issue, however, the fixed cost—and thus the average cost—of another voice does matter. When a voice is lost, its (fixed) cost is avoided, and resources become available to society for transmitting new voices or any other use. The considerable savings from pooling stations' fixed costs thus earn no credit in the First Amendment policy calculus.

That the First Amendment position eschews the natural concerns of auditors' welfare in the information market suggests a way to frame it, with economic consistency, in terms of the speaker's welfare, not the auditor's. Suppose that we define the function and social product of a "voice" in terms not of the increment that it provides to auditors' information stock but of the utility gained by the owner of the voice. That party may incur costs of disseminating its message, but those are internalized. Expressing one's views is taken as an important source of utility to the speaker, just the opposite of a costly use of the speaker's time and resources. Opportunities to give voice are not easily traded, although they can be pooled into advocacy groups. The First Amendment position then reduces to this: any voice that seeks to be heard should be heard, or else some amount of utility (assumed large) is denied to its owner. Costs may be imposed on other parties (those denied resource savings through consolidating station operations); for the speaker, being heard is a "merit good" excused from passing the test of offsetting the costs imposed on others.

This characterization can explain why First Amendment policy pays so little heed either to information as a marketed good or to the definition of the market through which it flows. It also explains why First Amendment policy tends toward positions of principle rather than quantitative resolutions. It is clear enough why First Amendment policy prefers an ownership cap of 35 percent to one of 45 percent, but not whether its adherents would abolish all multi-station ownership as their preferred outcome.

APPENDIXES

NOTES

SELECTED REFERENCES

INDEX

Determinants of Affiliates' Compensation

This appendix supplements Chapter 6 by presenting a statistical analysis of the determinants of compensation ("comp") paid by the network to its individual affiliates. In it we also consider some of the other terms that enter into networks' contracts with their affiliates and determine the resulting distribution of rents. Our data source pertains to the year 2000, when comp flowing to the affiliates was under aggressive attack by the Big 3 networks. Although contracts newly signed at that time commonly specified its curtailment over the life of the contract, this change had little affected the comp that actually flowed in 2000. Nevertheless, the determinants of comp will include both steady-state equilibrium factors and current and recent shifts in networks' and affiliates' relative bargaining power.

Framework for Explaining Compensation Patterns

We suppose that comp is determined in a bargaining process between the network and its affiliate. Each party has its reservation price, and comp (along with other terms) determines how the parties share their joint surplus. The parties' bargaining range is approached in two steps. First, assume that they have the local broadcast market to themselves (bilateral monopoly). The station's reservation price is the minimum flow of revenue that would sustain it as a local monopolist, and the network's maximum payment is the profit it would lose if it lacked an outlet in this market. Alternative deal partners impose a second set of limits on the bargaining range. The station might find a different network partner willing to pay more; the network might switch affiliation to a different local station with a lower opportunity cost. The deal struck within the bargaining range implicitly allocates the parties' combined rent. It reflects the flow of pecuniary compensation along with all other terms having any distributive consequences.

An ideal research design might be constructed by estimating each party's reservation price (conditioned on the other transaction partners who might be available), then invoking the elements of their respective bargaining power to explain how they split the joint surplus within the range. Even lacking a scalar measure of how the surplus is shared, one might treat each measurable contract term affecting the distribution of benefits as an endogenous variable determined by the same structural factors controlling of bargaining power. Such an approach suits a bargaining process in which all terms are simultaneously set and (presumably) adjusted so as to maximize the joint surplus.

The available data allow only a crude approach to this ideal design, but they give insight into the sources of bargaining power and the trade-offs among terms. We employ a database that reports comp paid by networks to stations, along with other useful features of their local broadcasting markets.[1] The BIA Financial Network's MEDIA Access Pro™ provides extensive data on financial, demographic, and general characteristics associated with all licensed U.S. commercial TV stations.[2] For the year 2000 we employed a sample of all TV stations affiliated with or owned by the ABC, CBS, and NBC networks.[3] We omitted stations that reported zero revenue in 2000; this occurred because the station either failed to report or had not begun operating (such stations tend to be in small markets). Joint affiliates of two networks were omitted. The missing affiliates numbered 43 for ABC, 56 for CBS, and 57 for NBC, leaving 565 franchisees of these networks for analysis.

Compensation and Its Determinants

The database suffers a major shortcoming for the measurement of comp. Rather than simply reporting each station's comp, the BIA aggregates comp payments over affiliated stations in each Designated Market Area (DMA) and expresses it as a ratio to total revenue of the network-affiliated stations in the market. We convert this to an estimated dollar value of comp for each station by multiplying this ratio by the station's dollar revenue. The fact that in each DMA comp is aggregated over the three comp-paying networks is less troubling than it might seem, because the close similarity of the Big 3 networks' affiliation contracts implies that affiliates in a given DMA likely receive quite similar amounts of comp. Of more concern is the fact that comp is expressed as a ratio to revenue of all affiliated stations, not just Big 3 affiliates. While all six networks have affiliates in nearly all large DMAs, some lack outlets in smaller markets. Even though a network's share of listeners appears to vary little among DMAs, a bias is introduced between large and small markets because of the smaller shares likely held by Fox, UPN, and The WB in smaller markets. This bias can be avoided by summing BIA's figures for Big 3 stations' revenues and using the ratio of that sum to total market revenue to adjust BIA's comp ratios. The disadvantage with this repair is that some stations' revenues go unreported, so observations are missing. We thus have two dependent variables, each defective in a different way.

$Comp1_i$ = (comp paid to stations in DMA/revenue of all
        stations in DMA) × revenue of ith station

$Comp2_i$ = $Comp1_i$ × (revenue of all stations in DMA/
        revenue of Big 3 affiliates)

For $comp1$ we have observations on 565 stations; for $comp2$, 450.

Determinants of Comp

A fundamental determinant of an affiliate's value to a network is the extra revenue obtainable from national advertisers due to access to consumers in its DMA. TV advertisements target household buyers, of course, and so the natural measure of potential ad revenue is the DMA's number of households multiplied by average personal disposable income per household. This measure of *spending power* should be a good (conditional) predictor of advertising revenue that a network can obtain by having a local outlet, and hence of its willingness to pay for affiliation.

The share of this revenue stream that the local affiliate can capture depends on the factors setting its bargaining power. The key limit should be the number of other stations in the DMA that might compete for affiliation with the network.[4] The measure used is the number of TV stations operating in the DMA (with or without network affiliation). That count is straightforward, but its own underlying determinants raise a vexing problem. At least some of a TV station's costs are both fixed and exogenous (technical equipment and its operation; general administration), implying that the free-entry equilibrium number of stations in a DMA market will be highly correlated with *spending power.*[5] This market equilibrium is vitally affected by decisions of the Federal Communications Commission (FCC) about how many stations to authorize in each DMA. The FCC may have restricted the typical DMA's number of stations below the free-entry equilibrium number, in its allocation of scarce spectrum frequencies, but it has not obviously distorted the economic forces underlying the positive relation between the DMAs' size and their number of stations. We cannot expect to measure accurately the independent influences of *spending power* and the number of stations when their correlation is destined to be high. We evade this problem by expressing the variable *station count* as the number of stations operating in a DMA divided by the DMA's number of TV households, so that the variable approximates the DMA's actual number of stations relative to its likely equilibrium number—a measure of excess supply.[6] The FCC has voiced a strong belief in the importance of the number of stations in a DMA relative to the number of networks. If the Big 3 plus Fox are taken as the relevant networks, and VHF outlets (channels 2–13) as the stations of choice, then only 4 percent of DMAs have more than four commercial VHF stations, implying bargaining strength for the stations. If, however, UHF stations (channels 14 and higher) are appropriately combined with VHF stations, then 49 percent of DMA markets sustain more stations than networks. If we count the competing networks as risen to six, the proportion of markets with "surplus" VHF plus UHF stations stands at 44 percent.[7]

Other limits on the station's bargaining power come from competing distributors of TV signals or of the entertainment product that they provide. The videocassette recorder (VCR) supplies a substitute distribution channel for broadcast entertainment, and so the higher the estimated proportion of the DMA's households with recorders (denoted *VCR prevalence),* the smaller should be the network's potential revenue from the DMA and the station's bargaining power. A possible counter to this prediction, though, lies in the VCR's potential for increasing the value of broadcast signals by letting the user view programs at more convenient times. Formally, the predicted sign of the coefficient of *VCR prevalence* should be judged indeterminate, but the small proportion of owners who program their VCRs suggests a sporting bet on a negative sign. A similar problem arises in cable systems, which distribute increasing numbers of cable networks that compete closely with the traditional over-the-air networks. In their early years, cable systems complemented over-the-air broadcasting by making signals (especially UHF stations) available to households that could receive them over the air either not at all or so poorly as to discourage viewing. Furthermore, the FCC promoted this complementarity by requiring each cable operator to carry the signals of all over-the-air broadcasters with a significant presence in its DMA. Cable systems have evolved, though, into transmitters of many cable networks whose programs substitute for those broadcast over the air. Since the importance of cable's two roles varies from place to place (apart from the time trend toward substitution), we need to control for variations in the proportion of households in a DMA subscribing to cable *(cable penetration).*[8] Like *VCR prevalence, cable penetration* comes with no formal sign prediction, although one might bet that the substitution role now dominates, lowering broadcast stations' value to the networks and reducing comp.[9]

Two variables indicate sources of bargaining power for a station negotiating comp with its network. First, many stations are members of chains, and it is common for many (if not all) of a chain's stations to be affiliated with the same network (Chapter 8). A chain negotiating an affiliation contract for one of its stations may enjoy access to bargaining ploys that a single station lacks. It can threaten to switch the affiliation not only of the station at the bargaining table but of its siblings as well. Or it can offer to switch to this network stations it owns with alien affiliations. The extent of this bargaining power should increase with the number of stations making up the group, a variable that we designate *group size.* Its coefficient should be positive.[10] As of 1994, 784 of 1,154 commercial stations were owned by entities that held more than one TV station license.[11] The other bargaining-power variable draws on the recent history of network-affiliate relations recounted in Chapter 6—the purchase of the New World chain by News Corp. and the switch of those stations' affiliations to the Fox network. This event set in motion a series of switches in affiliation in the affected markets and should have increased the bargaining power of each station in a DMA where any switch of affiliation occurred after 1993. That is, we suppose that a switched affiliation raised the bargaining power of all stations in a DMA (by rebutting the well-established presumption that these affiliations are set in stone), but that this perturbation did not spill over fully to DMAs where no shifts occurred. The dummy variable *affiliation switch* should take a positive coefficient.

A station's value to a network depends on its assignment to a VHF or UHF frequency. The first stations to receive FCC licenses were placed in the VHF frequencies. Those later assigned to the UHF band suffered substantial if declining disadvantages—in the ease of tuning the channel and the quality of the signal. An early study found that advertisers pay substantially less per household for messages on UHF than on VHF stations, with network affiliation controlled.[12] Although UHF and VHF signals received over cable lines are now generally equal in quality, a residue of the other disadvantages remains—along with whatever first-mover advantages the VHF stations have inherited and preserved.[13] We expect to find VHF stations worth more to networks: the coefficient of a dummy variable *VHF*, set equal to one for VHF stations, should be positive.[14]

A station that improves its audience ratings creates value both directly (local advertisers' greater willingness to pay) and through its effect on its network's revenues (by enticing more households to view the network's national ads). Some affiliation contracts contain incentives for the station to boost its ratings, and prime-time ratings have been found to be a statistically significant determinant of comp.[15] The BIA data include average ratings for each of several day parts. These ratings are very highly correlated with one another, so we settled on *prime-time ratings* to expose any explicit or implicit incentive element in affiliation contacts. Its coefficient should be positive.

The Big 3 networks, we saw in Chapter 6, follow closely parallel policies in dealings with their affiliates, down to using the same formula for comp. Payments of comp might differ among them for various reasons, however, notably differential rents extracted from the networks' differing long-run levels of excess profits. We therefore employ dummy variables to designate stations with *CBS* and *NBC* affiliations, treating ABC as the base case.[16] Similarly, the sample of stations includes both independently owned affiliates and O&Os. Casual evidence suggests that the networks have chosen to treat these two groups alike, but that conjecture can be tested statistically. As a first step we include an intercept shift for owned stations, *O&O,* expecting that its coefficient will prove insignificant.

A potentially important component of the reservation price of stations is the coverage of their fixed costs. Comp might be considered a payment that internalizes for the station the incremental national ad revenues that it generates for its partner network, at least when the station's fixed costs would otherwise not be covered. That a station has substantial fixed costs obviously accords with its technology. It is confirmed by the empirical observation that the ratio of stations' gross profits to their revenues increases strongly with the size of the market. Big-city TV stations regularly report gross profits around 50 percent of revenue, while small-city cousins achieve 20 percent or less.[17] On the one hand, with large fixed costs, comp could allow some stations (efficiently) to survive in small markets where they could not otherwise cover their costs. On the other hand, in larger markets the affiliate can flourish without comp, and the network would lack that reason for paying it. No good station-specific measure of exogenous fixed costs is available, but we can undertake an indirect statistical test. Consider the expected positive relation between comp (a dollar amount) and *spending power.* That large contributions might be needed to cover the fixed costs of stations in small markets implies that comp might diminish with market size, or increase only slowly. A simple test involves adding the squared value of *spending power* to the model, expecting (now) a negative coefficient on *spending power* but a positive coefficient on its square. Notice that this prediction depends strictly on the assumed exogenous character of a station's fixed costs. While the apparent fixed cost of a metropolitan station is very large, the unavoidable fixed costs of a hinterland station broadcasting ancient sitcoms and infomercials might be quite small. For example, the news anchor in a metropolitan station may be paid tenfold the salary of a small-town counterpart. While technical and administrative costs no doubt have some irreducible minimum, suppliers of syndicated programming themselves have near-zero variable costs and correspondingly low reservation values for their license fees.[18] Optimal spending on syndicated programs and in-house programs (local news) should increase markedly with market size, as should optimal selling costs for local advertising. The endogeneity of large components of fixed cost clearly weakens their expected influence on floor levels of comp.

Statistical Results

We can summarize the model to be estimated with data on individual stations (the sign preceding each coefficient indicates its expected sign):

$$\begin{aligned} Comp = a &- b_1 \times spending\ power + b_2 \times spending\ power\ squared \\ &- b_3 \times station\ count \pm b_4 \times VCR\ prevalence \\ &\pm b_5 \times cable\ penetration + b_6 \times group\ size \\ &+ b_7 \times affiliation\ switch + b_8 \times VHF \\ &+ b_9 \times prime\ time\ rating \pm b_{10} \times CBS \pm b_{11} \times NBC \\ &\pm b_{12} \times O\&O + e. \end{aligned}$$

The model is appropriately estimated by ordinary least squares except for one complication. Heteroskedasticity is expected to be present, because the conditional variance of *comp* will surely increase with the important variable *spending power*. The models in Table A.1 therefore are reported with robust standard errors.

Both models have substantial explanatory power and confirm a number of the hypotheses. Comp is larger, the fewer are the stations

TABLE A.1 Regression analysis of determinants of networks' compensation of affiliates

Exogenous variable	Endogenous variable	
	Comp1	Comp2
Constant	−599	714
	(1.19)	(0.84)
Spending power	2,200	3,910
	(6.32)	(7.51)
Spending power squared	−0.000000393	−0.000000663
	(4.96)	(5.37)
Station count	−2,935	−3,372
	(3.01)	(1.74)
VCR prevalence	−5.42	−19.1
	(0.97)	(2.12)
Cable penetration	10.1	7.38
	(2.66)	(1.36)
Group size	−0.273	−1.32
	(0.10)	(0.36)
Affiliation switch	22.3	−148
	(0.24)	(1.30)
VHF	192	249
	(4.66)	(3.71)
Prime time rating	44.2	49.0
	(6.57)	(4.72)
CBS	−43.1	−118
	(0.70)	(1.28)
NBC	99.1	143
	(1.46)	(1.32)
O&O	−226	−398
	(1.02)	(1.39)
$\overline{R}^2$	0.509	0.596
N	545	450

Note: t-statistics appear in parentheses beneath coefficients.

relative to the market's size (with *comp2*, the coefficient is significant at 5 percent only in a one-tail test). Comp is greater for the station occupying a VHF than a UHF channel. It is greater for stations that earn higher ratings, confirming that affiliation contracts carry a substantial incentive. While both *spending power* and its square take significant coefficients, the quadratic relationship is inverted from the one hypothesized. We discuss this perverse outcome subsequently. On the one hand, the prevalence of VCRs seems to reduce the value of local affiliates (significantly when the dependent variable is *comp2*). On the other hand, the penetration of cable tends to elevate the level of comp, significantly so with *comp1*. That result is consistent with cable complementing over-the-air broadcasting, though it could also point to survival problems for broadcast stations in areas relying heavily on cable. Two variables representing bargaining power, *group size* and *affiliation switch*, are quite insignificant. This is consistent with evidence that the station groups have been relatively cooperative in the networks' efforts to curtail comp (Chapter 6). With other variables controlled, no network is more generous or stingy than its peers, and O&Os apparently get treated the same as independent affiliates. To probe further whether the O&Os are treated like affiliates, we tested for the significance of slope shifts in each exogenous variable's coefficient associated with O&O stations. Significant shifts naturally occur for coefficients of the *spending power* variables, because the O&Os are concentrated in the largest markets. A significant negative slope shift appears for *station count* and a positive one for *cable penetration*. The former result plausibly indicates that O&Os do not gain bargaining power against their own parents from the presence of alternative affiliates. The latter result has no obvious explanation.

The inversion of the expected quadratic relation to *spending power* poses a puzzle. The estimated relation is strongly visible when comp values are plotted against *spending power*; they rise sharply with market size among small markets and become roughly flat among large ones. This is clearly no artifact. It is consistent with the conjecture previously offered about the endogeneity of stations' fixed costs, but that does not explain the sharpness of the rise of comp with market size among small markets. We divided the observations into two groups—those in DMAs with fewer than six stations, and those with six or more. Where there are not enough stations to "go around" for the networks, we conjectured that networks are more constrained to cover the fixed costs of small-market stations. The conjecture fails: the same quadratic form appears in both subsamples, although it is a good deal less significant statistically in the markets with few stations. When the dependent variable is changed to the *ratio* of comp to the station's revenue, we indeed find that it declines at a decreasing rate with increases of market size. But that does not fully square with the logic of (exogenous) fixed costs.[19] One clear conclusion survives: comp does *not* serve to cover the irreducible fixed costs of small-market stations.

Aside from this result, Table A.1 supports the main elements of a bargaining framework, with stations receiving more comp when they possess more bargaining power and deliver better performance in the eyes of the network. Their effective bargaining power lies in conditions within their individual DMAs and seems unaffected by membership in station groups. The groups' influence bears instead on the programming decisions made by networks and syndicators.

Comp and Contract Provisions

Comp is one of numerous terms set in contracts between networks and affiliates. Hence, what level of comp results from the parties' relative bargaining power is determined along with the choices that they make of other terms as well. We would like to know (for example) how much comp a station gives up when it negotiates stronger protection against contract termination by the network. This question is difficult to answer econometrically unless variables (instruments) can be found that are both exogenous and good predictors of terms that the parties will choose. Such instruments are not in good supply in the broadcasting markets.

We undertook only an exploratory analysis by adding to the model presented in Table A.1 several variables describing terms in the network-affiliate contracts. One of these is a dummy for a clause indicating conditions under which the network can terminate the affiliate's contract. Since affiliation with a major network substantially increases a station's market value, a compensating increase in comp is expected. The second addresses the station's rights to preempt network programs. While networks have used many strategies to restrict preemption, the most common and stringent is a cap on the number of hours of preemption permitted. Since preemption is a profit-increasing option for the station, a tighter cap should warrant higher comp. The third discretionary clause is a promotion requirement, which causes the station to expend some resources (such as its ad spots) to promote the network's programs. This cost to the affiliate should call for an offsetting increase in comp. The fourth variable is the duration of the contract. While there is no obvious general reason why one party to a network-affiliate contract should prefer a longer duration than the other, the New World shock supplied a strong particular reason: the station's newfound ability to make a credible threat to change its affiliation implied that the network would pay extra for a longer contract.

These dummy variables from our sample of contracts were combined with the database employed for Table A.1. Besides adding these contract variables, we employed a different measure of comp taken from the contracts. Rather than the approximated dollar value of comp, used in Table A.1, we used the single parameter in each affiliate contract which determines that station's comp relative to other stations' comp levels (the "network station rate"). Despite the different dependent variable and the much-reduced sample size, the substantive conclusions about the model change only a little.

When the contract terms are added as regressors, however, none is statistically significant except for the duration of the contract. Its positive coefficient confirms our hypothesis about parties' asymmetrical preferences for duration following the New World shock. Otherwise, this exploratory analysis suggests that the trade-offs built in to network-affiliate contracts will prove difficult to establish quantitatively.

Gains for Chains in Radio

For reasons explained in Chapter 8, radio stations provide a setting for testing the same hypotheses pertinent to the TV station chains. The two activities were reorganized owing to similar disturbances, and they possess similar technologies.

The key policy change for radio broadcasters came in 1996, when the Telecommunications Act removed all restrictions on the total number of stations a group could own nationwide. The limit had previously been twelve AM and twelve FM stations. The number of stations under common ownership in a given market remained restricted, however, the allowed number increasing with the total number of stations in a market. It may be as many as eight in a local market served by forty-five stations or more, fewer when the local population is smaller. The number may not exceed half the stations in a market. Additional conditions apply, depending on whether stations operate on the AM or FM band. Whatever the sources of advantage to larger groups, these revised rules bestirred a frenzy of ownership changes. Over the years from 1996 to 2000, stations changed hands in 1,483 transactions, with individual deals involving anywhere from one to four hundred stations. In the course of the 1,483 transactions, 3,528 stations changed owners (1,012 of them more than once). Thus, a large minority of the nation's ten thousand–plus commercial stations were affected.[1] The

273

consolidation process was by no means limited to rivals in a given market, since large nationwide groups emerged. By 2000 the largest group, Clear Channel Communications, had come to own 1,224 stations. The largest four groups accounted for 56 percent of total radio market revenue in 1999, the largest eight, 67 percent.[2] This burst of national concentration while the rules continued to constrain local-market concentration suggests that market power could hardly explain much of the consolidation wave. Several other hypotheses come to hand.

Hypotheses about Group Economies

The first hypothesis attributes common ownership to economies in administering multiple stations. These economies are presumed to increase with the geographic propinquity of stations under common ownership. Such economies obviously should accrue to stations located in a single market, where one headquarters facility and shared employees can serve several stations.[3] These economies may persist at a diminishing rate for stations located in nearby markets, especially since some stations' signals reach cities other than their base location. Several sorts of managerial and operating economies should persist, though attenuated, as the geographic distance between stations increases. Any practical test of propinquity and group economies obviously must rest on some simple assumption about the outer boundaries of these economies or the rate at which they decay with distance. We assume that a chain enjoys economies of geographic concentration among all stations that are located within a given state.

The second hypothesis rests on the fact that radio stations manage their programming by selecting a "format" or general style, then acquiring the specific inputs (talk, news, recorded music) to implement the format. The format is an intangible asset that can be transferred from station to station. Insofar as developing, imple-

menting, and sharing formats are tasks better accomplished between stations under common ownership than independent stations, a group's stations that share a format enjoy a straightforward
economy of spreading a fixed cost.[4] The key empirical prediction
then is that a group's stations will tend to concentrate on one or a
few formats. While we shall test the hypothesis of format specialization, we note some evidence casting doubt on it. First, concentration has increased rapidly within broadcasting markets, as permitted by the 1996 policy change, and this concentration of operators
has been associated with increased diversification of formats, as the
welfare economics of broadcast differentiation suggests.[5] This consideration presses groups to diversify rather than specialize their
format libraries. Second, strong economies from format specialization imply that a station's format is a sunk commitment costly to
reverse, and the empirical evidence on this point is mixed. Little evidence is available on the costs of devising a format or of transfer-
ring one between independent parties. Historically, formats have
appeared as innovations that then diffuse among stations.[6] Consultants stand ready to supply formats to independent stations and
groups.[7] One recent study by Charles Romeo and Andrew Dick
found that format changes are not uncommon, occurring in one-
sixth of the station-years observed in a panel data set covering
1988–1998. Groups are prone to change a station's format at the
time when it is acquired, consistent with the group having invested
in a library of formats. It takes a particularly grievous level of
underperformance, however, to provoke a format change by an acquiring station group. Format changes do not significantly improve
a station's listenership share in its market unless the new format
currently enjoys a high and/or growing level of general popularity.
The authors concluded that the pecuniary cost of shifting a station's
format is probably small, but the investment is a highly risky one,
with the station having little evidence for its ability to retain its current audience and/or attract a new one after a format change.[8]

The third hypothesis concerns stations' dealings with the advertisers who are the source of their revenue. National advertisers generally organize the physical distribution of their products nationwide and wish to distribute advertising messages so as to reach prospective purchasers simultaneously across the country. The advertising medium that can provide (or organize) this national reach clearly offers an advantage, one likely to command a premium in what the advertisers are willing to pay per household (Chapter 2 offered evidence from the TV syndication industry).[9] The largest station group, Clear Channel Communications, uses various strategies of bundled pricing to advertisers that are consistent with pursuing such an advantage of national coverage.[10] Station groups aiming to serve national advertisers would tend to acquire stations in all the largest cities: the bigger the city market, the more a given station purchase adds to its national coverage. This hypothesis could be specified in several ways, and the one we choose is quite unrestrictive. It holds simply that the proportion of the leading DMAs (market definitions widely used in broadcasting data) occupied by a group will on average be inflated relative to a null situation in which having several stations in one leading market is "just as good" as having one in each of several leading markets. Notice that this null hypothesis is entangled with the hypothesis of geographic concentration—undesirable but seemingly unavoidable.

Statistical Tests and Results

We now test each of these hypotheses in turn, starting with scale economies in geographic propinquity. Consider the set of station groups (two or more stations under common ownership) operating in the United States at any one time. To the extent that they pursue operating economies based on geographic propinquity, they should be more concentrated geographically than if their member stations had all been pooled and then assigned to group owners by random drawing. The first requirement is a way to measure the extent to which a group's stations are concentrated in one or a few states. We calculate the standard Hirschman–Herfindahl Index of concentration (HHI) among states for each station group. The average of HHIs over the groups then summarizes the actual degree of geographic concentration.[11] The next problem is how to construct a null hypothesis—a distribution of average HHI values that would emerge at random if the formation of station groups occurred with no heed to geographic propinquity. We pooled all the stations belonging to the station groups and drew from these at random to construct an alternative station-group population—the same numbers and sizes of groups but with stations randomly assigned to each group. The HHI for each artificial group was calculated and an average HHI over all these groups obtained. The construction of this contrafactual was repeated one thousand times and a statistical distribution obtained for the contrafactual HHI values. The actual mean HHI was then compared to the appropriate tail of the contrafactual distribution to determine whether it differs significantly from the randomly drawn distribution.

The preceding paragraph omits one important complication in the test. A heteroskedasticity problem arises because of the different numbers of stations contained in the actual groups—from 2 to Clear Channel's 1,224. With two stations the HHI value will be either 10,000 if they are in the same state or 5,000 if they are in different states. As the number of stations per group increases, the expected dispersion of the HHI values declines. For this reason, and because any variation of patterns in the different-sized station groups holds substantive interest, we perform the test for significant geographic concentration of station groups on each group size separately. The group breakdown that we employ distinguishes 2, 3, 4, 5, 6–10, 11–20, and 20+ stations per group. The numbers of groups falling into the size classes are respectively 45, 29, 25, 17, 43, 21, and 17. Because the consolidation of the radio industry oc-

TABLE B.1   Statistical test of geographic propinquity as a motive for organization of station groups

No. of stations in group	1997			2000		
	Constructed value	Significance level	Actual value	Constructed value	Significance level	Actual value
2	2,778	.01*	4,722	2,719	.01*	4,969
3	1,328	.01*	3,027	1,292	.01*	3,037
4	788	.01*	2,125	781	.01*	2,232
5	527	.01*	1,341	533	.01*	1,712
6–10	245	.01*	763	251	.01*	977
11–20	78	.01*	234	234	.01*	246
21+	16	.01*	45	8	.01*	19

Note: The value .01 indicates the relevant significance level, the asterisk (*) that the actual value significantly differs from (exceeds) the constructed value.

curred so quickly after the 1996 legislation, we obtained data for 1997, to pick up the early effects of the change, and 2000, when it seemingly had run much of its course.[12]

Table B.1 shows the statistical results for the hypothesis of geographic concentration. For each group size and year, it reports an appropriate significance level, the value of the contrafactual HHI distribution ("constructed value") corresponding to that significance level, and the actual mean HHI. The results are unambiguous: for each group size and year, the actual mean HHI indicates substantially more geographic concentration than the 1 percent level of the constructed distribution. The results are the same for both years, but in 2000 the actual concentration (relative to both the 1997 actual and the contrafactual) has risen somewhat in all but the largest-size groups. The expected heteroskedasticity of the distribution is sharply evident in the decline of the 1 percent point as size of the constructed groups increases.

The process of testing the hypothesis of economies of format specialization is similar to that for testing economies of geographic concentration. *Duncan's Radio Market Guide* classifies each station by the format it employs, and so a group's distribution of formats can be designated and concentration measured in just the same way as from classification by state of domicile. A complication arises, though, because *Duncan's Radio Market Guide* sometimes assigns several formats to a station; the first is supposed to be the principal format, and we assumed that to be the case.[13] There is room for skepticism about how clearly distinguished the formats are and how precisely they can be classified. Steven Berry and Joel Waldfogel probed this question by analyzing the Top 30 playlists of songs in various formats and measuring their overlap from format to format. They concluded that the formats can be regarded as spatially differentiated products with varying distances between pairs, making them appear quite suitable for our analysis.[14] With a few small-niche formats excluded, the formats in which *Duncan's* classifies stations used in our analysis number twenty-three.[15]

All group-member stations were pooled, one thousand sets of contrafactual format portfolios obtained, and HHI indexes calculated as before. Table B.2 reports the statistical results. For this hypothesis they do not yield easy interpretation. The larger station groups (six and above) do indicate significant format concentration in both 1997 and 2000. In the smaller groups statistical significance is erratic. The obvious a priori argument—the fewer entities available for bearing a fixed cost, the stronger the incentive to minimizing it—predicts that format specialization will prevail in the small rather than the large groups, and we find no plausible model to explain the actual result.

The third hypothesis concerns the potential advantages of national coverage of major-city markets in order to serve national advertisers. This hypothesis maintains that the proportion of leading markets in which the group is represented will exceed that of a contrafactual in which groups draw stations at random, with a new top-city station no better than a duplicate in a top market already

TABLE B.2 Statistical test of common format as a motive for organization of station groups

No. of stations in group	1997			2000		
	Constructed value	Significance level	Actual value	Constructed value	Significance level	Actual value
2	2,892	.05*	2,892	2,838	.05	2,804
3	1,481	.01*	1,506	1,376	.05	1,243
4	896	.05	875	859	.05*	879
5	631	.05	596	577	.05	535
6–10	313	.01*	356	322	.01*	418
11–20	117	.01*	124	118	.01*	146
21+	27	.01*	42	11	.01*	18

Note: The value .01 or .05 indicates the relevant significance level, the asterisk (*) whether the actual value significantly exceeds the constructed value.

occupied (or a station in a smaller market). We take the top fifty DMAs as the appropriate setting in which to test the national-coverage hypothesis. It clearly applies to the largest markets, since the fraction of the nation's consumers reached is at stake. We measured national coverage by the percentage of the top fifty DMAs in the group's portfolio. That fifty (making Buffalo the marginal market) is more appropriate than (say) twenty-five (Portland, Oregon) or seventy-five (Omaha) is purely judgmental; it does seem to possess strong focal power in the trade. To test the influence of national-coverage considerations, we constructed a contrafactual distribution as before, by pooling all the stations belonging to each station-group size in turn. Each random drawing from this pool reproduced the population of station groups. The mean national-coverage percentage was calculated for each drawing and added to the contrafactual distribution. The distribution of national-coverage percentages then provided a test for the actual mean as a statistically significant outlier. As in the previous two tests, because of heteroskedasticity, this one was carried out for each group size sep-

TABLE B.3 Statistical test of national coverage as a motive for organization of station groups

No. of stations in group	1997			2000		
	Constructed value	Significance level	Actual value	Constructed value	Significance level	Actual value
2	1.26	.01*	0.62	1.11	.01*	0.51
3	1.93	.01*	1.00	1.93	.01*	1.00
4	2.56	.01*	1.04	2.15	.01*	1.15
5	3.00	.01*	0.75	2.57	.01*	0.76
6–10	5.56	.01*	2.65	4.37	.01*	1.07
11–20	10.76	.01*	5.71	7.43	.01*	6.83
21+	28.65	.01*	14.24	30.94	.01*	17.79

Note: The value .01 indicates the relevant level of statistical significance, the asterisk (*) whether the actual value falls significantly short of the constructed value.

arately, for both 1997 and 2000. Note that the stations in the top fifty DMAs on which the test turns are only a minority of stations in the groups' portfolios: 32 percent in 1997, 28 percent in 2000.

The results appear in Table B.3. One might guess from the strong evidence of geographic concentration that the national coverage hypothesis was likely to fail. Indeed, its obverse—that station groups avoid diversifying among top fifty markets—is supported at the 1 percent level of significance for each size group in both years. The hypothesis might apply to Clear Channel and a few other large chains, but the observations on station groups in our sample are unweighted, and the national-coverage hypothesis clearly does not apply to the great bulk of small chains.[16] The result contrasts with the findings on TV station groups, where the evidence (implicitly sizeweighted) more clearly suggests that the largest groups (certainly the networks' O&Os) vigorously pursue national coverage. The difference between program supply sources for a network-affiliated TV station and the typical radio station (locally programmed within its selected format) is also important. Nonetheless, the TV and radio distributors do shed light on each other, with radio confirming the economies of geographic concentration that are present but less evident in TV, and identifying in format economies the same scale economies in program supply.

This statistical evidence on changes in radio has a comforting consistency with the explanations for TV broadcast groups, which we could test only from incident and distribution patterns. The general run of radio chains do not seem to pursue nationwide reach, as have some big-city TV groups, but the two sectors' quests for managerial and programming economies seem quite parallel.

Notes

Abbreviations

B&C   *Broadcasting & Cable*

BW   *Business Week*

EM   *Electronic Media*

JBEM   *Journal of Broadcasting and Electronic Media*

JME   *Journal of Media Economics*

MW   *Media Week*

NYT   *New York Times* (New England edition)

WSJ   *Wall Street Journal*

Introduction

1. This analysis of the organization and structure of the arts and entertainment industries was developed by Richard E. Caves, *Creative Industries: Contracts between Art and Commerce* (Cambridge, Mass.: Harvard University Press, 2000). TV broadcasting was omitted from that study solely to keep the book's length wieldy.
2. Carl Shapiro and Hal Varian, *Information Rules: A Strategic Guide to the Network Economy* (Boston: Harvard Business School Press, 1999), p. 3.
3. William Goldman, *Adventures in the Screen Trade: A Personal View of Hollywood and Screenwriting* (New York: Warner Books, 1984), p. 39.

4. John Sutton, *Sunk Cost and Market Structure* (Cambridge, Mass.: MIT Press, 1991). This mechanism had been recognized earlier by several economists who study the broadcasting and cinema film markets, e.g., Steven S. Wildman and Stephen E. Siwek, *International Trade in Films and Television Programs* (Cambridge, Mass.: Ballinger, 1988).

5. This pattern of imitative behavior, for reasons embedded in broadcasting's fixed cost, prompted extensive research. Welfare is lost owing to rival broadcasters' matching of programs appealing to the largest audience group rather than providing programs appealing to minority tastes. For a broad treatment of this issue, see Bruce M. Owen and Steven S. Wildman, *Video Economics* (Cambridge, Mass.: Harvard University Press, 1992).

1. The Market for Broadcast Network Programming

1. The organizational logic of program supply comes clearer if we start from its base rather than grope for its destination.

2. For example, the Writers Guild minimum price for an episode in a series is about two-thirds of the price for an episode plus "story" that sets the terms for a series. Todd Gitlin, *Inside Prime Time* (London: Routledge, 1994), p. 71.

3. Research by Berndt Ostendorf summarized by Todd Gitlin, *Media Unlimited: How the Torrent of Images Overwhelms Our Lives* (New York: Metropolitan Books, 2001), pp. 109–110.

4. Robert R. Faulkner, *Hollywood Studio Musicians: Their Work and Careers in the Recording Industry* (Chicago: Aldine Atherton, 1971), pp. 128–132.

5. Bernard Weinraub, "Two Mediums Make Like One," *NYT,* July 19, 1998, sec. 2, pp. 1, 20–21. Most scholarly accounts of broadcasting organization go back a decade or more, so we cite some recent trade periodical evidence that patterns continue to hold.

6. For a good account of the managerial task involved, see Emily Nelson, "Think You've Got a Tricky Staff? Try Herding Writers," *WSJ,* May 16, 2003, pp. A1, A6.

7. The organization of TV series production is described by Muriel G. Cantor, *The Hollywood TV Producer: His Work and His Audience* (New Brunswick, N.J.: Transaction Books, 1988); John W. Ravage,

Television: The Director's Viewpoint (Boulder, Colo.: Westview Press, 1978); and Horace Newcomb and Robert S. Alley, *The Producer's Medium: Conversations with Creators of American TV* (New York: Oxford University Press, 1983).

8. Ravage, *Television,* pp. 71, 105.

9. Ibid., pp. 75, 77, 142.

10. Ibid., pp. 19–20, 48, 119; Cantor, *Hollywood TV Producer,* pp. 108–110.

11. Ravage, *Television,* pp. 38–39; Newcomb and Alley, *The Producer's Medium,* p. 88.

12. Newcomb and Alley, *The Producer's Medium,* pp. 84, 130.

13. Ari Posner, "No Experience Required: 'The O.C.' Rewrites the Rules of TV Writing," *NYT,* Mar. 21, 2004, sec. 2, pp. 1, 35.

14. Michael Schneider, "One-hit Wonders?" *EM,* Nov. 9, 1998, pp. 1, 39.

15. Interview with David E. Kelley, *B&C,* June 12, 1995, pp. 16–19; Lynette Rice, "Heaven Can't Wait," *B&C,* Feb. 24, 1997, pp. 26–31.

16. Michael Schneider, "The MTM 'College,'" *EM,* Mar. 9, 1998, pp. 1, 37.

17. Joe Schlosser, "Carsey–Werner Company: Winning Both Ways," *B&C,* Jan. 18, 1999, p. 39.

18. Cynthia Littleton, "Big-Ticket Development at Big Ticket," *B&C,* Feb. 26, 1996, pp. 30–31.

19. Bernard Weinraub, "From Shoestring to Champagne," *NYT,* Sept. 4, 2001, pp. C1, C8.

20. Neal Koch, "Hey, Big Spender!" *Channels,* Sept. 1988, p. 63.

21. On the late 1980s, see Susan Tyler Eastman, *Broadcast/Cable Programming: Strategies and Practices,* 4th ed. (Belmont, Calif.: Wadsworth Publishing Co., 1993), p. 132.

22. Steve Coe, "Kelley's 20th Deal Includes ABC, Fox," *B&C,* Dec. 4, 1995, p. 42.

23. Steve Coe, "*E.R.* Producer Sews Up New Deal," *B&C,* Nov. 20, 1995, p. 12.

24. Michael Freeman, "Film Directors Zoom in on TV," *EM,* Oct. 28, 2002, pp. 1, 31.

25. Michael Schneider, "Saving Their Own Success," *EM,* July 13, 1998, pp. 1, 18; Joe Schlosser, "Fox's Split Personality," *B&C,* May 29, 2000, pp. 18–24. Fox by 2000 had accumulated nine such mini-studios. Joe Schlosser, "Lassner Sets Up His Own Shop," *B&C,* June 19, 2000, p. 28.

26. Alan James Frutkin, "Financing Each Other's Successes," *MW*, Mar. 27, 2000, pp. 48–56.

27. Bruce M. Owen and Steven S. Wildman, *Video Economics* (Cambridge, Mass.: Harvard University Press, 1992), tables 2.9, 2.10. Gitlin, *Inside Prime Time*, pp. 118–122, described these arrangements, which resemble the studios' multi-picture deals with cinema film producers.

28. Steve Coe, "Twentieth Corrals Comedy Writers," *B&C*, Oct. 23, 1995, p. 28.

29. David Tobenkin, "Stone Stanley Produces for New World," *B&C*, July 17, 1995, p. 22.

30. Gitlin, *Inside Prime Time*, pp. 134–135; Tom King, "A Very Rewarding Friendship," *WSJ*, Sept. 13, 2002, p. W4; Bill Carter, "Cadillac-Sized Hits by the VW of Producers," *NYT*, Jan. 22, 1996, pp. D1, D6; Robert Pekurny, "Coping with Television Production," in *Individuals in Mass Media Organizations: Creativity and Constraint*, ed. James S. Ettema and D. Charles Whitney (Beverly Hills, Calif.: Sage, 1982), pp. 138–139.

31. Betsy Sharkey, "Three Men and a Baby," *MW*, Nov. 9, 1998, pp. 32–36; Kyle Pope, "For TV's Hottest Team, It's Lets Make a Deal," *WSJ*, Apr. 5, 1999, pp. B1, B4.

32. Alec Foege, "Shades of Grey," *MW*, Oct. 4, 1999, pp. 34–44; Bernie Brillstein, *Where Did I Go Right?* (New York: Warner Books, 1999).

33. On United Talent Agency, see Alan James Frutkin, "The Art of the Deal," *MW*, July 31, 2000, pp. 32–36.

34. Joe Flint, "The Ovitz Show: Ex-Agent Scores Big for Fall TV," *WSJ*, July 17, 2000, pp. B1, B4; Tom King, "An Agent for Change in TV," *WSJ*, Dec. 8, 2000, p. W4.

35. Steve Coe, "NBC Gets First Look at Paramount, P&G Projects," *B&C*, Nov. 20, 1995, pp. 22–23.

36. Network Inquiry Special Staff, "An Analysis of Television Program Production, Acquisition, and Distribution," in U.S. Federal Communications Commission, *New Television Networks: Entry, Jurisdiction, Ownership, and Regulation*. II. *Background Papers* (Washington, D.C.: Federal Communications Commission, 1980), pp. 383–385, 394.

37. On made-for-TV movies, see Gitlin, *Inside Prime Time*, chap. 9, p. 158.

38. Betsy Sharkey, "ABC Movies: Top of the Lyne," *MW,* May 1, 1998, p. 8.

39. Kyle Pope, "A Profligate Producer Helps Hallmark Corner TV-Mini-series Market," *WSJ,* May 21, 1999, pp. A1, A6.

40. Greg Spring, "'Blind Date' Smiles on Scrappy Gold Coast," *EM,* Apr. 26, 1999, pp. 3, 27.

41. Owen and Wildman, *Video Economics,* pp. 196–199; Lynn Hirschberg, "Jamie Tarses' Fall, As Scheduled," *New York Times Magazine,* July 13, 1997, pp. 37–42.

42. Bruce M. Owen and Michael G. Baumann, "Economic Study E: Concentration among National Purchasers of Video Entertainment Programming," Federal Communications Commission, MB Docket no. 02–277 (2003). For the year 2001 they estimated a Herfindahl measure of buyer concentration (H) of 1120. For reference, markets with H<1000 are regarded as unconcentrated in antitrust policy practice while markets with H>1800 give rise to antitrust concern.

43. For an adroit demonstration, see William T. Bielby and Denise D. Bielby, "'All Hits Are Flukes': Institutionalized Decision Making and the Rhetoric of Network Prime Time Program Development," *American Journal of Sociology,* 99 (March 1994): 1287–1313.

44. Robert V. Bellamy, Daniel G. McDonald, and James R. Walker, "The Spin-Off as Television Program Form and Strategy." *JBEM,* 34 (Summer 1990): 283–297.

45. This sequence of steps pertains to scripted dramatic programs. For reality programs, a practice that reduces risk and development cost is to license formats that have already succeeded elsewhere (abroad or on cable). Edmund L. Andrews, "Europe's 'Reality' TV: Chains and Big Brother," *NYT,* Apr. 11, 2000, p. A4.

46. Michael Freeman, "Keeping Track of the Story Lyne," *EM,* Apr. 25, 2002, pp. 1, 20. A network riding a big success with a particular program or program type finds it difficult to manage its dependence so as to achieve a soft landing when viewers' interest falters. Even NBC faced the problem with sitcoms about "cute young single people quipping sardonically." Joe Flint, "How NBC, Out of Sync With Viewers' Tastes, Lost Top Ratings Perch," *WSJ,* Oct. 24, 2000, pp. A1, A16.

47. Mark Christensen and Cameron Stauth, *The Sweeps: Behind the Scenes in Network TV* (New York: William Morrow, 1984), pp. 34, 38; Gitlin, *Inside Prime Time,* pp. 20–26; Brooks Barnes, "Trusting

Gut Instincts, WB Network Stops Testing TV Pilots," *WSJ*, May 3, 2004, pp. B1, B7.

48. Rick Martin, "Loved the Pilot, Hated the Show," *Channels*, Sept. 10, 1990, pp. 43–45.

49. Gitlin, *Inside Prime Time*, pp. 20–21.

50. Joe Schlosser, "Wolf Says Shows Can Fly without Pilots," *B&C*, July 6, 1998, p. 30.

51. Alan Frutkin, "The Pilot Dilemma," *MW*, May 17, 1999, pp. 42–50.

52. Bernard Weinraub, "For TV's Vulnerable Shows, It's Fear-and-Lobbying Season," *NYT*, May 1, 2001, pp. B1, B7.

53. Other goodwill-related investments are commonly seen: Fox renewed *That '70s Show* for two years rather than the customary one in order to strengthen ties with the show's creative team and supplier, Carsey–Werner. Alan James Frutkin, "'70s Adds Two Years," *MW*, Nov. 29, 1999, p. 6.

54. Michael Schneider, "For Shows on Bubble, April Is Cruelest Month," *EM*, Apr. 12, 1999, pp. 1, 58.

55. "Aaron Spelling, TV's Over-achiever," *B&C*, Jan. 23, 1995, pp. 10–17.

56. Michael Schneider, "Is NBC Promising Producers Too Much?" *EM*, Jan. 12, 1998, pp. 3, 118. Studios have recently cooled in their former enthusiasm to lock successful producers into exclusive development deals; lightning seldom struck the same place twice. Chris Pursell and Michael Freeman, "Studios USA Will Stay the Course," *EM*, Oct. 29, 2001, pp. 1, 18.

57. Data are apparently from Writers Guild of America. See "Prime Time's Price Tag," *Channels*, Sept. 10, 1990, p. 50. We draw on this antiquated evidence because it predates the bargaining over ownership shares that began to affect negotiations in the early 1990s.

58. As mentioned previously, there resulted a sharp contraction of independent production companies as their proprietors sought alliances with better-financed studios. On the evolution of the syndication market, see Richard C. Block, "History of Syndie, A Short Look Back," *Variety*, Feb. 17, 1988, p. 77.

59. Joe Flint, "Studio Back in Broadcast TV," *WSJ*, Dec. 15, 2004, pp. B1, 7.

60. Christensen and Stauth, *The Sweeps*, especially pp. 34, 103–104. They quoted one producer on the dearth of objective judgment about the product of one's efforts: "Everything turns to shit over Denver."

61. Tom King, "I Love It, It's Perfect, Now Change It," *WSJ*, June 22, 2001, p. W9.

62. David Wild, *The Showrunners* (New York: HarperCollins, 1999).

63. David Carr, "Casting Reality TV, No Longer a Hunch, Becomes a Science," *NYT*, Mar. 28, 2004, pp. 1, 20.

64. Susan Tyler Eastman, Jeffrey Neal-Lunsford, and Karen E. Riggs, "Coping with Grazing: Prime-time Strategies for Accelerated Program Transitions," *JBEM*, 39 (Winter 1995): 92–108. Surveys report that 50 to 60 percent of a given show's audience may be inherited from its predecessor.

65. The costs of different programs do not enter directly in a major way into this calculation. The only important source of variation in pecuniary costs of different programs is rents passing to the talent (producer, actors) in successful shows.

66. Gitlin, *Inside Prime Time*, pp. 77–79; Joseph Turow, "Unconventional Programs on Commercial Television: An Organizational Perspective," in Ettema and Whitney, *Individuals*, pp. 107–129.

67. Ronald L. Goettler and Ron Shachar, "Spatial Competition in Network Television Industry," *RAND Journal of Economics*, 32 (Winter 2001): 624–656. Compare William J. Adams, "TV Program Scheduling Strategies and Their Relationship to New Program Renewal Rates and Rating Changes," *JBEM*, 37 (Fall 1993): 465–474.

68. ABC was consciously trying to reduce the cost of pilots by stretching the process out over time. Steve McClellan, "Remixing the Network Formula for Success," *B&C*, Dec. 21, 1998, pp. 18–23. Fox was cutting into the problem by moving more original programming into the summer and seeking to diffuse the fall opening season. Bill Carter, "Forget Bang; Fall TV Lineup Barely Musters a Whimper," *NYT*, July 27, 1998, pp. D1, D9.

69. James Sterngold, "For All the TV Pilots, There's Just Not Enough Youth To Go Around," *NYT*, May 17, 1999, pp. B1, B4.

70. Michael Schneider, "Networks Get Jump on Drama," *EM*, Sept. 6, 1999, pp. 3, 25.

71. Alan Frutkin, "The Pilot Dilemma," *MW*, May 17, 1999, pp. 42–50.

72. The advertising contracts guarantee a certain level of viewership to the advertiser. If a program flops and viewers' attention is undersupplied, the network later gives the advertiser additional spots to make up the promised total viewership.

73. The scatter market gives advertisers flexibility in dealing with unex-

pected variations in their demands over the season. Buyers and networks also are able to speculate based on their expectations about prices that will prevail in the scatter market relative to the up-front. Market-wide disturbances, however, tend to destabilize prices in the scatter market. When all parties expect a year of lowered demand for ad spots, the proportion of spots sold in the up-front market tends to fall, augmenting the supply and further depressing prices in the scatter market. On these dynamic processes, see John Consoli, "Turning Hits into Dollars," *MW*, Oct. 16, 2000, pp. 9–10; idem, "4th-Qtr. Scatter Is in Tatters," *MW*, Nov. 20, 2000, pp. 6–7.

74. On the evolution of the up-front market and its relationship to the scheduling game, see Erwin Ephron, "The Fifth Season: The Fascinating History of the Upfront," Apr. 2003, found at *www.ephrononmedia.com*. The competitiveness of the national TV advertising market and the closeness of substitution for other media have been subject to a controversy that is not relevant to this study.

75. Newcomb and Alley, *The Producer's Medium*, pp. 108–109; Pekurny, "Coping with Television Production," pp. 131–143.

76. Bill Carter, "Fall Schedules: Scientific Proof That Chaos Is Not Just Theory," *NYT*, June 8, 1997, sec. 2, pp. 29–30; idem, "The Art and Craftiness of TV Scheduling," *NYT*, Sept. 12, 1996, pp. C13, C18.

77. Steve Coe, "Counterprogramming in the Air for Fall," *B&C*, May 22, 1996, pp. 8–14.

78. Bill Carter, "A Rising ABC Rediscovers Its Inner Regular Slob," *NYT*, June 23, 2003, pp. C1, C5.

79. Bill Carter, "The Thursday Night Fights," *NYT*, Jan. 18, 2001, pp. C1, C13.

80. Thursday's traffic jam is not unique, however, as Sunday evening has recently attracted the same congestion. Tom King, "Tune In: The Day of Rest Gets Busy," *WSJ*, Jan. 31, 2003, p. W6.

81. These special programs represent aggressive moves because they are substantially more costly to prepare than series programs, disruptive of schedules, and difficult to promote. David Bianculli, "The Roots of the Problem," *Channels*, Jan. 1987, pp. 32–33.

82. Bill Carter, "Who Needs the Sweeps?" *NYT*, Apr. 24, 2000, pp. C1, C17.

83. Warner and UPN, with their affiliated stations concentrated in large metropolitan areas, initially leaned strongly toward programming

that appeals to urban minorities. Stuart Elliott, "A TV Season When Image Is Everything," *NYT,* Sept. 20, 1996, pp. D1, D5; Bill Carter, "Two Upstart Networks Courting Black Viewers," *NYT,* Oct. 7, 1996, pp. C11, C16.

84. Michael Freeman, "When 39 Weeks Just Aren't Enough," *EM,* Sept. 9, 2002, pp. 1, 28.

85. Bill Carter and Jim Rutenberg, "Networks Try Reality Cure for Summer Rerun Blues," *NYT,* June 19, 2003, pp. C1, C10; Paige Albiniak, "Catch the Fever," *B&C,* May 17, 2004, p. 16; Scott Robson, "TV's Bold New Concept: Summer," *NYT,* May 25, 2004, sec. 2, pp. 1, 32.

86. Michael Schneider, "Every Night a Showdown," *EM,* Sept. 6, 1999, pp. 12–13.

87. Emily Nelson, "NBC To Launch Its Fall Lineup Early," *WSJ,* Jan. 15, 2004, p. B6; Bill Carter, "Following HBO, Networks Test Short-Run Series," *NYT,* Jan. 19, 2004. pp. C1, C5.

88. Emily Nelson and Brian Steinberg, "'Upfront' Market Loses Its Appeal," *WSJ,* Jan. 20, 2004, p. B5.

89. Neal Koch, "It's Show Biz, Trust Me," *Channels,* Oct. 1988, p. 64. An econometric analysis of program costs and license fees in the 1977–78 season concluded that the fees respond significantly and substantially to indicators of the excess of actual over expected or predictable audience for a program. The authors conclude that substantial renegotiation occurs, for both hits and flops, and that the network's adjusted payment to the supplier is reflected in adjusted costs of the supplier—presumably bonuses to the program's talent. These adjustments are particularly evident after the first year. Part of this ex post settlement may be due to annual budget increases written into the contract, although the research design seeks to isolate the "surprise" element. See John R. Woodbury, Stanley M. Besen, and Gary M. Fournier, "The Determinants of Network Television Program Price: Implicit Contracts, Regulation, and Bargaining Power," *Bell Journal of Economics,* 14 (Autumn 1983): 351–365. Also see Sora K. Park, "Determinants of Renewal and Adjustment of License Fees of Network Prime Time Programs," *JME,* 9, no. 3 (1996): 1–19.

90. Richard E. Caves, *Creative Industries: Contracts between Art and Commerce* (Cambridge, Mass.: Harvard University Press, 2000), pp. 15, 62–64, 88–89.

91. Bill Carter, "Networks' Choice of Fall Programs Begins with Let's

Make a Deal," *NYT,* May 25, 1998, pp. D1, D6. See Chapter 7 for recent changes.

92. Greg Spring, "Networks Drain Thin Talent Pool," *EM,* Jan. 26, 1998, p. 9. A network executive observed that the number of comedies in production rose from about thirty-five in 1993 to about eighty in 1998, causing the available talent to be spread very thin. Bill Carter, "As Their Dominance Erodes, Networks Plan Big Changes," *NYT,* May 11, 1998, pp. A1, A14. The effects of this dilution of talent fed back to lower the threshold for renewing incumbent shows. Scotty Dupree, "Slow Starters Get Reprieve," *MW,* Nov. 18, 1996, pp. 6–8.

93. Don Aucoin, "Deluge of Programs, Drought of Ideas," *Boston Globe,* Jan. 19, 1998, pp. C6, C12. Large rents to creative talents in TV writing seem to have their usual effect of eventually drawing forth an ample supply response. See James Sterngold, "Looking For Laughs? Call a Harvard Grad," *NYT,* Aug. 26, 1997, pp. B1, B6. This process also works in reverse. In 2004 the collapse of the sitcom market in the face of reality programming led the premium cable channel HBO to start its own comedy shop with the unemployed writers. Bill Carter, "HBO Moves To Develop and Show New Situation Comedies," *NYT,* June 3, 2004, p. C7.

94. Bill Carter, "Back to the Storyboard for Sitcoms," *NYT,* Aug. 29, 1996, pp. C13, C20.

95. Neal Koch, "TV's New Ruling Class," *Channels,* May 1989, pp. 30, 35.

96. Alan Frutkin, "Agents of Change," *MW,* Mar. 22, 1999, pp. 34–40.

97. Mark Litwak, *Dealmaking in the Film and Television Industry: From Negotiations to Final Contracts* (Los Angeles: Silman–James, 1994), p. 139.

98. Bill Carter, "Seinfeld Says It's All Over, And It's No Joke for NBC," *NYT,* Dec. 26, 1997, pp. A1, A34.

99. Bill Carter, "Could NBC Live Without 'E.R.'?" *NYT,* Nov. 3, 1997, pp. D1, D10; idem, "Outbid on Pro Football, NBC Retains 'E.R.' in Record Pact," *NYT,* Jan. 15, 1998, pp. A1, A10.

100. Steve McClellan, "NBC: Must-See or Must-Pay?" *B&C,* Jan. 5, 1999, pp. 6, 10.

101. Bill Carter, "'Friends' To Keep Bond Alive for One More Season on NBC," *NYT,* Dec. 21, 2002, pp. B1, B2. Two other factors affect the

levels of renewal fees: (1) many episodes are now in stock for syndication, so the expected marginal syndication revenue is declining; (2) stars may be happy to settle for a reduced number of new episodes, given the high price per episode. Also, see Emily Nelson and Joe Flint, "Deal for 'Friends' Offers NBC Time to Seek New Hit," *WSJ*, Dec. 23, 2002, p. B3.

102. Bill Carter, "Good Sitcom Is Rare, and Actors Know It," *NYT*, Aug. 25, 2003. An epidemic of holdups in the 2003 season was attributed to the networks' success in the May 2003 up-front market.

103. Bernard Weinraub, "D'oh! Am I Underpaid?" *NYT*, Apr, 14, 2004, pp. B1, B7.

104. A producer once passed up a major star's offer to appear for one year only in a faltering network series because all the rents would pass to the star when renewal time came around. Brown, *Television*, p. 124.

105. Charles Goldsmith, "British TV Executives Bemoan Creativity Deficit," *WSJ*, Aug. 26, 2002, p. B4.

106. Chad E. Dell, "The History of 'Travelers': Recycling in American Prime Time Network Programming," *JBEM*, 47 (June 2003): 260–275.

107. On the deal angles involved, see Michael Freeman, "Turner Link May Help WB Slay 'Buffy' Suitors," *EM*, Mar. 26, 2001, pp. 3, 35.

108. Lynette Rice, "Playing Musical Networks," *B&C*, Feb. 10, 1997, p. 14; Marc Berman, "Changing Channels," *MW*, Apr. 24, 2000, pp. 76–80; Ronald Grover, "Must-See TV for Left-Handed Men under 30," *BW*, Dec. 14, 1998, p. 104.

109. Each is assumed to have the same fixed and no variable cost. Owen and Wildman, *Video Economics,* chaps. 3, 4.

110. For an empirical investigation that illustrates this point, see Hyuhn-Suhck Bae, "Product Differentiation in Cable Programming: The Case in the Cable National All-News Networks," *JME*, 12, no. 4 (1999): 265–277. Also see Goettler and Shachar, "Spatial Competition."

111. Sterngold, "For All the TV Pilots," p. B4.

112. In 1998 CBS had on average more viewers than ABC or NBC, but its average ad spot brought in $92,000, while theirs earned $171,000 and $176,000, respectively. Richard Siklos, "CBS: Can Mel Karmazin Reinvent Network TV?" *BW*, Apr. 5, 1999, pp. 75–82.

113. James Sterngold, "Ushering Out a Sitcom and a Television Era," *NYT,* May 6, 1999, pp. A1, A24.

2. Syndication

1. The assumptions being made about viewers' behavior are worth stating precisely: (1) those who enjoyed a program on its first showing grow more likely as time passes to watch a repeat, though they may ultimately forget it; (2) as time passes after the first showing, some viewers whose tastes did not embrace the program on its inaugural appearance mature into potential viewers (this stock of potential new viewers need not grow without limit).

2. Economists, Inc., *An Economic Analysis of the Prime Time Access Rule,* Federal Communications Commission, MM Docket no. 94–123 (1995).

3. Mara Einstein, "Program Diversity and the Program Selection Process in Broadcast Network Television," Federal Communications Commission, Media Ownership Working Group, no. 2002–5, accessed at *www.fcc.gov/ownership/studies.html.*

4. This consolidation process was reviewed by Joe Schlosser, "Shrinking the Playing Field," *B&C,* Aug. 23, 1999, pp. 18–20.

5. Paige Albiniak, "Small Fry Find Spots in Syndie Market," *B&C,* Jan. 19, 2004, p. 16.

6. For example, in 2001 strong international demand for dramas coincided with a substantial increase in such shows on U.S. prime time (U.S. cops-and-robbers programs "travel" readily internationally, but sitcoms do not). Joe Flint, "TV's Criminal Streak," *WSJ,* May 18, 2001, p. W9.

7. This highly profitable program pioneered in treating entertainment news as serious information, and still achieves ratings more than twice those of its closest competitor. Suzanne Ault, "ET: The Business Behind the Buzz," *B&C,* July 2, 2001, pp. 14–18.

8. Joe Schlosser, "The Kings: Who'll Stop the Reign?" *B&C,* Jan. 12, 1998, pp. 48–49; Neal Koch, "The Paramount Challenge: Make Hits New Ways," *Channels,* Feb. 1989, pp. 44–56.

9. Greg Spring, "Syndication Executives As Busy As Ever," *EM,* Oct. 5, 1998, pp. 32, 35; David Tobenkin, "'Dr. Quinn' Pays Call on Family, MTM," *B&C,* Dec. 19, 1994, p. 19.

10. David Tobenkin, "Carsey–Werner Arms for Syndication," *B&C*, Dec. 19, 1994, p. 14; Joe Schlosser, "Carsey–Werner To Sell 'Profiler,'" *B&C*, Nov. 16, 1998, p. 11; Joe Schlosser, "Raleigh Looks To Keep Laughs," *B&C*, Jan. 15, 2001, p. 60. Several examples from the 1980s were cited by David Kalish, "The Haves and the Have-nots," *Channels*, Nov. 5, 1990, pp. 26–27.

11. David Tobenkin, "Sitcoms: On a Laugh Track to Profitability," *B&C*, Apr. 4, 1994, pp. 15–18.

12. Greg Spring, "With Cash and Creativity, Syndication Ages Gracefully," *EM*, June 7, 1999, pp. 14, 22; idem, "Carsey–Werner Will Tell Ya Who's on '3rd,'" *EM*, Aug. 30, 1999, pp. 3, 25.

13. Greg Spring, "Not Quite Yet," *EM*, Nov. 16, 1998, pp. 1, 66.

14. Michael Freeman and Claude Brodesser, "Where Station Groups Stand," *MW*, Jan. 13, 1997, pp. 20–28. "Access" refers to late afternoon/early evening.

15. Betsy Sharkey, "A Change Is in the Air," *MW*, Jan. 13, 1997, pp. 14–19; Joe Schlosser, "CBS Crowns Its King World," *B&C*, Jan. 24, 2000, p. 10.

16. Spring, "Not Quite Yet"; Chris Pursell, "NBC Mulls Its Own Syndication Unit," *EM*, May 22, 2000, pp. 1, 40; idem, "Syndie Wings for Peacock," *EM*, Sept. 11, 2000, pp. 1, 62.

17. Joe Schlosser, "Mitch Stern: Carrying the Big Sticks," *B&C*, Jan. 25, 1999, pp. 32–44; Chris Pursell, "Fox Puts Syndic on Top of List," *EM*, Aug. 21, 2000, pp. 1, 31.

18. Jim McConville, "Film Packages: Still Selling After All These Years," *B&C*, Jan. 15, 1996, p. 74; Greg Spring, "Columbia Revisits Past to Create 'Screen Gems,'" *EM*, Jan. 11, 1999, pp. 1, 82; Joe Schlosser, "CTTD Pitches Classic TV," *B&C*, Jan. 11, 1999, p. 10.

19. Greg Spring, "Back in the Movie Biz," *EM*, July 19, 1999, pp. 4, 32.

20. In 1973 the Big 3 networks were required by the FCC to divest their program libraries. After various changes of ownership, all three of these wound up in the hands of Paramount's syndication unit. Guy Spring, "Paramount's Syndication Nation," *EM*, Aug. 2, 1999, pp. 3, 29.

21. David Tobenkin, "New World Buys into Cannell for $3 Million," *B&C*, Mar. 27, 1995, p. 16.

22. Greg Spring, "Tribune Taps into NBC–Engel Franchise," *EM*, Dec. 15, 1997, p. 3.

23. Chris Pursell and Jim McConville, "NBC in Syndie Pact with Station Groups," *EM,* Dec. 11, 2000, p. 1A.

24. Cynthia Littleton, "Twentieth Begins New World Takeover," *B&C,* Oct. 21, 1996, p. 22.

25. "Generating Generations of Execs," *B&C,* Jan. 15, 2001, pp. 22–30.

26. Joe Schlosser, "All's 'Squared' between King World and Sony," *B&C,* Sept. 22, 1997, pp. 23–24.

27. Steve Coe, "NBC/New World Take Aim at 'ET,' 'Extra,'" *B&C,* Aug. 28, 1995, p. 8; Steve McClellan, "It's the Mergers, Stupid," *B&C,* Jan. 29, 1996, pp. 26–27; Cynthia Littleton, "Tough Reality for Magazine Shows," *B&C,* Jan. 6, 1997, pp. 44, 50; Joe Schlosser, "Entertainment Magazine Shows Hold Their Own," *B&C,* Jan. 19, 1998, p. 52; Michael Freeman, "Newsmag War Heats Up," *MW,* Apr. 27, 1998, p. 8; idem, "Confidence Vote for 'AH,'" *MW,* Nov. 3, 1997, p. 9; Greg Spring, "NBC Seeking New 'Access' Partner," *EM,* Dec. 7, 1998, pp. 2, 62.

28. Joe Schlosser, "ET Calls Paramount Home," *B&C,* May 31, 1999, p. 14.

29. Michael Freeman, "Strength in Numbers," *MW,* Apr. 22, 1996, p. 9.

30. Verne Gay, "World Domination," *MW,* Jan. 24, 2000, pp. 40–50.

31. John McManus, "Grid Lock," *MW,* Jan. 12, 1998, pp. 52–58; Chuck Larson, "It's Not What It Used To Be," *MW,* Jan. 25, 1999, pp. 38–39.

32. In 1998, 43 percent of NATPE exhibitors and 20.5 percent of persons registered were from outside the United States. The main transactors (both sellers and buyers) tended to dwell in the lower reaches of the vertical differentiation *(A-list/B-list)* ranking. Greg Spring, "Changes Clear at NATPE '98," *EM,* Jan. 26, 1998, pp. 1, 33.

33. Chris Pursell, "NATPE Pulls Out of '03, '04," *EM,* Nov. 26, 2001, pp. 1, 27; Alex Ben Block, "Rooms with a View of the Future," *EM,* Jan. 27, 2003, p. 2; Marc Berman, "Slim Pickings," *MW,* Jan. 20, 2003, pp. 22–24.

34. Cynthia Littleton, "For Syndicators, Access Is Key," *B&C,* Jan. 27, 1997, pp. 8–9.

35. Greg Spring, "What Is a Contract? Syndicators Wonder," *EM,* Oct. 12, 1998, pp. 1, 51; Greg Spring and Jon Lafayette, "Paramount Sues WSVN," *EM,* Oct. 26, 1998, p. 2.

36. Melissa Grego, "Syndie Goes a Court-ing," *B&C*, Nov. 8, 1999, p. 12; Mark Berman, "Awaiting the Verdict," *MW*, Jan. 18, 2000, pp. 40–48.

37. Cynthia Littleton, "The Times They Are A-Changin'," *B&C*, Jan. 29, 1996, pp. 8–9.

38. Cynthia Littleton, "'Dr. Quinn' Moves in Five Markets," *B&C*, May 6, 1996, pp. 2, 22.

39. Michael Freeman, "Slow Going for Action Shows," *MW*, Sept. 29, 1997, p. 8.

40. Cynthia Littleton, "'Walberg' Exit Makes It Seven Down," *B&C*, Mar. 25, 1996, p. 34.

41. In an interview with a Tribune Broadcasting Group executive: Don West and Steve McClellan, "On the Leading Edge of Television's New Wave," *B&C*, Jan. 22, 1996, pp. 18–26.

42. Cynthia Littleton, "Show Hopes Hinge on February Books," *B&C*, Feb. 26, 1996, pp. 31–32; Suzanne Ault, "Syndie Market Slump," *B&C*, Feb. 12, 2001, p. 12.

43. Michael Freeman, "Top Markets Choke Access," *MW*, Sept. 8, 1997, p. 12.

44. E.g., see Carol Hall, "Deal Makers Pull the Purse Strings," *Channels*, Feb. 1989, pp. 82–83.

45. Tobenkin, "Sitcoms"; Greg Spring, "It's Now or It's Later," *EM*, Sept. 6, 1999, p. 28. Spring also discusses options offered by some syndicators to loosen the constraints associated with barter. Also see Cheryl Heuton, "Dealing with Barter," *Channels*, Sept. 10, 1990, p. 55.

46. Cynthia Littleton, "Guerrilla Warfare at Rysher," *B&C*, Nov. 18, 1996, p. 100; Steve McClellan, "Barter Boom Continues in Off-Net," *B&C*, Apr. 4, 1994, p. 27.

47. David Tobenkin, "Warner Touts Young-Skewing Shows," *B&C*, July 31, 1995, p. 21.

48. Cynthia Littleton, "Action Breaks Out of Formulas," *B&C*, Nov. 13, 1995, pp. 50–54.

49. Cynthia Littleton, "NATPE Newcomers. Made to Order," *B&C*, Jan. 15, 1996, p. 8; Greg Spring, "Syn City Secrets," *EM*, Jan. 11, 1999, pp. 22–26.

50. As with off-network sitcoms, movie packages entitle the station to a

certain number of runs of each film over a period of several years. Cynthia Littleton, "NATPE at the Movies," *B&C*, Jan. 13, 1997, p. 52.

51. Spring, "Syn City Secrets"; Greg Spring, "Syndicators' 'Dirty Little Secret' Out in the Open," *EM*, Mar. 22, 1999, pp. 1, 53; idem, "Sellers' New View of N.Y.C.," *EM*, Mar. 29, 1999, pp. 3, 28.

52. Michael Freeman, "Pay-for-Play Paxson Profit?" *MW*, June 2, 2001, pp. 9–12. This source also documents the effect of adding a seventh station to New York's syndication market.

53. Michael Freeman, "CBS O&Os Paid for Play," *MW*, Jan. 25, 1999, p. 6. Large advertising agencies may similarly receive equity positions in programs for bringing their clients along. Cynthia Littleton and Steve Coe, "Ad Dollars: Syndication's Not-so-hidden Persuaders," *B&C*, Feb. 19, 1996, pp. 21–24.

54. Spring, "Syndicators' 'Dirty Little Secret.'" For another example, see Chris Pursell, "Future in Jeopardy for 'Jenny Jones,'" *EM*, Mar. 4, 2001, pp. 1, 20; idem, "'Jenny' Saved by Tribune Deal," *EM*, Apr. 22, 2001.

55. Greg Spring, "Rent-A-Slot: Sinclair Sells Time Periods," *EM*, Jan. 18, 1999, p. 5; Joe Schlosser, "Do I Hear $1 Million," *B&C*, Jan. 18, 1999, pp, 3, 140–141.

56. Jean Bergantini Grillo, "The Cautious Survivors," *Channels*, Jan. 1988, pp. 64–65.

57. Statistical evidence on decisions about syndication and the determinants of a program's syndication potential appears in Steven Wildman and Kala Salomon Robinson, "Network Programming and Off-Network Syndication Profits: Strategic Links and Implications for Television Policy," *JME*, 8, no. 2 (1995): 27–48.

58. These contracts roll ahead six to nine months for each year's renewal of the program in its first run. One contract capped its duration for the licensee at six years and nine months. Mike Freeman, "Big 3 Affils Cool to Sitcoms," *MW*, Jan. 6, 1997, pp. 2–3.

59. Steve McClellan, "PTAR Fall Adds Spring to Off-Net," *B&C*, Jan. 22, 1996, pp. 62–63. These agreements also create risks for the syndicator obligated to supply a minimum number of episodes, as with NBC's program *In the House*. Broadcast for two years on NBC and syndicated by Warner Bros. for fall 1999, the program was first transferred from NBC to the UPN network, then cancelled by UPN, com-

pelling NBC to produce enough additional episodes to fulfill the syndication contract. See Greg Spring, "NBC Goes In-House To Save Deal," *EM*, July 6, 1998, pp. 4, 26.

60. Michael Freeman, "It's No Laughing Matter," *MW*, June 23, 1997, pp. 9–12; Mark Berman, "No Laughing Matter," *MW*, Jan. 24, 2000, pp. 68–69. Also see Cynthia Littleton, "'Nanny,' 'Moesha' Step Out," *B&C*, May 12, 1997, pp. 31–32.

61. Michael Freeman, "Suddenly Off-Net Is Hot Again," *MW*, Apr. 20, 1998, pp. 4–5.

62. Michael Freeman, "2001: A Sitcom Odyssey," *MW*, Jan. 4, 1999, pp. 4–5.

63. Cynthia Littleton, "Tribune Buys 'Friends' for '98," *B&C*, Nov. 6, 1995, p. 16; Greg Spring, "Will Viewers Like Old 'Friends' Now?" *EM*, Sept. 21, 1998, pp. 3, 44.

64. Betsy Sharkey, "*Profiler* Will Break Early," *MW*, Nov. 16, 1998, p. 6.

65. Greg Spring, "'Suddenly' on Cable," *EM*, June 15, 1998, pp. 2, 48.

66. Cynthia Littleton, "'Walker,' 'Sister, Sister' Head for Off-net Runs," *B&C*, May 27, 1996, pp. 20–21; Danielle Parker, "*Moesha* Has What Advertisers Want," *EM*, May 22, 2000, pp. 14, 23.

67. Joe Schlosser, "Twentieth Rolls Out the Hours," *B&C*, Sept. 21, 1998, p. 75.

68. Greg Spring, "Columbia Moves Fast on 'NewsRadio' Deal," *EM*, July 6, 1998, p. 15.

69. Steve McClellan, "Off-Net Sitcoms Are the Stars of Access," *B&C*, Jan. 15, 1996, pp. 35–36.

70. Cynthia Littleton, "Syndicated Magazines Fight for Shares," *B&C*, Sept. 2, 1996, pp. 22–26.

71. Also, the Big 3 network affiliate has less flexibility than other stations to shuffle an underperforming off-network program around in its schedule, because of its obligation to clear network programs. See McClellan, "Off-Net Sitcoms."

72. Cynthia Littleton, 'Grace,' 'Frasier' Pace Race for '97," *B&C*, Sept. 18, 1995, pp. 31–32.

73. Cynthia Littleton, "No 'Mad' Rush," *B&C*, Nov. 6, 1995, p. 16; Spring, "Syn City Secrets."

74. Neal Koch, "No Laughing Matter," *Channels*, Feb. 1988, pp. 48–49. Assume that the popular program attracts every viewer in the station's market, the advertiser's message does not benefit from repetition, and

all local advertisers can be accommodated by the popular program's ad spots. Then there is no more ad revenue to be realized from the local market, and the station has no willingness to pay for other syndicated programs.

75. Don West and Steve McClellan, "On the Leading Edge of Television's New Wave," *B&C*, Jan. 22, 1996, pp. 18–26.

76. Alex Ben Block, "Picking on the Little Guys," *Channels*, Feb. 1989, pp. 76–79.

77. Joe Schlosser, "The Funny Money in Off-Net," *B&C*, Feb. 23, 1998, pp. 18–23. The Pax stations previously showed infomercials and religious broadcasts.

78. Joe Mandese, "Off-Network Series Pull Top Ad Dollars," *EM*, Jan. 18, 1999, p. 68; Greg Spring, "Second Cycle Strong for 'Seinfeld' Sales," *EM*, Jan. 19, 1998, p. 5. The claim that the top early-evening syndicated shows enjoy an entry barrier is right in one sense. The majority of these programs are co-owned by the broadcast networks and cleared primarily on those networks' O&Os; an entrant directly challenging these clearances could not be sanguine about elbowing into the O&Os' schedules. Michael Freeman, "Top Markets Choke Access," *MW*, Sept. 8, 1997, p. 12

79. This mechanism was tested and confirmed in another context by Marvin B. Lieberman, "The Learning Curve, Technological Barriers to Entry, and Competitive Survival in the Chemical Processing Industries," *Strategic Management Journal*, 10, no. 5 (1989): 431–447. It also appeared in Chapter 1 as the "Thursday night problem" facing NBC's competitors.

80. An overall failure rate of 85 to 90 percent has been cited for new syndicated programs. Don West and Steve McClellan, "On the Leading Edge of Television's New Wave," *B&C*, Jan. 22, 1996, pp. 18–26.

81. Daniel Frankel, "Action Fights Back," *MW*, Feb. 28, 2000, p. 18; Alan Frutkin, "Pamela Lee . . . Please Call Home," *MW*, Jan. 25, 1999, pp. 26–29; Joe Schlosser, "Rough Times for Action Shows," *B&C*, Jan. 11, 1999, pp. 30, 36.

82. For a good general treatment, see Steven S. Wildman and Stephen E. Siwek, *International Trade in Films and Television Programs* (Cambridge, Mass.: Ballinger, 1988).

83. Steve McClellan, "RTL Deal Shapes MCA's Future," *B&C*, Aug. 12, 1996, p. 48.

84. Barbara Osborn, "First-run Fantasy/Sci-fi: Scoring with Unreality," *B&C*, Oct. 5, 1998, pp. 36–43; Greg Spring, "Too Many Chefs Can Spoil Co-Ventures," *EM*, Jan. 25, 1999, p. 100.

85. Greg Spring, "Turner Books 'L.A. Heat' in U.S.," *EM*, Mar. 22, 1999, p. 2.

86. Debra Johnson, "Europe Still Hot for U.S. Shows," *B&C*, Jan. 13, 1997, pp. 92–94.

87. Debra Johnson, "Hallmark Takes TV Movies on World Tour," *B&C*, Jan. 13, 1997, p. 104.

88. Greg Spring, "Pearson Maneuvering Its Game Pieces," *EM*, Jan. 5, 1998, pp. 1, 41. Pearson was later expanded to include European interests as well. Stanley Reed et al., "A Media Star Is Born," *BW*, Apr. 24, 2000, pp. 136–137.

89. Chris Pursell, "Picture Gets Smaller for Syndication," *EM*, Feb. 12, 2001, pp. 1, 28; Michael Freeman, "Many Pieces of the Action," *MW*, Nov. 24, 1997, p. 9; Joe Schlosser, "Where the Action Is at NATPE," *B&C*, Jan. 12, 1998, p. 52; idem, "Can New Hours Stand Test of Time?" *B&C*, Nov. 13, 1997, pp. 36–38; John Consoli, "Dramatic Pauses," *MW*, Jan. 31, 2000, pp. 19–22.

90. Alan Frutkin, "Land of the Rising Shows," *MW*, Apr. 12, 1999, pp. 9–12.

91. Michael Freeman, "Goldberg Enjoys Reality of Success at Endemol," *EM*, Feb. 25, 2002, pp. 3, 19.

3. The Public Broadcasting System

1. Richard E. Caves, *Creative Industries: Contracts between Art and Commerce* (Cambridge, Mass.: Harvard University Press, 2000), chap. 14.

2. Accounts of the system's history include James Day, *The Vanishing Vision: The Inside Story of Public Television* (Berkeley: University of California Press, 1995); Ralph Engelman, *Public Radio and Television in America: A Political History* (Thousand Oaks, Calif.: Sage Publications, 1996); William Hoynes, *Public Television for Sale: Media, the Market, and the Public Sphere* (Boulder, Colo.: Westview Press, 1994); and Marilyn Lashley, *Public Television: Panacea, Pork Barrel, or Public Trust?* (Westport, Conn.: Greenwood Press, 1992).

3. "As a National System, Public TV Struggles with Weak Decision-making Powers," *www.current.org/ptv/ptv1.html.*

4. CPB's weak governance and preoccupation with the short-run political game were described by David Stewart, "The Emperor's Old Clothes: It's Time to Retailor CPB," *Current,* Sept. 8, 1997.

5. "Statement of Mr. Robert Coonrod, President and CEO of Corporation for Public Broadcasting, before House Subcommittee on Television and the Internet," July 10, 2002, p. 8.

6. "Dead End for Sesame Street," *BW,* June 19, 1995, pp. 66–69.

7. *PBS 2001 Annual Report, www.pbs.org/insidepbs/annualreport/text/fiscal_text.html.*

8. For a detailed chronicle of the ideological conflicts over PTV, see James Ledbetter, *Made Possible by . . . : The Death of Public Broadcasting in the United States* (London: Verso, 1997).

9. Twentieth Century Fund Task Force on Public Television, *Quality Time?* (New York: Twentieth Century Fund Press, 1993), pp. 150–151 (hereafter *Quality Time);* Aaron Barnhart, "The Little Picture: In Public TV We Trust," *EM,* July 22, 2002, p. 10.

10. For recognition of these problems within the system, see (for example) "APTS Launches Governance Reviewing Leading to 'Constitutional Convention,'" *Current,* Apr. 8, 1996; "National Forum for Public Television Executives," *Public Broadcasting PolicyBase, www.current.org/pbpb/forum/forumphase1.html;* "As a National System, Public TV Struggles with Weak Decision-making Processes," *Current Online, www.current.org/ptv/ptv1.html.*

11. See esp. Lashley, *Public Television,* chaps. 3–5.

12. Ibid., pp. 62–63.

13. CPB's discretionary program funds were whittled down from 49 percent of its budget in 1973 to 9 percent in 1986. Ibid., table 5.2. For the detailed rules that govern the allocation of CPB's funds, see "CPB Budget Allocation Formula," *Public Broadcasting PolicyBase, www.current.org/pbpb/statistics/CPBformula.html.*

14. Caves, *Creative Industries,* chaps. 14, 15.

15. Laurie Mifflin, "For WNET, A New Fund and a New Security," *NYT,* Nov. 17, 1997, pp. B1, B7.

16. "PBS Links Video Rights to Production Funding," *Current,* Sept. 7, 1992, *www.current.org/pbs/pbs216v.html.*

17. Chris McConnell, "PBS Keeps Its Head Above Cable," *B&C,* Aug.

10, 1998, pp. 20–28; Karen Everhart Bedford, "Hull Dived into the PBS Archives, Found Himself among Old Friends," *Current Online, www.current.org/prog/prog70gh.html.*

18. Dan McGraw, "Is PBS Too Commercial?" *U.S. News & World Report,* June 1, 1998, p. 42.
19. Daniel Golden, "Spin-offs, Corporate Tie-ins a Precarious Path for WGBH," *Boston Globe,* June 24, 1997, pp. A1, A12.
20. Lawrie Mifflin, "Public Broadcasting Head, Noted for Fund-Raising, Quits," *NYT,* Sept. 10, 1999, p. A13.
21. "PBS Invites Stations To Become Equity Partners," *Communications Daily,* Dec. 1, 1995, p. 6.
22. Elizabeth A. Rathbun, "Burns' Jazz Is Hot," *B&C,* Feb. 5, 2001, p. 36.
23. Steve Behrens, "Public TV Evenly Split on 30-Second Underwriting Credits," *Current,* April 5, 1999, *www.current.org/mo/mo906u.html.* The rules are quoted in *Quality Time,* pp. 153–155.
24. Michael Oneal and Richard A. Melcher, "Dead End for Sesame Street," *B&C,* June 19,1995, p. 66.
25. Debby Garbato Stankevich, "Public Interest: Underwriting PBS Cooking Shows Stretches the Advertising Dollar," *Business and Industry,* July 24, 1995, p. 45.
26. Corporate sponsors are said to show little interest in ads appearing in program breaks on PTV relative to program sponsorship. "Should Public Broadcasting Go More Commercial?" *Current Online, www .current.org/cm/cm1.html.*
27. For an example from an outgoing head of PBS, see "Duggan Goes Out Swinging against Policies that Commercialize PTV," *Public Broadcasting Report,* Oct. 8, 1999 (hereafter *PBR).*
28. David Hatch, "PBS Group Finds a Way to Snag Ads," *EM,* Sept. 7, 1998, pp. 27, 28.
29. Brendan Christie, "The ABCs of PBS," *Realscreen,* Feb. 1, 1998, p. 24.
30. "Make It for the US," *Televisual,* Aug. 1, 2001, p. 18. PBS and the British producer Carlton contribute equally to fund programs produced by Carlton, with PBS holding the U.S. domestic rights and Carlton the international rights. The produced material is to be split equally between U.S. and U.K. content. See Broadcast News by Produxion.com, June 21, 2001.

31. For public TV's absorption with prizes awarded for its programs, see Beth Pinsker, "Cash, With Strings, for Documentaries," *NYT,* Jan. 14, 2002, p. C7.
32. Lashley, *Public Television,* p. 57 and chap. 4 generally.
33. Furthermore, critics of PTV's choice of target audiences regularly focus on the unfairness of ignoring the unserved and disadvantaged and make no claim that PBS passes up opportunities to enhance its ratings overall.
34. Frederick Wiseman, "What Public TV Needs: Less Bureaucracy," *NYT,* Nov. 27, 1988, sec. 2, p. 35.
35. "As a National System, Public TV Struggles with Weak Decision-Making Processes," *www.current.org/ptv/ptv1.html.*
36. "Duggan: PBS Exists To Serve Stations," *PBR,* June 28, 1996; "Swope Sets Ambiguous Goal: Restoring Trust in PBS," *PBR,* Nov. 5, 1999.
37. Without this attitude an economist presumes that an organization pursuing some goal other than profit will nonetheless maximize its profit from all activities that do not impair that goal (a museum's shop, for example) and apply the surplus to its furtherance.
38. "Mitchell Discounts Ratings as Measure of Success of PBS Programs," *PBR,* March 22, 2002.
39. "PBS Should Consider Revised Governance Structure, Mitchell Says," *Communications Daily,* June 25, 2002.
40. "PBS Appoint Kathy Quattrone Chief Programming Executive," *PBR,* June 28, 1996.
41. The conflicts and tensions between PBS and the stations resemble the relationships between National Public Radio (NPR) and the public radio stations. NPR serves as the news-gathering arm of the stations, in the same way PBS functions as a collective supplier of programs. In 2004 NPR received a large charitable bequest of $236 million, which set off a chorus of concern over how the stations would benefit from this bounty, and whether NPR would pursue investments outside its domain (such as dealing with newly launched satellite radio). Lynette Clemetson, "All Things Considered, NPR's Growing Clout Alarms Member Stations," *NYT,* Aug. 30, 2004, pp. B1, B4.
42. Around 1990 the stations were supplying 42.1 percent of PBS programs, independent producers 19.4 percent, Children's Television Workshop 16.1 percent, foreign producers and co-producers 14 percent, and other sources 8.4 percent. *Quality Time,* pp. 138–139.

43. Daniel Golden, "Channel 2's Challenge: Local Programming Doesn't Rate," *Boston Globe,* June 23, 1997, pp. A1, A8.

44. B. J. Bullert, *Public Television: Politics and the Battle over Documentary Film* (New Brunswick, N.J.: Rutgers University Press, 1997), p. 15.

45. Natan Katzman and Ken Wirt, "Program Funding in Public Television and the SPC," in *The Future of Public Broadcasting,* ed. Douglass Cater (New York: Praeger, 1976), pp. 251–273.

46. Jeremy Gerard, "Public TV Is Seeking To Centralize Programs," *NYT,* June 21, 1990, p. C22; Lawrie Mifflin, "Reprieve for PBS But Hunt for Funds Continues," *NYT,* Jan. 2, 1996, pp. A9, A13. The old system made no changes in nationally scheduled series during its last four years; in the first year the chief program executive added eight and dropped seven. *Quality Time,* p. 132.

47. Lawrie Mifflin, "As the Pendulum Swings at PBS," *NYT,* Feb. 27, 1995, p. D8.

48. Barnhart, "The Little Picture," p. 10.

49. Elizabeth A. Rathbun, "Too Good To Be 2.0," *B&C,* June 12, 2000, p. 14; Mark Jurkowitz, "WGBH Wonders What's in Store for the Future," *Boston Globe,* Feb. 11, 2000, pp. M1, M4.

50. Joe Flint, "Louis Rukeyser of 'Wall $treet Week' Needs a New Address," *WSJ,* Mar. 22, 2002, p. B2.

51. An account of this screening process was provided by Bullert, *Public Television,* pp. 10–35.

52. Brendan Christie, "The ABCs of PBS," *Realscreen,* Feb. 1, 1998, p. 24.

53. Jack Gardner, "Sponsorship: Digging Deep into the Foundations, Jon Else Finds Water," *Realscreen,* Jan. 1, 1998, p. 26.

54. Stuart Sucherman, "Old Enough To Get Its Act Together," *Channels,* Oct. 1987, pp. 68–70.

55. Elizabeth Jensen, "Changing the Documentary Landscape," *Los Angeles Times,* July 14, 2001, sec. 6, p. 18; Jenny Hazan, "Championing the Public Voice," *Realscreen,* June 1, 2001, p. 38.

56. David Stewart, *The PBS Companion: A History of Public Television* (New York: TV Books, 1999); Daniel Golden, "Winds of Change Buffet WGBH," *Boston Globe,* June 22, 1997, pp. A1, A24. Stewart's book comprises chapter-length studies of the production of major PBS series.

57. Alan James Frutkin, "A Los Angeles Station Tries To Be a Player for PBS," *NYT,* June 3, 2001, sec. 2, pp. 25, 29; Karissa S. Wang, "L.A. PBS Station Enters a New Era," *EM,* Aug. 27, 2001, p. 26.

58. David Hatch, "Can PBS Stave Off Its Preschool Competitors?" *EM,* Feb. 9, 1998, pp. 28, 34.

59. A group of stories on how-to programs appeared in *EM,* July 13, 1998, pp. 29–36.

60. Aaron Barnhart, "The Little Picture: PBS Needs Local Focus," *EM,* July 3, 2000, p. 9.

61. Beth Pinsker, "Cash, With Strings, for Documentaries," *NYT,* Jan. 14, 2002, p. C7.

62. Richard Somerset-Ward reported such a survey result in *Quality Time,* pp. 140–141.

63. Brendan Christie, "Investigating Bill Kurtis," *Realscreen,* May 1, 1998, p. 14; Edward Wong, "Hard Times for TV Documentaries," *NYT,* Jan. 4, 2001, pp. B1, B5.

64. Elizabeth Jensen, "In Funding Squeeze, PBS Cozies Up to Madison Avenue 'Sponsors,'" *NYT,* July 3, 1996, pp. B1, B5; Brendan Christie, "Public Stations, Private Money," *Realscreen,* June 1, 1999, p. 45.

65. *Quality Time,* p. 16.

66. Elizabeth A. Rathbun, "Merge or Perish?" *B&C,* May 22, 1995, pp. 46–48; Steve Behrens, "Beyond Public TV's Single-channel Habit," *Current,* July 22, 1995, *www.current.org/ptv/ptv613o.html.*

67. By 1998 four had been sold. "Public TV Stations Sell Second Channels in Albany/Schenectady and Oklahoma City," *Current,* July 27, 1998, *www.current.org/ptv/ptv813s.html.*

68. "As a National System, Public TV Struggles."

69. "What Pubcasters Are Doing To Increase Impact and Reduce Operating Costs," *Current Online,* Aug. 6, 2001, *www.current.org/mo/mo3.html.*

70. "Dead End for Sesame Street."

71. *Quality Time,* pp. 127, 143.

72. Bill Carter, "Public Television Stations Propose Merging Operations," *NYT,* Aug. 1, 2001, p. A17.

4. The Squeeze on Broadcasters' Rents

1. *B&C,* Dec. 30, 2002, p. 8.

2. At the beginning of the 2003–4 season, the leading audience survey reported viewership down 12 percent for males eighteen to thirty-four and down 20 percent for men eighteen to twenty-four. John Schwartz, "Leisure Pursuits of Today's Young Men," *NYT,* Mar. 29, 2004,

pp. C1, C2. These declines were widely thought too large to be credible, but the general process is clearly real.

3. Kevin J. Delaney, "Ads in Videogames Pose a New Threat to Media Industry," *WSJ*, July 28, 2004, pp. A1, A8.

4. Ronald Grover, "Off the Island and into the Outback," *BW*, Sept. 11, 2000, p. 48; Bill Carter, "Final Answer: Quiz Show Put in ABC Lineup," *NYT*, Dec. 1, 1999, pp. C1, C22; Bernard Weinraub, "Sudden Explosion of Game Shows Threatens Old TV Staples," *NYT*, Feb. 9, 2000, pp. B1, B3.

5. An incidental advantage of reality shows is their immunity to strikes by the Writers Guild of America. These conflicts over "residuals"—rents from reused programs that were not anticipated and contracted upon when programs were first filmed—have a long, bitter history in Hollywood. TV underwent a serious strike in 1989 and anticipated but avoided one in 2001. Jim Rutenberg, "'Reality' Shows May Undercut Writers' Strike," *NYT*, Apr. 23, 2001, pp. C1, C4.

6. Paige Albiniak, "Does Reality Have an Afterlife?" *B&C*, Oct. 11, 2004, p. 20. To be viable in syndication, a program's episodes must be self-contained and independent of one another. Networks licensing reality shows pay the producer's full cost, which implies that expected off-network value is not significantly greater than zero.

7. "Reality 1994: Special Report," *B&C*, May 9, 1994, pp. 29–42.

8. Stefan Fatsis, "TV Networks Add More Sports to Prime Time," *WSJ*, Mar. 20, 2001, pp. B1, B4.

9. Bill Carter, "The Man Reshaping Prime Time," *NYT*, June 8, 1998, pp. D1, D9. The program's average cost is two-thirds that of an hour drama, but an episode, being time-sensitive, cannot be reused as a summer repeat.

10. Diane Mermigas, "'Millionaire' Could Make a Billion," *EM*, Oct. 23, 2000, p. 18.

11. Bill Carter, "Fox Pursuing a Gentler Reality," *NYT*, Oct. 16, 2000, pp. C1, C6; idem, "Can ABC Kick the Regis Habit?" *NYT*, Feb. 5, 2001; Joe Flint, "ABC Takes Chance on New Sitcom With Gritty Edge," *WSJ*, Mar. 14, 2001, pp. B1, B6.

12. Brooks Barnes, "Reality Checks: Unscripted Shows Become a Money Pit," *WSJ*, July 27, 2004, pp. A1, A12.

13. Bill Carter, "ABC's 'Millionaire' May Not Survive Beyond the Current Season," *NYT*, Nov. 28, 2001, pp. C1, C5.

14. Lisa Napoli, "Camcorders and PC's Shape Aesthetics of 'Reality' TV," *NYT,* Mar. 13, 2003, pp. C1, C4.

15. Steve McClellan, "Liar Liar Ransom Ransom," *B&C,* Mar. 6, 2000, p. 52.

16. With fresh episodes doled out over a nine-month season and aired during the sweeps months, reruns had to start popping up within the main season, even while potent miniseries sat in the vault waiting for May. Bill Carter, "Where Did the Reliable Old TV Season Go?" *NYT,* Apr. 20, 1997, sec. 2, pp. 1, 30.

17. Susan Tyler Eastman, *Broadcast/Cable Programming: Strategies and Practices,* 4th ed. (Belmont, Calif.: Wadsworth Publishing Co., 1993), pp. 123–124.

18. Joe Flint, "Fresh Episodes Are Latest Victims in TV Cutbacks," *WSJ,* Jan. 31, 2002, pp. B1, B4. It was argued that similar increases in reruns during the 1960s reflected collusion among the networks; see Bruce M. Owen, Jack H. Beebe, and Willard G. Manning, Jr., *Television Economics* (Lexington, Mass.: Lexington Books, 1974), pp. 106–110. Since the more recent reductions were apparently rational for each network acting independently, it seems impossible either to confirm or reject collusion.

19. Steve McClellan, "ABC Faces Affiliates, Problems Head On," *B&C,* June 10, 1996, pp. 8–10.

20. Chris Pursell and Michael Freeman, "Fox's Off-Net Solution," *EM,* Aug. 6, 2001, pp. 1, 29.

21. In 2004 NBC acquired Universal Studios.

22. Bill Carter, "ABC Reverses TV Pattern and Schedules Cable Rerun," *NYT,* Aug. 7, 2002, p. C5.

23. Bill Carter, "TV's Loneliest Night of the Week Is Starting To Look Very Familiar," *NYT,* June 21, 2004, pp. C1, C9.

24. Andrew Ross Sorkin and Bill Carter, "NBC Is Said To Be Close to Acquiring Bravo," *NYT,* Nov. 4, 2002, p. A15.

25. Geraldine Fabrikant with Andrew Ross Sorkin, "Disney Is Said To Be Close to Acquisition of Fox Family," *NYT,* July 23, 2001, pp. C1, C8; Nikhil Deogun and Bruce Orwall, "Disney Is Close to Buying Fox Family Worldwide," *WSJ,* July 23, 2001, p. A3. Joe Flint and Bruce Orwall, "Play It Again, Goofy . . . Recycled Shows Are Central to Disney–Fox Deal," *WSJ,* July 23, 2001, pp. B1, 6; Bill Carter, "Disney Discusses Strategy Behind Buying Fox Family," *NYT,* July 24, 2001,

p. C9. ABC was widely judged to have overpaid for Fox Family, but that does not impugn the principle of the deal.

26. Interview, "Eye to Eye with Moonves," *B&C,* Jan. 21, 2002, pp. 26–30.

27. Jim McConville, "Peaking at the Future Through a Shared Window," *EM,* Jan. 8, 2001, p. 31.

28. Michael Freeman, "ABC Gets Syndie Slice of 'Whose Line,'" *EM,* Nov. 3, 2000, pp. 8, 41.

29. Joe Flint, "ABC and Warner Bros. Click on a Deal To Recycle Shows Through Many Outlets," *WSJ,* Nov. 1, 2001, p. B9; Michael Freeman, "Forging a Model for Profitability," *EM,* Jan. 28, 2002, pp. 1, 13–15.

30. Diane Mermigas, "WB Hits To Replay on TNT," *EM,* May 14, 2001, pp. 1, 25.

31. This effect was recognized by David Atkins and Barry Litman, "Network TV Programming: Economics, Audiences, and the Ratings Game, 1971–1986," *Journal of Communication,* 36 (Summer 1986): 32–51.

32. Amy Harmon, "Skip-the-Ads TV Has Madison Ave. Upset," *NYT,* May 23, 2002, pp. A1, A3; Bill Carter, "Skipping Ads? TV Gets Ready To Fight Back," *NYT,* Jan. 10, 2003, pp. C1, C4.

33. See John Consoli, "Clutter Climbs Higher," *MW,* Apr. 12, 1999, pp. 6–8; Chuck Ross, "Peacock Clutters Up Airwaves," *EM,* Aug. 7, 2000, p. 38.

34. Bruce M. Owen and Steven S.Wildman, *Video Economics* (Cambridge, Mass.: Harvard University Press, 1992), p. 125.

35. Networks and national advertisers objected strenuously. Michele Greppi, "CBS Time Squeeze Scandal Widens," *EM,* Nov. 12, 2001, pp. 1, 43.

36. Joe Flint, "Disappearing Act: The Amount of TV Screen Devoted to Show Shrinks," *WSJ,* Mar. 29, 2001, pp. B1, B6.

37. Matthew Rose and Suzanne Vranica, "Prolonged Advertising Slump Puts Media in Mood To Pander," *WSJ,* May 9, 2002, pp. A1, A10.

38. Grover, "Off the Island"; Marc Gunther, "Now Starring in Party of Five—Dr Pepper," *Fortune,* Apr. 17, 2000, pp. 88–90; Anna Wilde Mathews, "Ford Motor Gets Starring Role on WB Network," *WSJ,* Mar. 21, 2001, pp. B1, B4.

39. Joe Flint and Emily Nelson, "'All My Children' Gets Revlon Twist,"

WSJ, Mar. 15, 2002, pp. B1, B4; Suzanne Vranica, "Coming: Jay Leno and the Lincolns," *WSJ,* Apr. 1, 2002, p. B1.

40. Brian Steinberg and Emily Nelson, "Unit of WPP Will Own Stake in ABC Shows," *WSJ,* Dec. 1, 2003, pp. B1, B4.

41. Evelyn Nussenbaum, "Products Slide Into More TV Shows, With Help From New Middlemen," *NYT,* Sept. 6, 2004, pp. C1, C7; Suzanne Vranica, "Product-Placement Sheds Its Cozy Trappings," *WSJ,* Sept. 23, 2004, pp. B1, B6.

42. The practice has spread, with consultants emerging to match music to program. Daniel Frankel, "Synergy Sings at The WB," *B&C,* July 29, 2002, pp. 20–22.

43. Jonathan Levy, Marcelino Ford-Livene, and Anne Levine, *Broadcast Television: Survivor in a Sea of Competition,* OPP Working Paper Series 37 (Washington, D.C.: Office of Plans and Policy, Federal Communications Commission, 2002), pp. 3–10.

44. John M. Higgins and Allison Romano, "Cheaper by the Dozen," *B&C,* Feb. 4, 2002, pp. 20–28.

45. Bill Carter, "Even As Executives Scorn the Genre, TV Networks Still Rely on Reality," *NYT,* May 19, 2003, pp. C1, C7.

46. We take no position on whether networks, advertising agencies, or both enjoy some bargaining power. We do assume that ad prices respond normally to disturbances.

47. Because the networks are rolled into larger enterprises, their separate profits are not disclosed.. The statement in the text is based on analysts' estimates reported in *B&C,* Mar. 25, 1996, p. 6; Mar. 3, 1997, p. 4; Mar. 2, 1998, p. 4; and Mar. 8, 1999, p. 11.

48. See Thomas G. Krattenmaker and Lucas A. Powe, Jr., *Regulating Broadcast Programming* (Cambridge, Mass.: MIT Press, 1994), pp. 157–174.

49. For an excellent study of the supply and demand determinants of violent programming, see James T. Hamilton, *Channeling Violence: The Economic Market for Violent Television Programming* (Princeton, N.J.: Princeton University Press, 1998).

50. Ken Auletta, *Three Blind Mice: How the TV Networks Lost Their Way* (New York: Random House, 1991), esp. pp. 285, 340–347, 472.

51. Steve McClellan, "The Ax Man Cometh," *B&C,* Sept. 21, 1998, pp. 6–7.

52. Bill Carter and Jim Rutenberg, "CNN's Parent May Postpone News Merger with ABC," *NYT,* Nov. 11, 2002, pp. C1, C2. The expected

economies were discussed by John Consoli, "Buyers Back CNN/ABC Pact," *MW,* Jan. 27, 2003, pp. 5–6.

53. The motion picture studios were similarly wrung out when their profitability came under major assault from the rise of television as a competing, low-cost entertainment medium. See Robert H. Stanley, *The Celluloid Empire: A History of the American Movie Industry* (New York: Hastings House, 1978), esp. chap. 5.

54. For an example (reduction of cost and improved incentives in ABC's owned-and-operated stations), see Jack Loftus, "How They Do It," *Channels,* Apr. 1989, pp. 44–46.

55. James T. Hamilton, *All the News That's Fit To Sell: How the Market Transforms Information into News* (Princeton, N.J.: Princeton University Press, 2004).

56. Daniel Boorstin, *The Image, or What Happened to the American Dream* (New York: Atheneum, 1962), p. 57; Leo Lowenthal, *Literature, Popular Culture, and Society* (Englewood Cliffs, N.J.: Prentice-Hall, 1961), chap. 4.

57. John Consoli, "See You Next Year," *MW,* July 31, 2000, p. 7.

58. Bill Carter, "Fox TV Studio Creates a Unit To Produce Cheaper Shows," May 5, 2004, pp. C1, C9.

59. Michael Freeman, "NBC Lowers the Bar with $500,000 Hours," *EM,* Jan. 14, 2002, p. 1A; idem, "NBC Targets Family Fare for Sundays," *EM,* Mar. 19, 2002, pp. 1, 28.

60. Eastman, *Broadcast/Cable Programming,* p. 133; Michael Freeman, "Networks Cut Back on Development," *EM,* Nov. 12, 2001, pp. 3, 42.

61. Alan Frutkin, "Pilots Fly New Routes," *MW,* Oct. 25, 1999, p. 5; Ari Posner, "No Experience Required: The O.C. Rewrites the Rules of TV Writing," *NYT,* Mar. 21, 2004, sec. 2, pp. 1, 35.

62. Chris Pursell, "Programming Warner's Future," *EM,* Jan. 21, 2002, p. 26.

63. To be more precise, in light of declining average audiences, the condition pertains to a constant coefficient of variation.

64. Tom King, "When Every Show's a Survivor," *WSJ,* Nov. 16, 2001, pp. W1, W15; Bill Carter, "Not a TV Hit? This Season, Not a Problem," *NYT,* Nov. 18, 2002, pp. C1, C9.

65. See Chapter 1 for a brief discussion of the welfare economics of programming.

66. Steve McClellan, "Audiences Lost to Network Errors, CBS Strategist Says," *B&C,* Dec. 15, 1997, p. 71.

67. Brooks Barnes, "NBC Unveils Plan To Launch Shows All Year Round," *WSJ,* May 18, 2004, p. B11.
68. Lynette Rice, "Moonves Urges Broadcast Solidarity," *B&C,* Sept. 30, 1996, pp. 27–28; Michael Schneider, "Networks Abandoning Fall Premiere Stunts," *EM,* Aug. 10, 1998, pp. 3, 10; Alan Frutkin, "Nets Hold Back More for Midseason," *MW,* May 24, 1999, p. 6; John Consoli, "Meet You in Midseason," *MW,* May 31, 1999, pp. S40–S42; Joe Schlosser, "Summer Surge Is On," *B&C,* June 12, 2000, p. 8.

5. Cable Networks and Upgraded Cable Programming

1. U.S. Department of Commerce, *Statistical Abstract of the United States, 2001* (Austin, Tex.: Hoover's Business Press, 2001), table 1126; National Cable & Telecommunications Association Web site; Nielsen Media Research, *2000 Report on Television* (New York: Nielsen Media Research, 2000), p. 17. Nielsen (p. 14) reports on another form of demand expansion that is at least partly exogenous: the increase in the average household's daily usage from 6 hours 48 minutes in 1981–82 to 7 hours 24 minutes in 1998–99.
2. National Cable & Telecommunications Association, *2003 Year-End Industry Overview,* found at *www.ncta.com.*
3. Aaron Barnhart, "Cable, Cable Everywhere But Not a Thing to Watch," *NYT,* Dec. 28, 1996; Donna Petrozzello, "New Cable Networks," *B&C,* Feb. 22, 1999, pp. 18–19.
4. Jim McConville, "Fox Ready To Roll Dice in All-News Gamble," *B&C,* Oct. 7, 1996, pp. 52–54.
5. Joe Schlosser, "Cable's Little Engines That Could," *B&C,* Mar. 31, 1997, pp. 62–63; Rich Brown, "Turning Up the Volume," *B&C,* Oct. 9, 1995, pp. 40–42.
6. Jim McConville, "New Nets: Tough Act To Open," *B&C,* Nov. 27, 1995, p. 74.
7. Joe Schlosser, "CBS Set To Open New Eye," *B&C,* Mar. 31, 1997, p. 10; Jim McConville, "Toon Disney Ready To Roll," *EM,* Apr. 6, 1998, p. 8; interview, "An Animated Conversation with Betty Cohen," *B&C,* June 2, 1997, pp. 26–32.
8. Steve McClellan, "CNBC Gets Down to Business," *B&C,* Dec. 15, 1997, p. 15. The deal also consolidated competing business TV services that the two firms operated in Europe and Asia.

9. Jim McConville, "CNNSI Readies for December Launch," *B&C,* Nov. 18, 1996, p. 68.

10. Donna Petrozzello, "The A Team," *B&C,* Nov. 30, 1998, pp. 6, 10; Jim McConville, "Oxygen Fills In Money, Content Gaps," *EM,* June 21, 1999, pp. 4, 27.

11. Megan Larson, "Odyssey Swings for a Homer," *MW,* July 24, 2000, pp. 11, 14.

12. Sally Beatty, "Rainbow Media Still Expects Pot of Gold," *WSJ,* Mar. 27, 2001, p. B8.

13. Interview, "Building NBC's Future," *B&C,* May 5, 1997, pp. 28–34.

14. Allison Romano, "The Final Frontier," *B&C,* May 3, 2004, p. 28.

15. John Higgins, "E! Has Original Vision," *B&C,* Oct. 20, 1997, p. 46.

16. Steve McClellan, "NBC, Liberty Say No to CNNfn/Court TV Merger," *B&C,* Mar. 10, 1997, p. 7; Jon Lafayette, "Court TV Near a Divorce Pact," *EM,* Jan. 12, 1998, pp. 8, 119; Jim McConville, "Court TV Parties Make Peace Pact," *EM,* Feb. 23, 1998, pp. 34, 35; John M. Higgins, "Time Warner Looks To Have Day in Court," *B&C,* May 25, 1998, p. 14. For a similar episode involving USA Network, see Michael Bürgi, "USA, Now In Play?" *MW,* Nov. 4, 1996, pp. 4–5.

17. For example, Joe Flint, "Under Viacom, Comedy Central Finds Its Groove," *WSJ,* June 23, 2004, pp. B1, B10.

18. John M. Higgins, "A Call to Arms," *B&C,* Feb. 22, 1999, pp. 22–24, provided an example of a frustrated entrant with assets closely matching those of its incumbent competitor but unable to surmount the first-mover advantage.

19. Lawrie Mifflin, "Clash of the Old-Movie Titans," *NYT,* Mar. 19, 1995, sec. 2, pp. 38–40.

20. Jim McConville, "New Cable Networks Scramble for Space," *B&C,* Dec. 30, 1996, pp. 36–37.

21. Megan Larson, "For Big Cable, the World's Flat," *MW,* July 3, 2000, pp. 4–5.

22. Joe Flint, "It Isn't Sex or City, But It's Hot on Cable TV," *WSJ,* Aug. 11, 2003, pp. B1, B3.

23. "Interview with Robert L. Johnson," *B&C,* July 3, 1995, pp. 16–19. Viacom continued its planning off and on, facing difficulties such as a shortage of appropriate off-network material that could be recruited for syndication. Joe Flint, "Viacom Plans a Gay Channel, But Reception Isn't Clear," *WSJ,* Mar. 29, 2004, pp. B1, B6.

24. Bill Carter, "MTV and Showtime Plan Cable Channel for Gay Viewers," *NYT*, Jan. 10, 2002, pp. C1, C5. Viacom continued its planning off and on, facing difficulties such as a shortage of appropriate off-network material that could be recruited for syndication. Joe Flint, "Viacom Plans a Gay Channel, But Reception Isn't Clear," *WSJ*, Mar. 29, 2004, pp. B1, B6.

25. Jim Cooper, "The Road More Traveled," *MW*, Jan. 26, 1998, p. 8.

26. Jim McConville, "New Nets Seek Right Launch Mix," *B&C*, Mar. 4, 1996, pp. 38–40.

27. Michael Bürgi, "Fox Cable Kicks Off Today," *MW*, Oct. 7, 1996, p. 9; Steve McClellan, "Murdoch Changing Basic Equation," *B&C*, July 28, 1997, p. 59.

28. Price Colman, "TCI May Carry Fox News," *B&C*, June 3, 1996, p. 50.

29. The Sci-Fi Channel was offering $2 to $3 per subscriber. Jim Cooper, "New Bosses Shake Up USA," *MW*, Sept. 14, 1998, p. 16.

30. E.g., Price Colman, "Lifetime Takes a Hit with FNC Launch," *B&C*, Oct. 14, 1996, p. 50.

31. Price Colman, "War Looms Over Program Prices," *B&C*, Dec. 16, 1996, p. 11; John M. Higgins, "Programming Costs: Cable's Catch-22," *B&C*, Dec. 8, 1997, p. 7. On disputes with satellite broadcasters, see Joe Flint and Andy Pasztor, "DirecTV Threatens To Cut Channel," *WSJ*, Mar. 10, 2003, p. B3; Joe Flint, "They've Killed Kenny! And Sponge Bob!" *WSJ*, Mar 11, 2004, p. B3.

32. Federal law requires cable networks in which MSOs hold ownership stakes to offer satellite operators the same subscriber charges they offer their MSO owners. See John M. Higgins, "License to Kill," *B&C*, July 19, 2004, p. 8.

33. McClellan, "Murdoch Changing Basic Equation," p. 59.

34. Jim McConville, "It's Slow Going for Fox Family, Odyssey," *EM*, Mar. 29, 1999, pp. 3, 38; Joe Flint, "Odyssey Cable Network To Change Its Name to Hallmark Channel," *WSJ*, Mar. 29, 2001, p. B15.

35. Since cable networks carry few if any programs of specific local interest, one would expect profit-maximizing cable operators to transmit all broadcast stations with substantial local viewership. Indeed, in 1988, when retransmission was not required, the only omitted stations tended to be those located at some distance from the system and/

or in a different city, or those that achieved only minimal viewership. Michael G. Vita and John P. Wiegand, "Must-Carry Regulations for Cable Television Systems: An Economic Policy Analysis," *JBEM*, 37 (Winter 1993): 1–19; George D. Ford and John D. Jackson, "Preserving Free Television? Some Empirical Evidence on the Efficiency of Must-Carry," *JME*, 13, no. 1 (2000): 1–14.

36. For examples, see Rich Brown, "Fox's fX Unveils Programming Lineup," *B&C*, Apr. 25, 1994, pp. 29–30; Michael Bürgi, "Eye on More Subscribers," *MW*, June 9, 1997, p. 5.

37. Rich Brown, "New Networks Jockey for Channel Position," *B&C*, May 23, 1994, pp. 42–44; Steve McClellan, "The Remaking of CBS," *B&C*, July 15, 1996, pp. 4–5. In 2004 a new issue of retransmission payments arose over broadcast stations' digital signals; see Peter Grant and Joe Flint, "Some HDTV Sets Won't Get a Super Picture of Super Bowl," *WSJ*, Jan. 29, 2004, pp. B1, B8.

38. On the plausibility of this assumption, see Donna Petrozzello, "Cable Gets With the Program," *B&C*, Nov. 30, 1998, pp. 60–68.

39. Jim McConville, "TCI Move Not So Super for Superstations," *B&C*, Dec. 9, 1996, pp. 92–94; Price Colman, "VH1, MTV Get Reprieve from TCI," *B&C*, Jan. 27, 1997, p. 10.

40. See, for example, Steve Donahue, "ESPN Fee Hike Irksome to Cable Operators," *EM*, June 15, 1998, pp. 1, 49; Joe Flint, "TNT Upsets Cable Operators with a New Bill," *WSJ*, Oct. 14, 2002, pp. B1, B3. Nonetheless, some sports leagues and teams have investigated starting their own sports networks, motivated by a suspicion that some rents are sticking to ESPN that could be captured by displacing that network.

41. The theory of bundling also suggests the case in which the seller (cable operator) offers both bundled and separate prices to two groups of customers. Bundling of cable networks may be an artifact of technical constraints on letting each household freely select its own bundle from a menu.

42. Peter Grant, "It's Yankees 1, Cablevision 0, In TV-Fee Fight," *WSJ*, Mar. 25, 2004, pp. B1, B6.

43. Anne Marie Squeo and Joe Flint "Should Cable Be à la Carte, Not Flat Rate?" *WSJ*, Mar. 26, 2004, pp. B1, B2; Bill McConnell, "Against à la Carte," *B&C*, May 10, 2004, p. 6.

44. The same problem arises in music publishers' process of collecting

royalties from performance venues. Copyright collectives such as ASCAP in effect employ the all-or-nothing strategy, in the face of venues' attempts to lower their outlays by a pick-and-choose strategy. Richard E. Caves, *Creative Industries: Contracts between Art and Commerce* (Cambridge, Mass.: Harvard University Press, 2000), chap. 19.

45. Lee Hall, "CMT Ready To Deal To Stop Defections," *EM,* June 15, 1998, pp. 1A, 49.

46. Turner Broadcasting had previously announced a women's channel in cooperation with *Time* magazine and Condé Nast publishers, but it was aborted. Richard Siklos et al., "Oxygen: Inflated Expectations?" *BW,* Feb. 7, 2000, pp. 114–119.

47. Diane Brady, "'Television for Women': No One's Laughing Now," *BW,* Dec. 24, 2001, pp. 56–57; Sally Beatty, "Oxygen Media, After Long Lag, Shows New Life," *WSJ,* Dec. 24, 2001, pp. B1, B4; Jim Rutenberg, "Poor Showing for Oxygen in Ratings," *NYT,* Apr. 22, 2002, pp. C1, C10.

48. Jack Banks, *Monopoly Television: MTV's Quest to Control the Music* (Boulder, Colo.: Westview Press, 1996), pp. 31–43.

49. Ibid., chap. 3. MTV left some room for entrants by gravitating from an outlet for videos to a more general youth/lifestyle channel. David Tobenkin, "Cable: More Than Just MTV," *B&C,* Sept. 2, 1996, pp. 37–46.

50. Bill Carter, "After Years of Being Off Track, VH1 Hits Its Groove," *NYT,* June 22, 1998, pp. D1, D8.

51. Jim McConville, "ESPNNEWS, CNN/SI To Square Off," *B&C,* June 17, 1996, pp. 57–58.

52. Banks, *Monopoly Television,* pp. 63–76; Martin Peers, "Fed Up With MTV's Clout, Record Labels Use the Web to Fight Back," *WSJ,* Dec. 16, 1999, pp. B1, B4.

53. Joe Schlosser, "Showtime Fights for Screentime," *B&C,* Apr. 14, 1997, pp. 58–62; Tim Carvell, "You'll Want Your Starz! TV," *Fortune,* Nov. 24, 1997, p. 55. Would-be competitors of Black Entertainment Television were reviewed by Jim McConville, "Competition Getting Fierce," *EM,* Feb. 21, 2000, p. 25.

54. The data source is Kagan World Media, *Economics of Basic Cable Networks, 2002* (Carmel, Calif.: Kagan World Media, 2001), pp. 30–31.

55. Rich Brown, "Turner Unveils New Roster of Movies," *B&C,* July 5, 1995, p. 21; John M. Higgins, "Court TV Likes the Verdict," *B&C,* Mar. 20, 2000, p. 38; P. J. Bednarski and Allison Romano, "Make No Small Plans," *B&C,* Mar. 18, 2002, p. 14.

56. John Higgins, "Big-Ticket Originals Pay Off for Cable," *B&C,* Oct. 20, 1997, pp. 28–34.

57. Kagan World Media, *Basic Cable Networks,* pp. 24–26.

58. For a similar interpretation of this history, see Joe Flint, "Cable Nets Trying To Make Basic Original," *B&C,* Nov. 29, 1993, pp. 48–50; Jean Bergantini Grillo," What's Up with Originals," *B&C,* May 28, 2001, pp. 18–22.

59. Joe Flint, "Sci Fi Channel Hopes Aliens Will Nab Viewers," *NYT,* Nov. 29, 2002, pp. A11, A13.

60. Kathy Haley, "The Journey to Mainstream," *B&C,* Nov. 3, 1997, pp. 48–51.

61. Tom King, "The Demise of the TV Movie," *WSJ,* Feb. 2, 2001, p. W6; Daisy Whitney, "TV Movies Switch to Cable," *EM,* Oct. 22, 2001, pp. 10, 12.

62. A simple way to do this is to recruit better-known stars. Tom King, "Nickelodeon Comes of Age," *WSJ,* Mar. 15, 2002, p. W9.

63. Rich Brown, "When It Works, It Really Works Well," *B&C,* Feb. 21, 1994, pp. 34–40.

64. Mike Menechini, "Originals Drive Networks' Brand," *EM,* July 19, 1999, pp. 16, 21; Bernard Weinraub, "Little Screen, Big Ambition," *NYT,* Jan. 3, 2001, pp. B1, B6; Jim Rutenberg, "Cable Networks Look for Ways To Stand Out," *NYT,* Aug. 20, 2001, pp. C1, C9.

65. Jim Cooper, "Now at Networks Near You," *MW,* Apr. 13, 1998, pp. 6–8; Jim McConville, "Cable Goes to Hollywood," *EM,* July 19, 1999, pp. 14, 20.

66. Joe Schlosser, "The 'B'—As in Broadcast—List?" *B&C,* Jan. 11, 1999, p. 52; Jim McConville, "Window Openings Narrow," *EM,* July 19, 1999, p. 14.

67. Jim Cooper, "Chao Plays His First Hand," *MW,* Nov. 9, 1998, pp. 9–12; Lewis Beale, "A Cable Channel Seeks New Life Beyond Its Niche," *NYT,* Aug. 26, 2001, sec. 2, pp. 23, 27.

68. Bernard Weinraub, "Police Show Has Humans, Not Heroes," *NYT,* Apr. 3, 2002, pp. B1, B4. A warm critical reception supported the strategy.

69. Beth Pinsker, "Putting on the Hits," *B&C,* May 28, 2001, pp. 14–16.

70. Allison Romano, "MTV: Operating without a Net," *B&C,* May 27, 2002, pp. 21–26.

71. Michael Katz, "TLC Snags 'How'd They Do That,'" *B&C,* Dec. 9, 1996, p. 102; Cynthia Littleton, "E! Buys, Co-Finances 'Night Stand,'" *B&C,* Aug. 26, 1996, pp. 27–28; Anne Becker, "New Lease on Life,"*B&C,* Oct. 5, 2004, p. 20.

72. Patricia E. Bauer, "Hollywood's New Low-End Market," *Channels,* Dec. 1986, pp. 13–15; Betsy Sharkey, "There *Is* Life after Death," *MW,* Feb. 9, 1998, p. 9.

73. Caryn James, "Afterlife for TV's Quirky Flops? Sometimes," *NYT,* Apr. 18, 2001, pp. B1, B8.

74. Chris Pursell, "'VIP' Treatment: $500,000 per Episode," *EM,* Nov. 20, 2000, pp. 1A, 29.

75. Lynette Rice, "Lifetime Buys the Show," *B&C,* Aug. 19, 1996, p. 60; Joe Schlosser, "The Funny Money in Off-Net," *B&C,* Feb. 23, 1998, pp. 18–23. Also see Suzanne Ault, "*West Wing* Could Fly to Cable," *B&C,* Feb. 19, 2001, p. 36.

76. Jim Cooper, "Big Money for Nothing," *MW,* Sept. 21, 1998, p. 9; Jim McConville, "Shopping at Home," *EM,* June 14, 1999, pp. 3, 53.

77. Jon Lafayette, "Bartering to Cable," *EM,* Jan. 10, 2000, p. 22.

78. Bill Carter, "NBC Executive Raises Issues on 'Sopranos,'" *NYT,* May 2, 2001, pp. C1, C7.

79. Jim Rutenberg, "Seamy or Serious, It's Now Center Stage," *NYT,* Mar. 21, 2001, pp. B1, B4.

80. John Higgins, "South Park: An Original Original," *B&C,* Oct. 20, 1997, p. 44.

81. Anne Marie Squeo and Joe Flint, "FCC Tells Cable Industry To Clean Up Content—or Else," *WSJ,* Feb. 11, 2004, pp. B1, B9.

82. Bill Carter, "Cable and Broadcast Networks Clinch Over Wrestling Ad Revenue," *NYT,* Aug. 17, 1998, pp. D1, D6.

83. Sally Beatty, "ESPN To Produce Made-for-TV Movie, Sports Soap Opera," *WSJ,* July 13, 2001, p. B2; Bruce Orwall, "ESPN Adds Entertainment Shows to Its Playbook," *WSJ,* Mar. 6, 2002, pp. B1, B4; Jim McConville, "HGTV Plot Thickens," *EM,* Apr. 10, 2000, p. 58.

84. Jim Cooper, "TNT Seeks Broader Appeal," *MW,* Apr. 12, 1999, p. 5.

85. Jim McConville, "Amid New Competition, Nickelodeon Ups Spending," *EM,* Dec. 14, 1998, pp. 4, 56.

86. Sally Beatty, "What Are Space Aliens and Lingerie Doing on Learning Channel?" *WSJ*, Mar. 27, 2001, pp. A1, A6.
87. Jim McConville, "Competition Driving HBO," *EM*, Oct. 25, 1999, pp. 1, 31; Sally Beatty, "Unconventional HBO Finds Its Own Success Is a Hard Act to Follow," *WSJ*, Sept. 29, 2000, pp. A1, A8.
88. John Motavalli, "Cable Enters the Mix," *Channels*, Feb. 1988, pp. 53–57.
89. Rich Brown, "'Politically Incorrect' Mainstreams on ABC," *B&C*, Jan. 15, 1996, p. 6.
90. Cynthia Littleton, "'Atlantis' Surfaces on Cable," *B&C*, Dec. 9, 1996, p. 104.
91. T. L. Stanley, "Goodbye, National Launch?" *MW*, Apr. 28, 1997, p. 9.
92. Steve McClellan, "Big-Ticket Sitcoms Top Off-Net-Cable First-Run Fare," *B&C*, Jan. 23, 1995, pp. 76–82.
93. J. Max Robins, "Shandling's Foxy Deal," *Channels*, Apr. 1988, p. 61.
94. Rich Brown, "Nick Makes Syndication Push," *B&C*, Oct. 30, 1995, p. 50.
95. Chris Pursell, "Cable Series Consider Syndication Arena," *EM*, May 8, 2000, pp. 1A, 68.
96. Hugh Hart, "All the Drama of TV News, Including a Cancellation," *NYT*, July 14, 2002, sec. 2, p. 30.
97. Jim Rutenberg and Andrew Ross Sorkin, "Networks Embrace Cable, Their Longtime Threat," *NYT*, Nov. 5, 2002, pp. C1, C7; Michael Freeman, "Nets Keep It in the Family," *EM*, May 20, 2002, pp. 3, 31.
98. Jim Cooper, "Nets Want Bigger Piece of Action," *B&C*, Feb. 21, 1994, p. 40; Greg Spring, "'Call of Wild' Lands on Animal Planet," *EM*, Jan. 18, 1999, pp. 4, 58.
99. Allison Romano, "Table Scraps," *B&C*, July 26, 2004, p. 1. Cable program suppliers enjoy a non-pecuniary benefit in the fact that cable networks do not meddle continuously in the production of series under license, as do the broadcast networks. See Allison Romano and Paige Albiniak, "Funny Business," *B&C*, June 28, 2004, p. 1.
100. Donna Petrozello, "Only on Cable," *B&C*, Oct. 26, 1998, pp. 42–44; Rich Brown, "Original Cable Programming," *B&C*, Feb. 19, 1996, pp. 32–44.
101. Joe Flint, "Studio Back in Broadcast TV," *WSJ*, Dec. 15, 2004, pp. B1, B7.

102. Suzanne Ault, "It's Not Just for Broadcast," *B&C*, Sept. 24, 2001, pp. 16–20; Michael Freeman, "Jonas Navigates Tough Programming Landscape," *EM*, Nov. 19, 2001, pp. 3, 22.

103. John Motavalli, "Albrecht: Life on the Edge," *EM*, June 17, 2002, pp. 1, 22.

104. David D. Kirkpatrick and Bill Carter, "AOL Time Warner and Disney Revive Talks on News Ventures," *NYT*, Sept. 23, 2002, pp. C1, C2.

6. Broadcast Networks, Stations, and Rents

1. Bruce M. Owen and Steven S. Wildman, *Video Economics* (Cambridge, Mass.: Harvard University Press, 1992), pp. 166–172.

2. FCC Network Inquiry Special Staff, "An Analysis of the Network-Affiliate Relationship on Television," U.S. Federal Communications Commission, *New Television Networks: Entry, Jurisdiction, Ownership, and Regulation. II. Background Papers* (Washington, D.C.: Federal Communications Commission, 1980), pp. 105–292 (esp. pp. 144–149); Stanley M. Besen and Ronald Soligo, "The Economics of the Network-Affiliate Relationship in the Television Broadcasting Industry," *American Economic Review,* 63 (June 1973): 259–268.

3. Accordingly, stations' total revenue is more highly leveraged on their audiences in hours adjacent to prime time than during that peak period for viewers. Franklin M. Fisher, John J. MacGowan, and David S. Evans, "The Audience-Revenue Relationship for Local Television Stations," *Bell Journal of Economics,* 11 (Autumn 1980): 694–708.

4. FCC Network Inquiry Special Staff, "An Analysis," pp. 163–170. Of course, there were then fewer stations to be switched.

5. Marianne Barrett, "The Relationship of Network Affiliation Changes to Prime Time Program Ratings," *JBEM,* 43 (Winter 1999): 91–109.

6. KION (1995). Affiliation contracts are cited by the station's call letters and the year. More detail on which contracts contain or omit various provisions can be found in Matthew Rosenberg, "The Television Broadcasting Network Affiliate Relationship" (senior honors thesis, Harvard College, 2002), pt. 2.

7. KLST (1995); KGPE (1996); WCPO (1996).

8. Exceptions were WCMH (1994), KTAL (1996), and KQCD (1996).

9. After 1993 ABC also required that reports be delivered within five days of a request.

10. Interview, "It's Come to This," *B&C*, Apr. 9, 2001, pp. 18–22.

11. KHMT (1995) and WLUK (1998) are the only exceptions.

12. KTRV (1996), WTNZ (1996), WUPW (1996), WPMT (1997), KDF (1997), KPDX (1997), WHNS (1997), WLUK (1998), WVFX (1999), WSVN (1999), and WACH (1997).

13. Doug Halonen, "Networks Say Affiliates Abuse Pre-emptions," *EM*, July 30, 2001, pp. 2, 21.

14. KVIQ (1985), WJSU (1985), KLBK (1990), KCCW (1991), and KCCO (1991).

15. Stations have long been distinguished between VHF (channels 2–13) and UHF (14 and higher). VHF stations, the first in place, long held a major advantage of better reception and easier tuning. Especially with distribution by cable, this advantage has disappeared, but the UHF stations, latecomers into the local markets and mostly without Big 3 network affiliations, still suffer a disadvantage.

16. Steve Coe, "FOX Pushes News, Blasts Nielsen," *B&C*, Jan. 29, 1996, pp. 30–31; Steve McClellan, "Fox to Affiliates: Show Me the Money," *B&C*, Jan. 26, 1998, pp. 26–27.

17. KOKI (1992), KFXA (1995), KHMT (1995), KFXA (1995), WUPW (1996), WFFF (1997), WTGS (1997), WPMT (1997), KDF (1997), KPDX (1997), WHNS (1997), and WVFX (1999).

18. Steve McClellan and Paige Albiniak, "It's Getting Ugly," *B&C*, Jan. 18, 1999, pp. 11, 24–25.

19. Exceptions are WJSU (1989), WFSB (1993), and WJXT (1993).

20. KHSL (1995), WWNY (1995), WTOC (1995), WHBF (1995), WGCL (1994), WMAZ (1994), WHNT (1994), and KLFY (1994).

21. After 1993 NBC affiliates' contracts obligated the network to fulfill all contractual terms in the event of a change in the network's ownership.

22. Jon Lafayette, "ABC: No Assured Affiliation Transfers," *EM*, Jan. 18, 1999, pp. 1A, 39.

23. Katy Bachman, "Affiliates Stand Firm vs. FOX," *MW*, Apr. 24, 2000, p. 7.

24. For early efforts to limit comp, see Steve Behrens, "Will Temptation Undo the Tie That Binds?" *Channels*, May 1987, pp. 41–43.

25. "CBS Affiliates Take $30 Million Compensation Hit," *Broadcasting*, Nov. 26, 1990, p. 30.

26. Interview, "The Brass at Cap Cities/ABC: Rethinking TV," *Channels*,

Feb. 1989, pp. 93–95; Max Robins, "Bang the Drum Loudly," *Channels,* Dec. 1989, pp. 72–73.

27. Behrens, "Will Temptation Undo the Tie That Binds?"

28. Interview, "In the Eye of the Storm," *B&C,* Dec. 19, 1994, pp. 31–36; David Tobenkin, "Nets Want Clearance Bang for Buck," *B&C,* Nov. 7, 1994, p. 20.

29. Steve Coe, "ABC Drops Plans for Compensation Cuts," *B&C,* June 13, 1994, p. 6; Steve McClellan, "NBC Still Considering Offers, Wright Says," *B&C,* Oct. 24, 1994, pp. 20, 22.

30. Another investment made by the networks in keeping control of their affiliates was to take minority ownership positions—not large enough to tangle with FCC rules but large enough to block shifts of affiliation. Christopher Stern, "Small Investments Yield Big Benefits," *B&C,* Oct. 17, 1994, pp. 26–28.

31. KKTU (1996), KRIS (1996), KCEN (1997). KTAL (1996) dropped the comp formula and specified a flat payment.

32. Steve McClellan, "Remixing the Network Formula for Success," *B&C,* Dec. 21, 1998, pp. 18–23; Diane Mermigas, "ABC's Iger: Compensation Changes Loom," *EM,* Dec. 21, 1998, pp. 1A, 27.

33. Jon Lafayette, "NBC Affiliates Chew Over Comp Proposal," *EM,* May 25, 1998, pp. 3, 30.

34. Steve McClellan, "NBC, Affils Talking Joint Venture," *B&C,* Nov. 24, 1997, p. 15.

35. For example, see Steve McClellan, "Nothing Much Ventured," *B&C,* June 18, 2001, p. 16.

36. Jon Lafayette, "Cosmos Chief Alleges ABC Tough Tactics," *EM,* Jan. 11, 1999, pp. 2, 83; idem, "ABC: No Assured Affiliation Transfers," *EM,* Jan. 19, 1999, pp. 1A, 109; idem, "Station Group Riled by ABC Comp Change," *EM,* Oct. 9, 2000, pp. 1A, 35.

37. Steve McClellan and John M. Higgins, "Battle by the Bay," *B&C,* Oct. 18, 1999, p. 6; Joe Flint, "NBC Makes Offer of About $700 Million For San Francisco Television Station," *WSJ,* Nov. 3, 1999, p. B8; Elizabeth A. Rathbun, "The King of KRON," *B&C,* Nov. 22, 1999, pp. 22–26.

38. Diane Mermigas, "Station Economics Rocked," *EM,* Feb. 28, 2000, pp. 1, 47.

39. Jon Lafayette, "Granite's Rocky Dealing," *EM,* Feb. 21, 2000, pp. 1, 23; idem, "ABC Affils Man Battle Stations," *EM,* Mar. 20, 2000,

pp. 3, 38. NBC was simultaneously making another investment that would increase its leverage against affiliates—purchasing a 32 percent interest in the Pax network, which covered 58 percent of U.S. households and could be used as a supply of alternative NBC affiliates. Steve McClellan, "NBC, Paxson in Mating Dance," *B&C*, Sept. 13, 1999, p. 4.

40. Jon Lafayette, "NBC Eyes Gannett Comp Cut," *EM*, Jan. 24, 2000, pp. 1A, 120; idem, "NBC to Pay Gannett Affils," *EM*, Feb. 28, 2000, pp. 3, 47; idem, "Hearst, NBC Ink 10-yr. Deal," *EM*, July 24, 2000, pp. 6, 28.

41. Diane Mermigas, "Affiliates Facing Big Trouble Ahead," *EM*, May 31, 1999, p. 21.

42. ABC, for example, feared that it would otherwise slip into fourth place among the networks in ratings among the eighteen to forty-nine age group most preferred by advertisers. Steve McClellan, "The New NFL Ticket Price: $18 Billion," *B&C*, Jan. 19, 1998, pp. 4, 8.

43. Steve McClellan, "ABC Cuts Monday Night Football Compensation," *B&C*, Sept. 14, 1998, p. 12.

44. Creating new ad spots is an odd solution, because it would increase the revenue to be shared only if the current "clutter" was suboptimal. Chapter 4 suggested some reasons why the number might be below the profit-maximizing level and subject to increase only in times of apparent stringency.

45. Steve McClellan, "War at NBC, ABC at Peace," *B&C*, July 5, 1999, pp. 4–6; Jon Lafayette, "ABC Deal 'Fair,' Say Affiliates," *EM*, July 5, 1999, pp. 3, 24.

46. Sandy Brown, "ABC's Push-me Pull-you," *MW*, Oct. 7, 2002, pp. 5–6; Tony Case, "Still Nasty after All These Years," *MW*, Nov. 11, 2002, pp. 20–24.

47. Michael Schneider, "CBS, Affiliates Reach Deal to Pay for NFL," *EM*, June 1, 1998, pp. 1, 29; Michael Stroud, "CBS Affils Meet on Gridiron," *B&C*, June 1, 1998, p. 6.

48. Jon Lafayette, "Incomplete Pass on NFL Deal, Fox Affiliates Say," *EM*, May 25, 1998, pp. 1, 31; Steve McClellan, "Fox Stations on the Goal Line," *B&C*, July 20, 1998, p. 15.

49. Fox contracts permit the network to determine the allocation of ad spots. Bill Carter, "TV Networks' Tough Talk Leaves Local Stations Fuming," *NYT*, Apr. 12, 1999, pp. C1, C10; Jon Lafayette, "Fox,

ABC Stagger Affiliates," *EM*, Apr. 12, 1999, pp. 1, 55; Kyle Pope, "Fox Affiliates Preparing to Battle Plan That Would Cut Ad Revenue," *WSJ*, Apr. 27, 1999, p. B15.

50. Fox also experimented with short-run trading of ad spots, offering affiliates spots it could not sell in several National Football League divisional playoff games. The affiliates would pay Fox half the revenue received if the spots were sold locally, nothing if they could not be sold. Michele Greppi, "Fox Spots Affiliates Extra Ad Time," *EM*, Jan. 21, 2002, pp. 1, 51.

51. Steve McClellan, "Affils Reject Fox Spot Grab," *B&C*, May 10, 1999, p. 10; idem, "Fox Affils Yield on Take-Backs," *B&C*, May 31, 1999, p. 7; Jon Lafayette, "Fox and Its Affils Reach Accord," *EM*, May 31, 1999, pp. 3, 30. Its expiration was welcomed by the stations, for whom the recession in ad demand spoiled the plan's benefit. Steve McClellan and Joe Schlosser, "4Kids Win-Win Deal," *B&C*, Jan. 28, 2002, p. 17.

52. Jon Lafayette, "Affils Holding Fox's Money," *EM*, Jan. 10, 2000, pp. 1A, 61.

53. Steve McClellan, "210 Seconds over NBC," *B&C*, May 17, 1999, p. 16; Michael Freeman and Alicia Mundy, "Mutually Assured Destruction?" *MW*, June 14, 1999, pp. 6–7; Katy Bachman, "Affils Stand Firm vs. Fox," *MW*, Apr. 24, 2000, p. 7.

54. Steve McClellan, "ABC Faces Affiliates, Problems Head On," *B&C*, Feb. 24, 1997, p. 14.

55. Rich Brown, "NBC Cable Moves Vex Affiliates," *B&C*, June 17, 1996, p. 15. NBC also recycled substantial amounts of programming on its joint-venture MSNBC cable network.

56. Michael Freeman, "Fox, ABC Fail to Settle," *MW*, June 8, 1998, p. 5.

57. Jon Lafayette, "NBC's 15% Exclusivity Price Tag," *EM*, June 21, 1999, pp. 1, 27.

58. Sally Beatty, "ABC, Affiliates Reach Accord On 'Reairing,'" *WSJ*, June 29, 1999, p. B8; Steve McClellan, "Can These Marriages Be Saved?" *B&C*, Jan. 14, 2002, pp. 6–7.

59. Joe Flint, "NBC Yields to Affiliates, Ending Plan To Rebroadcast News Show on PAX TV," *WSJ*, May 1, 2000, p. B25.

60. Michele Greppi, "What Went Wrong with Paxson, NBC?" *EM*, Dec. 10. 2001, pp. 1, 22.

61. With some exceptions: WCMH (1994), KCRA (1995).

62. For example, see Steve McClellan and Paige Albiniak, "It's Getting Ugly," *B&C*, Jan. 18, 1999, pp. 11, 24–25; Steve McClellan, "It's War," *B&C*, Mar. 12, 2001, pp. 6–10.

63. Jon Lafayette, "Wright Roils NBC Affiliates with Cable Talk," *EM*, Mar. 29, 1999, pp. 1A, 39.

64. Dan Trigoboff, "Preparing to Say Nay to Eye," *B&C*, Nov. 5, 2001, p. 5; idem, "The Hard Way," *B&C*, June 17, 2002, pp. 29–31.

65. Steve McClellan, "It's War!" *B&C*, Mar. 21, 2001, pp. 6–10.

66. When a station switched from independent status to CBS affiliation, its ratings rose 42 to 62 percent. Switches from Big 3 affiliation to Fox lowered the station's ratings while raising Fox's. Steve McClellan, "Fox UP, CBS Down in Switched Markets," *B&C*, Jan. 9, 1995, p. 12.

7. Program Supply, Integration, and the Fin-Syn Rules

1. If the seller sets a price which the buyer takes as given, the resulting "double marginalization" leaves both producers and ultimate consumers worse off. The same conclusion is reached if the monopolistic buyer ("monopsonist") sets a buying price to maximize its own profit and the seller reacts passively.

2. "Syndication" here refers to the licensing of program series to individual stations for rebroadcast after their first-run network showings.

3. For background on these regulations, see Stanley M. Besen et al., *Misregulating Television: Network Dominance and the FCC* (Chicago: University of Chicago Press, 1984); and Franklin M. Fisher, "The Financial Interest and Syndication Rules in Network Television: Regulatory Fantasy and Reality," in *Antitrust and Regulation: Essays in Memory of John J. McGowan*, ed. Franklin M. Fisher (Cambridge, Mass.: MIT Press, 1985), pp. 263–298.

4. Advertising agencies had once been important suppliers of TV programs, but their role was being phased out in the 1960s for reasons unrelated to fin-syn.

5. Until 1990 the networks were also constrained by consent decrees imposed by the Department of Justice in the early 1970s; these were effectively identical to the fin-syn rules, and their expiration made worthwhile the networks' political investment in ending fin-syn.

6. For detailed chronicles of this deregulation process, see Tamber Chris-

tian, "The Financial Interest and Syndication Rules—Take Two," *CommLaw Conspectus: Journal of Communications Law and Policy,* 3 (Summer 1995): 107–119; William G. Covington, Jr., "The Financial Interest and Syndication Rules in Retrospect: History and Analysis," *Communication and the Law,* 16 (June 1994): 3–21.

7. Little recent and systematic research exists on program license fees. Their close relationship to production costs and the dependence of both on expected advertising revenues were shown in Network Inquiry Special Staff, "An Analysis of Television Program Production, Acquisition and Distribution," in U.S. Federal Communications Commission, *New Television Networks: Entry, Jurisdiction, Ownership, and Regulation. II. Background Studies* (Washington, D.C.: Federal Communications Commission, 1980), pp. 627–640. Also, changes in license fees for continuing shows are closely related to changes in their production costs. See Sora K. Park, "Determinants of Renewal and Adjustment of License Fees of Network Prime Time Programs," *JME,* 9, no. 3 (1996): 1–19.

8. Susan Tyler Eastman et al., "Accelerating the Flow: A Transition Effect in Programming Theory?" *JBEM,* 41 (Spring 1997): 265–283; James T. Tiedge and Kenneth J. Ksobiech, "The 'Lead-in' Strategy for Prime-Time TV. Does It Increase the Audience?" *Journal of Communication,* 36 (Summer 1986): 51–63.

9. Networks regard the cost of promoting a new prime-time show as important enough to make these outlays depend closely on the contract's duration and/or the network's equity share. See Steve McClellan, "Feeding the Peacock," *B&C,* Feb. 9, 1998, p. 22.

10. Daniel Frankel, "Life after Cancellation," *EM,* Sept. 27, 1999, pp. 8, 40. The origin and rationale of this threshold are unclear. One hundred episodes stripped without repeats would last for just under five months, but repeats commonly carry syndication cycles along for years.

11. Joe Schlosser, "Why CBS Loves Raymond," *B&C,* Dec. 7, 1998, p. 42.

12. Bengt Holmstrom, "Moral Hazard in Teams," *Bell Journal of Economics,* 13 (Autumn 1982): 324–340.

13. The structure of contracts in the broadcasting industry, where the optimal allocation of decision rights is a close call, can be compared to other creative industries in which it is clear. Consider a cinema film

that is assembled in stages: the screenwriter passes the script to the producer, who completes the film and passes it to a distributor (studio) for promotion and license to exhibitors. At each stage decision rights are completely or largely transferred by means of a real option contract to the party about to sink a further investment in the project, and with maximal incentive to make a value-maximizing choice. Richard E. Caves, *Creative Industries: Contracts between Art and Commerce* (Cambridge, Mass.: Harvard University Press, 2000), pp. 15, 88–91, 104–106.

14. William T. Bielby and Denise D. Bielby, "'All Hits Are Flukes': Institutionalized Decision Making and the Rhetoric of Network Prime-Time Program Development," *American Journal of Sociology,* 99 (March 1994):1287–1313.

15. Doug Halonen, "He Told You So: Valenti's Fin-Syn Warnings Come True," *EM,* June 8, 1998, p. 1.

16. Networks held financial interests in 31.9 percent of their programs in 1957, rising to 65.4 percent in 1967. The proportion in which they held domestic syndication rights rose from 15.9 to 23.8 percent. Thomas L. Schuessler, "FCC Regulation of the Network Television Program Procurement Process: An Attempt To Regulate the Laws of Economics," *Northwestern University Law Review,* 73, no. 2 (1978): 227–306.

17. "Prime time" in broadcasting practice is defined as covering twenty-two hours a week—7 to 11 P.M. on Sunday, 8 to 11 P.M. the other days; because our sample picked up very few programs shown on Sunday before 8 P.M., those were dropped.

18. In 1994–95, 20 of 108 series pilots were already in-house productions or had network equity. See Michael Freeman, "The Wages of Fin-Syn," *MW,* May 9, 1994, p. 14.

19. The source of the basic sample is Quigley Publishing Co., *International Television & Video Almanac* (annual). The ownership status of shows not included in the *Almanac* was found in "Internet Movie Database" (imdb.com). Another Web site, "Epguides" (epguides.com), provided detailed listings of the exact years in which each show was aired, for identifying its initial and final years, premiere date, and annual renewal decision. Other Internet databases such as Infoplease (infoplease.com), Jump the Shark (jumptheshark.com), and Zap2It (zap2it.com) filled in information missing from other sources.

20. Bernard Weinraub and Bill Carter, "TV Networks Favor Pilots They've Made," *NYT*, Apr. 1, 2002, pp. C1, C8.

21. For a related analysis, see Bruce M. Owen and Steven Wildman, *Video Economics* (Cambridge, Mass.: Harvard University Press, 1992), pp. 52–59.

22. Bill Carter, "Disney To Join Operations of Studio and ABC Units," *NYT*, July 9, 1999, p. C6; idem, "Ailing ABC Turns to HBO in Search of TV Hits," *NYT*, Aug. 5, 2002, pp. C1. C6.

23. Bob Woletz, "On to 1990: Can the Next Fin-Syn War Be Averted?" *Channels*, Feb. 1988, pp. 82–85; Doug Halonen and Thomas Tyrer, "Judge Keeps Fin-Syn Phase-Out on Track," *EM*, July 18, 1994, p. 2.

24. Michael Freeman, "Producers Fight for Fin-Syn," *MW*, Dec. 5, 1994, p. 10.

25. Among explicit references to sticky fee-to-cost ratios, see Cynthia Littleton, "Broadcast Networks Face Fin-Syn Trade-off," *B&C*, June 3, 1996, pp. 35–36; Michael Schneider, "Networks, Studios Still in Rights War," *EM*, Oct. 26, 1998, pp. 1, 48. Also see Park, "Determinants of Renewal."

26. Caves, *Creative Industries*, pp. 56–59.

27. It seems clear why new programs (pilots) are not auctioned. Each program is developed as a joint venture between a network and a producer, and thus styled to the network's needs and interests (Chapter 1). An auction would be efficient only if the networks' idiosyncratic preferences were minor or if they comprised information strategically concealed from the producers.

28. Greg Spring and Michael Schneider, "Producers: Networks Milk Fin-Syn Clout," *EM*, Mar. 10, 1997, p. 1; Lynette Rice and Jon Feltheimer: "Leading Television's Prolific Producer," *B&C*, May 26, 1997, p. 20.

29. Greg Spring, "In the Thick of It," *EM*, July 20, 1998, pp. 1, 38; Joe Schlosser, "Twentieth Topples Warner," *B&C*, May 24, 1999, p. 19. Robert W. Crandall, "FCC Regulation, Monopsony, and Network Television Program Costs," *Bell Journal of Economics and Management Science*, 3 (Autumn 1972): 483–508, found that in 1960–1965 the prices networks paid for programs were negatively related to the ownership shares they obtained, whereas the standard contract approach implies a positive relationship. He conjectured the same mechanism that we propose for 1995–1999.

30. Michael Freeman, "Financial Stakes Raised," *MW,* May 31, 1999, p. 12.
31. Michael Freeman, "20th Century Fox Still at Top of Heap," *EM,* Dec. 4, 2000, pp. 1A, 34.
32. Lynette Rice, "NBC Pushes for Piece of Prime Time," *B&C,* Apr. 7, 1997, pp. 14–15; John Consoli and Betsy Sharkey, "On-the-Job Training at NBC," *MW,* Nov. 2, 1998, pp. 9–12. NBC might have argued that assigning it some decision rights could lead to more value created for network and studio together than equity assigned to a less successful studio.
33. Michael Schneider, "Studios Feel Networks' Strong-Arm," *EM,* May 25, 1998, p. 26.
34. Michael Schneider, "Fall TV Prix Fixe: Stakes, Well Done," *EM,* May 24, 1999, pp. 1, 38; Marc Gunther, "War Breaks Out in TV Land," *Fortune,* June 1, 1999, pp. 35–36.
35. *EM,* June 1, 1998, p. 2.
36. Bill Carter, "NBC Faces Prospect of Losing 'Frasier' in Contract Talks," *NYT,* Dec. 7, 2000, pp. C1, C15.
37. Schlosser, "Why CBS Loves Raymond."
38. Mike Freeman, "Victimized by Synergy," *MW,* Oct. 4, 1999, p. 6.
39. Johnnie L. Roberts, "Suing Hollywood's Suits," *BW,* Oct. 11, 1999, pp. 62–63.
40. Ronald Grover, "The Art of the TV Deal," *BW,* June 2, 1997, p. 121.
41. Karen Guo and Richard E. Caves, "The End of Fin-Syn and the Reorganization of the Television Broadcast Programming Market," working paper, Harvard University, 2001.
42. The study did not control for the type of competing program—whether other networks match or counter-program the show at hand. See James T. Tiedge and Kenneth J. Ksobiech, "CounterprogrammingPrimetime Network Television," *JBEM,* 31 (Winter 1987): 41–55.
43. David Barth, "Assessing the Value of Vertical Integration in Television Program Supply," working paper, Northwestern University, 2002.
44. Steve McClellan, "ABC Makes High-Profile Production Leap," *B&C,* Dec. 5, 1994, p. 18. Robert W. Crandall argued that the studios' support of fin-syn was aimed at denying the independent producers access to joint ventures with the networks: "Who's Afraid of the TV Networks?" *WSJ,* Sept. 9, 1999, p. A30.
45. Cynthia Littleton, "Charting a New World for Fox," *B&C,* Jan. 13, 1997, pp. 30–31.

46. Joe Flint, "Networks Win, Hollywood Winces, and Fin-syn Barriers Fall," *B&C*, Nov. 22, 1993, pp. 6, 16; Steve Coe and Mike Freeman, "Networks' Gain Could be Indies' Loss," *B&C*, Nov. 22, 1993, pp. 20–21.

47. Laurie Thomas and Barry R. Litman, "Fox Broadcasting Company, Why Now? An Economic Study of the Rise of the Fourth Broadcasting Network," *JBEM*, 35 (Spring 1991): 139–157; Alex Ben Block, *Outfoxed: Marvin Davis, Barry Diller, Rupert Murdoch, Joan Rivers, and the Inside Story of America's Fourth Television Network* (New York: St. Martin's Press, 1990), pp. 96–102.

48. Greg Spring, "Paramount Strategy Builds a Growing Station Group," *EM*, Dec. 8, 1997, pp. 1A, 67.

49. Howard J. Blumenthal and Oliver R. Goodenough, *This Business of Television,* 2nd ed. (New York: Billboard Books, 1998), pp. 6–10

50. Steve McClellan, "WB Woos and Wins Sinclair," *B&C*, July 21, 1997, pp. 4, 8.

51. Steve Coe, "Five More for Warner's Fifth," *B&C*, Apr. 4, 1994, pp. 6–7.

52. Damiel M. Kimmel, *The Fourth Network: How Fox Broke the Rules and Reinvented Television* (Chicago: Ivan R. Dee, 2004), pp. 97–100.

53. Larry Collette and Barry R. Litman, "The Peculiar Economics of New Broadcast Network Entry: The Case of United Paramount and Warner Bros.," *JME*, 10, no. 4 (1997): 3–22.

54. Lynette Rice and Steve McClellan, "The WB Gets New Legs," *B&C*, Aug. 11, 1997, pp. 20–24.

55. Alex Ben Block, "Twenty-First Century Fox," *Channels,* Jan. 1990, pp. 36–39; Lynette Rice, "Fox's One-Two Punch," *B&C*, Nov. 18, 1996, pp. 24–27.

56. Karissa S. Wang, "UPN Wants To Take Affils by the Hand," *EM*, Jan. 22, 2001, pp. 24–27.

57. *B&C*, Apr. 18, 1994, p. 6; Lynette Rice, "10 Years from Wannabe to Big Four," *B&C*, Sept. 22, 1997, pp. 36–38.

58. Claude Brodesser et al., "UPN Gets Leap-Frogged," *MW*, July 21, 1997, pp. 2–3; Joe Flint, "Will Viacom's Big Bet on 'Buffy' Become UPN's Savior or Slayer?" *WSJ*, July 12, 2001, pp. B1, B4.

59. Block, "Twenty-First Century Fox."

60. Wang, "UPN Wants To Take Affils by the Hand."

61. Steve McClellan, "The Fight To Be Fifth," *B&C,* May 12, 1997, p. 5; Michael Freeman, "UPN's Fate Hangs in Balance," *MW,* Aug. 21, 2000, pp. 3, 32; Flint, "Viacom's Big Bet."

62. A current theoretical literature on the problem is more sophisticated than the argument made in the text, because it makes the determination of the market price explicit and endogenous (whereas we appeal to casual evidence of limited price flexibility). These theoretical models, however, cannot readily deal with price determination where fixed costs and *infinite variety* both prevail. See Y. Chen, "On Vertical Mergers and Their Competitive Effects," *RAND Journal of Economics,* 32 (Winter, 2001): 667–685; and Volker Nocke and Lucy White, "Do Vertical Mergers Facilitate Upstream Collusion," working paper, University of Pennsylvania, 2003.

63. Caves, *Creative Industries,* pp. 47–48, 158–159.

64. Steve McClellan, "X Fin-Syn," *B&C,* Jan. 24, 2000, p. 30.

65. Kim Masters, *The Keys to the Kingdom: How Michael Eisner Lost His Grip* (New York: William Morrow, 2000), p. 348. The stock market cheered this acquisition with a 24 percent increase in Disney's value.

66. CBS had previously been acquired by Westinghouse, and that firm's chain of major TV stations was folded into CBS while unrelated businesses of Westinghouse were spun off.

67. Jim Rutenberg and Bill Carter, "NBC Ponders Its Options: Grow or Else," *NYT,* May 14, 2001, p. C1.

68. NBC's owner General Electric turned down or discouraged several bids for the network (Disney, Paramount, Turner Broadcasting). Steve McClellan, "Aggressive Disney Goes after NBC," *B&C,* Oct. 31, 1994, p. 6.

69. Lynette Rice, "Jon Feltheimer: Leading Television's Prolific Producer," *B&C,* May 26, 1997, pp. 20–24; Joe Schlosser, "Sony: No Time for Prime Time," *B&C,* Oct. 22, 2001, pp. 5–8.

70. Deborah Starr Seibel, "Inside the Fluff Factory," *B&C,* Nov. 22, 2004, p. 1.

71. "Managing Creativity," *B&C,* Sept. 22, 1997, pp. 40–42.

72. Schlosser, "Why CBS Loves Raymond."

73. Michael Freeman, "Touchstone Throws Its Weight around Fall Skeds," *EM,* June 4, 2001, pp. 3, 30.

74. Weinraub and Carter, "TV Networks."

75. Michael Schneider, "ABC Fare Won't Be All-Disney, Say Execs," *EM,* Aug. 2, 1999, p. 31.

8. Broadcast Stations

1. Harvey D. Shapiro, "Sale of the Century," *Channels,* Apr. 1987, pp. 48–52. VHF stations occupy channels 2 through 13 and have enjoyed several sorts of advantages over the later-developed UHF stations using channels 14 and above. These disadvantages have diminished over the years and are absent when local stations are received via cable.

2. Steve McClellan, "One-Stop Shopping," *B&C,* July 16, 2001, p. 10.

3. Ben Yagoda, "McStations," *Channels,* Sept. 1986, pp. 27–31; Harry A. Jessell and Elizabeth A. Rathbun, "Striking It Rich with Sinclair," *B&C,* Aug. 19, 1996, pp. 27–32.

4. For example, *B&C,* Apr. 5, 1999, p. 27; Apr. 12, 1999, p. 16; May 10, 1999, p. 23; May 31, 1999, p. 66.

5. Michele Greppi, "Hubbing Is the Word for the NBC O&Os," *EM,* Jan. 15, 2001, pp. 8, 123.

6. Steve McClellan, "Sinclair's $2.3B Powerhouse," *B&C,* Apr. 15, 1996, pp. 8–9. Also see Elizabeth Rathbun, "Allbritton Gives ABC a Boost in Alabama," *B&C,* Nov. 20, 1995, p. 29.

7. E.g., "Gray to Buy 22 TV Outlets of Station Holdings," *WSJ,* Apr. 3, 2002, p. B2.

8. Jon Lafayette, "Hearst–Argyle Buying Won't End with Pulitzer," *EM,* June 1, 1998, p. 4; Shapiro, "Sale of the Century."

9. Michael Freeman, "Welcome to the Big Time," *MW,* Mar. 2, 1998, pp. 4–5.

10. Lafayette, "Hearst–Argyle Buying."

11. Donna Petrozello, "$4.4 Billion and Counting," *B&C,* Sept. 4, 1995, pp. 6–7.

12. Also, Fox's acquisition of the Chris–Craft chain gave it the option to kill off the UPN network—an action that would have been severely impolitic though quite possibly profitable. Michael Freeman, "UPN's Fate Hangs in Balance; News Corp. Could Cut Network's Affiliation," *EM,* Aug. 21, 2000, p. 3.

13. Jon Lafayette, "Ownership Ranks Rapidly Thinned by Consolidation," *EM,* May 18, 1998, pp. 1A, 12.

14. Ibid.; Rathbun, "Allbritton Gives ABC a Boost"; Claude Brodesser,

"Hicks, NBC Eye $1 Bil. Link," *MW,* Sept. 15, 1997, p. 7; Steve McClellan, "Lund Outlines Likely Structure of CBS/Maxam/Group W," *B&C,* Jan. 29, 1996, p. 28; Freeman, "Welcome."

15. Richard Katz, "Program Balancing Acts," *Channels,* Apr. 9, 1990, pp. 42–44. The practice of decentralization was partly a "perk" bestowed on station managers at little evident cost to stations' high profit rates. The practice was curbed as a result of rising real costs of programming and (probably) tighter governance constraints imposed on and by the station groups.

16. Cynthia Littleton, "Tribune Broadens Development Slate," *B&C,* Sept. 23, 1996, p. 28.

17. Elizabeth A. Rathbun, "Tribune's Renaissance," *B&C,* July 8, 1996, pp. 4–9; Jon Lafayette, "Consolidation: They May Be Giants," *EM,* Oct. 5, 1998, pp. 30, 34.

18. Cynthia Littleton, "Renaissance Buy Should Boost Tribune Entertainment," *B&C,* July 8, 1996, p. 9; idem, "Tribune/Worldvision Team," *B&C,* Oct. 23, 1995, p. 28.

19. David Tobenkin, "New World, Tribune Team Up," *B&C,* July 17, 1995, p. 16.

20. Paige Albiniak, "Strategic Battle for Ali & Jack Time Slot," *B&C,* Feb. 2, 2004, p. 5.

21. Steve McClellan, "Renaissance Breaks into Top 25," *B&C,* July 10, 1995, p. 10; Lafayette, "Consolidation."

22. For pre-1990 interactions of policy and group ownership, see Herbert H. Howard, "The 1996 Telecommunications Act and TV Station Ownership: 1 Year Later," *JME,* 11, no.. 3 (1998): 21–32. The absence of a trend toward concentration was shown by David Waterman, "A New Look at Media Chains and Groups: 1977–1989," *JBEM,* 35 (Spring 1991): 167–178.

23. The rules for calculating this constraint discount UHF stations' shares by 50 percent for their systematic disadvantage, so the constraint is compared to the sum of household shares of the group's VHF stations plus half the sum of the shares of its UHF stations. The constraint applies alike to networks and other owners of groups of stations.

24. The former transaction was effected by Westinghouse (Group W) acquiring CBS. Harry A. Jessell, "Getting Ahead of the Curve," *B&C,* July 31, 1995, p. 12.

25. Elizabeth A. Rathbun, "Hearst Stocks Up on Argyles," *B&C,* Mar. 31, 1997, pp. 6–7.

26. Data from *Broadcasting & Cable Yearbook, 2001* (New Providence, N.J.: Bowker, 2001), p. 1A, 89.

27. Donna Petrozzello, "Trading Market Explodes," *B&C*, Feb. 3, 1997, pp. 18–19; Sara Brown, "The Big Get Bigger," *B&C*, Apr. 6, 1998, pp. 8, 26.

28. Mark. C. Rainey, "The Cost Effect of Television Local Marketing Agreements," working paper, MIT, 2000.

29. Steve McClellan, "As LMAs Grow, So Do Concerns," *B&C*, June 5, 1995, pp. 8–9; Chris McConnell and Sarah Brown, "FCC Finds 70 In-Market LMAs," *B&C*, Aug. 11, 1997, pp. 6–7.

30. Contrary to the standard economic definition: a market containing (only) two independent competitors. The 1999 rules permit a top-rated station to merge with a low-rated one so long as eight independent stations remain in the market. More liberal terms are permitted for failing or authorized but unbuilt stations.

31. Karissa S. Wang, "UPN Wants to Take Affils by the Hand," *EM*, Jan. 22, 2001, pp. 6, 94. Still larger economies are cited by Steve McClellan, "Fox Duops in Chicago," *B&C*, July 1, 2002, p. 8. A joint marketing agreement similarly was reported to cut the two stations' sales staff costs by one-third and their program costs by one-fourth. Steve McClellan, "Making Most of Duopolies," *B&C*, Apr. 17, 1995, pp. 50–51.

32. Suzanne Ault, "Duops Do Deals," *B&C*, Aug. 20, 2001, p. 10; Chris Pursell, "Duopolies Share the Wealth," *EM*, Sept. 10, 2001, pp. 1, 41.

33. In one instance a station's payment for an off-network sitcom fell by two-thirds. Lynette Rice, "Distributors Identify Local TV Threats," *B&C*, Jan. 20, 1997, p. 36.

34. "Television Stations, Two by Two," *NYT*, Apr. 8, 2002, p. C8.

35. Bill McConnell and Suzanne Ault, "Fox's TV 'Triopoly' Strategy," *B&C*, July 30, 2001, pp. 5–6; Dan Trigoboff, "Fox Swaps for a Pair of Duops," *B&C*, Aug. 13, 2001, p. 9; Steve McClellan, "Fox Duops in Chicago," *B&C*, July 1, 2002, p. 8.

36. Diane Mermigas and Jon Lafayette, "What Is Delaying Duop Deals?" *EM*, Oct. 18, 1999, pp. 1, 28; Diane Mermigas, "News Corp. Plays Duopoly Game," *EM*, Aug. 21, 2000, pp. 1, 30.

37. Seth Schiesel, "F.C.C. Rules on Ownership under Review," *NYT*, Apr. 3, 2002, pp. C1, C10.

38. Bill McConnell, "Review, Relax, Relieve," *B&C*, Feb. 5, 2001, p. 16.

39. *B&C*, July 10, 1995, pp. 8–9.

40. Warren Communications, *Television & Cable Factbook 2002*, pp. A1701–28, lists all owners of commercial TV stations in the United States. For each owner this section gives the number of stations owned and a list by call letters and location. To calculate shares of TV households reached, we turned first to pp. A1–A4 of the *Factbook*, which give the number of households in each of the 210 standard DMA markets. These are divided by total U.S. TV households to obtain each market's (and thus each station's) share, and the sum of a group's stations' shares yields the share for a station group. This basic procedure needed several refinements. (1) In 2002 restrictions on "duopolies" had been relaxed, so some groups owned two stations in the same DMA; the duplicated signal was left out of the group's calculated share. (2) The DMA is not the relevant market for two types of stations, and their shares were determined in a different way. For stations in isolated small towns not reached by distant signals, we used the station's own estimate of the number of households it reaches (appearing in the *Factbook*, Part A). For a station transmitting on the edge of a DMA, with its signal reaching only part of the market, we again used the station's estimate of the number of households reached by its signal. (3) In a few cases a group holds less than 100 percent equity in a station; we assumed that any share greater than 40 percent conveys effective control. (4) A few groups hold stations in U.S. territories (such as Puerto Rico); these were ignored owing to lack of household count data. (5) For some groups the *Factbook* shows a discrepancy between the summary number of stations and the count of stations individually listed (usually the former exceeds the latter by one or two); for lack of a convenient way to resolve the discrepancy, we defined the group as the sum of its listed stations. (6) The *Factbook* does not state an exact date to which the information pertains; we presume it to be 2001 and not necessarily the same for all groups.

41. The head of Viacom (CBS and UPN networks) would have liked to acquire more big-city affiliate stations, but would avoid ownership in small markets. *EM,* Feb. 25, 2002, p. 20.

9. Cable Networks and Cable Operators

1. Data came from National Cable and Telecommunications Association, *Industry Overview 2003 (www.ncta.com).*

2. David Waterman and Andrew A. Weiss, *Vertical Integration in Cable Television* (Cambridge, Mass.: MIT Press and AEI Press, 1997), p. 46.

3. There is no case for cable operators to provide local programming, because they transmit the full program streams of all local broadcast stations, which perform this task.

4. In 2001 basic networks received $7.1 billion in fees from cable operators, $10.1 billion from advertisers. Many operators, especially in large urban and suburban markets, have arrangements with networks to sell local advertising on the network's programs, like the broadcast networks and their affiliates. In some cases, the MSO retains all local sales revenues but pays the network a higher monthly price to carry its programming.

5. Maricris Briones, "A Funny Thing Happened on Turner's Way to Building a Network—a TV Revolution," *Marketing News,* March 29, 1999, p. 52.

6. "How TCI Builds a Cable Empire," *BW,* Nov. 23, 1981, p. 74. We ignore the recent changes of ownership among the MSOs, notably TCI's acquisition first by AT&T and then by Comcast.

7. See Mark A. Zupan, "Cable Franchise Renewals: Do Incumbent Firms Behave Opportunistically?" *RAND Journal of Economics,* 20 (Winter 1989): 473–482.

8. Geraldine Fabrikant and Bill Carter, "Cable's New Giant Flexes His Muscles," *NYT,* Oct. 20, 2003, pp. C1, C7.

9. National Cable and Telecommunications Association, *2001 Cable TV Handbook (www.ncta.com/industry-overview).* Data on the competitiveness of cable systems' market for inputs of programming and outputs of video services are provided in "Annual Assessment of the Status of Competition in the Market for the Delivery of Video Programming," CS Docket no. 01–129, 17 FCC Rcd 1244 (2002).

10. Thomas W. Hazlett and Matthew L. Spitzer, *Public Policy toward Cable Television: The Economics of Rate Controls* (Cambridge, Mass.: MIT Press, 1997). Some networks lowered their subscriber fees and quality and shifted their revenue dependence toward advertising. Rich Brown, "New Networks Jockey for Channel Position," *B&C,* May 23, 1994, pp. 42–44.

11. Stanley M. Besen et al., "Vertical and Horizontal Ownership in Cable TV: Time Warner–Turner (1996)," in *The Antitrust Revolution: Economics, Competition, and Policy,* ed. John M. Kwoka and Lawrence J. White (New York: Oxford University Press, 1999), pp. 452–475.

12. Waterman and Weiss, *Vertical Integration,* chap. 3.
13. A major explanation for this concentration was economies in jointly operating cable systems serving a large region. The causation does not appear to run from economies of vertical linkage to concentration of cable networks.
14. This research includes Waterman and Weiss, *Vertical Integration;* idem, "The Effects of Vertical Integration between Cable Television Systems and Pay Cable Networks," *Journal of Econometrics,* 72 (May 1996): 357–395; and Bruce M. Owen and Steven S. Wildman, *Video Economics* (Cambridge, Mass.: Harvard University Press, 1992), chap. 5.
15. For example, minority investments are sometimes sold as liquid assets when the holder wishes to reduce its debt or mobilize cash for a large transaction. For example, see Geraldine Fabrikant, "MGM to Sell Its Stake in Three Cable Channels, *NYT,* July 1, 2003, p. C2.
16. Robert Frank, Emily Nelson, and Peter Grant, "Cablevision Nears Agreement to Sell Bravo to NBC," *WSJ,* Oct. 7, 2002, pp. A3, A14; Martin Peers and Joe Flint, "Viacom To Buy Full Ownership of Comedy Central," *WSJ,* Apr. 22, 2003, pp. A3, A14.
17. David Waterman, "A Model of Vertical Integration and Economies of Scale in Information Product Distribution," *JME,* 6 (Fall 1993): 23–35.
18. George S. Ford and John D. Jackson, "Horizontal Concentration and Vertical Integration in the Cable Television Industry," *Review of Industrial Organization,* 12 (August 1997): 501–518.
19. One exception, though, is a premium network that charges MSOs on the basis of their numbers of basic cable subscribers—potential customers for premium networks—rather than actual premium subscribers. Price Colman, "John Sie: All the Right Movies," *B&C,* Nov. 24, 1997, pp. 28–31.
20. Welfare problems with vertical ownership links are discussed extensively by Waterman and Weiss, *Vertical Integration,* chap. 5. A parallel welfare issue arises in the availability of vertically integrated cable networks to direct broadcast satellites. Cable MSOs with ownership stakes in cable networks might find their interests better served by denying the satellites access to these channels. In 1992 Congress acted to require the networks to deal with satellite operators.
21. Steve McClellan, "The New Name in News: MSNBC," *B&C,* Dec. 18, 1995, pp. 8–12.

22. See Jack Banks, *Monopoly Television: MTV's Quest to Control the Music* (Boulder, Colo.: Westview Press, 1996), chap. 6.

23. Owen and Wildman, *Video Economics,* pp. 245–250.

24. Benjamin Klein, "The Competitive Consequences of Vertical Integration in the Cable Industry," report on behalf of the National Cable Television Association (Washington, D.C., 1989).

25. Robert W. Crandall, "Vertical Integration and q Ratios in the Cable Industry," appended to TCI Reply Comments, FCC Mass Media Docket 89–600 (1990).

26. Waterman and Weiss, "Effects of Vertical Integration"; Waterman and Weiss, *Vertical Integration,* pp. 87–127.

27. Hoekyun Ahn and Barry R. Litman, "Vertical Integration and Consumer Welfare in the Cable Industry," *JBEM,* 41 (Fall 1997): 453–477.

28. Tasneem Chipty, "Vertical Integration, Market Foreclosure, and Consumer Welfare in the Cable Television Industry," *American Economic Review,* 91 (June 2001): 428–453.

29. Richard J. Wegener and Richard E. Caves, "Cable Networks and Cable Operators: Ownership Stakes and Decisions to Carry," manuscript, Harvard University (2003).

30. In the end, twenty independent systems (no MSO ownership) were dropped when we discovered that all vertical ownership stakes belong to MSOs.

Epilogue

1. Charles H. Ferguson, *The Broadband Problem: Anatomy of a Market Failure and a Policy Dilemma* (Washington, D.C.: Brookings Institution, 2004). Each mode has a severe drawback, cable's being its poor suitability to serve central business districts.

2. See Ruth Towse, ed., *Baumol's Cost Disease: The Arts and Other Victims* (Cheltenham, England: Edward Elgar, 1997).

3. Joe Flint, Martin Peers, and Andy Pasztor, "Viacom Signals It May Want To Buy a Cable System," *WSJ,* Mar. 10, 2004, pp. A1, A8.

4. Consider, however, one antitrust case described by Stanley Besen et al., "Vertical and Horizontal Ownership in Cable TV: Time Warner–Turner (1996)," in *The Antitrust Revolution: Economics, Competition, and Policy,* ed. John E. Kwoka and Lawrence J. White, 3rd ed. (New York: Oxford University Press, 1999), 452–475.

5. *General Motors Corporation and Hughes Electronics Corporation, Transferors, and The News Corporation Limited, Transferee, for Authority To Transfer Control, Memorandum Opinion and Order,* Federal Communications Commission, MB Docket no. 03–124, December 19, 2003.

6. Comcast's shareholders, however, either disbelieved this strategic value or doubted that Comcast's management could run Disney better than its incumbent executives, since they bid down Comcast's shares enough to make the merger offer worthless to Disney.

7. Patrick Parsons, "The Evolution of the Cable-Satellite Distribution System," *JBEM,* 47 (March 2003): 1–13.

8. Comcast, recently bulked up by acquiring AT&T's cable assets, voiced the hope of beating down its programming costs by $270 million in 2003. Joe Flint and Peter Grant, "Comcast: Newfound Clout, Bare-Knuckle Tactics," *WSJ,* June 27, 2003, pp. B1, B4.

9. For an extensive (if now dated) treatment, see Bruce M. Owen, *Economics and Freedom of Expression: Media Structure and the First Amendment* (Cambridge, Mass.: Ballinger, 1975).

10. The effective maximum percentages are understated, because the calculation discounts by 50 percent the households reached by UHF stations.

11. Yochi J. Draezen and Joe Flint, "In Blow to FCC, House Votes To Reverse Media Deregulation," *WSJ,* July 24, 2003, pp. A1, A6. The rollback did not affect the other policy changes in the FCC's package.

12. If only to acknowledge its absence from this study, we should note the regulation of indecency in broadcast content. Broadcast stations (TV and radio) are subject to fines and possible loss of license if found to violate decency standards. (Cable and satellite are not, because they are not deemed to use the public airwaves and pervade the nation's homes.) The decency policy of course encounters an important frontier of conflict with the First Amendment position. In early 2004 Congress was considering legislation imposing a manifold increase in these penalties. Anne Marie Squeo, "Indecent Proposal?" *WSJ,* Mar. 24, 2004, p. A4.

13. Some research has checked for statistical associations between stations' local programming and their ownership. The networks' O&Os were found to offer significantly more minutes of local news than independent stations and not to differ on average measures of news quality. Bruce M. Owen et al., "Effect of Common Ownership or Op-

eration on Television News Carriage, Quantity, and Quality," Economic Study B; and Bruce M. Owen et al., "News and Public Affairs Programming: Television Broadcast Owned and Operated Stations Compared to Network Affiliated Stations," Economic Study N, Federal Communications Commission, MB Docket no. 02–277 (2003).

Appendix A

1. The market units here are Designated Market Areas (DMAs), commonly used in broadcasting statistics. They are devised by aggregating counties into coherent media markets made up of a metropolitan area and its hinterland.
2. A referee suggests that the stations' reported data might be distorted strategically to influence their negotiations with the networks.
3. As explained in Chapter 6, the networks' practice of writing contracts with their fully owned stations (O&Os) identical in features to those with independent affiliates caused us provisionally to pool the two groups.
4. The number of networks seeking affiliates also matters, but of course the U.S. networks operate nationwide, so the same number come seeking affiliates in every DMA.
5. The concept of a free-entry equilibrium assumes an unlimited number of firms, all with identical costs, standing ready to enter a market. With every firm's costs containing some fixed component (or otherwise subject to some economies of scale) and the market of finite size, free-entry equilibrium exists when n firms competing in the market can all earn at least normal profits, but with $n + 1$ present all would earn less than normal profits. Depending on scale economies and the market's size, n could be either small or large. Given the firms' identical cost structures, n should increase closely with market size. The rate of increase may not be strictly linear, however, because it also depends on the vigor with which the incumbents compete—and that also should increase with n.
6. In a study of comp payments done a quarter-century ago, the presence of an independent (unaffiliated) UHF or VHF station was found to increase comp significantly. We measured total stations rather than just independents, because the New World shock demonstrated to all that long-standing affiliations can be upset. See FCC Network Inquiry

cial Staff, "An Analysis of the Network–Affiliate Relationship in Television," in U.S. Federal Communications Commission, *New Television Networks: Entry, Jurisdiction, Ownership, and Regulation. II. Background Reports* (Washington, D.C.: Federal Communications Commission, 1980), pp. 231–268.

7. Federal Communications Commission, *Notice of Proposed Rule Making: In the Matter of Review of the Commission's Regulations Governing Programming Practices of Broadcast Television Networks and Affiliates,* Docket no. 95–92 (1995), paragraphs 12, 13; found at *http://www.fcc.gov/Bureaus/Mass_Media/Notices/fcc95254.txt.*

8. The influence of cable penetration may be difficult to detect because of its small variance among DMAs. The mean in our sample is 66.5 percent, the standard deviation only 8.5 percent.

9. The receipt of broadcast signals via direct broadcast satellites (DBS) grows increasingly important, but we were unable to secure data on DBS subscription rates by DMA.

10. It was insignificant, however, in FCC Network Inquiry Special Staff, "Network–Affiliate Relations."

11. Federal Communications Commission, *Regulations Governing Programming Practices,* paragraph 16.

12. Franklin M. Fisher, John J. McGowan, and David S. Evans, "The Audience–Revenue Relationship for Local Television Stations," *Bell Journal of Economics,* 11 (Autumn 1980): 694–708.

13. For evidence on the decline of the UHFs' disadvantage, see Patricia L. Pacey, "Cable Television in a Less Regulated Market," *Journal of Industrial Economics,* 34 (September 1985): 81–91.

14. Scholarly evidence was provided by Harvey J. Levin, *Fact and Fancy in Television Regulation: An Economic Study of Policy Alternatives* (New York: Russell Sage Foundation, 1980), p. 128.

15. Fisher, McGowan, and Evans, "The Audience–Revenue Relationship." In the 1980s, before the disturbances to comp patterns occurring in the 1990s, it was observed that networks' comp payments in the aggregate were closely correlated with their overall average ratings.

16. Keep in mind the previously explained peculiarity of the BIA measure of comp, which averages out the variance among networks within a DMA.

17. For example, see Steve McClellan, "Small Towns, Big Problems," *B&C,* Aug. 6, 2001, pp. 20–22.

18. An FCC study analyzed stations' ratios of cash flow to total revenue in 2000 by size of DMA. It was higher for stations in cities ranked by size from 1 through 30, but showed no systematic variation among smaller markets. This pattern is inconsistent with any substantial nondiscretionary fixed cost per station. Jonathan Levy, Marcelino Ford-Livene, and Anne Levine, *Broadcast Television: Survivor in a Sea of Competition,* OPP Working Paper Series no. 37 (Washington, D.C.: Office of Plans and Policy, Federal Communications Commission, 2002), table 14.

19. These results closely resemble those of a similar model estimated on 1970s data—FCC Network Inquiry Special Staff, "An Analysis of the Network–Affiliate Relationship." Prime-time ratings, specified so as to pick up most of the influence of market size, carried a great deal of explanatory power in that study. A significant influence was found for the presence of independent UHF and VHF stations in the DMA. Station group ownership was similarly found not significant.

Appendix B

1. These tabulations were prepared from the rosters of transactions in station ownership reported in the trade publication *Broadcasting & Cable.* Some transactions apparently go unreported, but we have no indication of the size of the undercount.

2. James H. Duncan, Jr., ed., *Duncan's Radio Market Guide, 2000* (Cincinnati: Duncan's American Radio, 2000), p. 8.

3. Before 1996 the FCC had permitted common ownership of several stations in a city served by a sufficiently high total number. A previous burst of radio station consolidations hence had joined several stations within a market. Julie A. Zier, "Station Sales Rebound in '93," *B&C,* Mar. 7, 1994, pp. 33–36.

4. At least one value of having a library of formats is being able to buy a station trapped in local head-to-head rivalry and switch its format. Eben Shapiro, "A Wave of Buyouts Has Radio Industry Beaming with Success," *WSJ,* Sept. 18, 1997, pp. C1, C6.

5. For example, see Anna Wilde Mathews, "In San Diego, Legal Quirks Help a Radio Empire," *WSJ,* Oct. 4, 2002, pp. A1, A8.

6. A current example is hip-hop, which emerged as a format in the mid-1990s and by 2002 was employed by 150 stations (twenty-three cities

have two hip-hop stations). Lynette Holloway, "Hip-Hop Transforms Radio As Stations Seek Ad Dollars," *NYT,* July 22, 2002, pp. C1, C7.

7. Formats appeared as an innovation to replace broadcast networks, as a cost-effective source of radio programming when television overwhelmed radio as a transmitter of scripted programming. Geoffrey P. Hull, *The Recording Industry* (Needham Heights, Mass.: Allyn and Bacon, 1998), pp. 96–103.

8. On the riskiness of format-change investments, see Charles J. Romeo and Andrew R. Dick, "The Effect of Format Changes and Ownership Consolidation in Radio Station Outcomes," Discussion Paper, Economic Analysis Group, Antitrust Division, U.S. Department of Justice (2001).

9. Press reports on major radio mergers mention all three of these hypotheses, but especially the role of national advertising. See Shapiro, "A Wave of Buyouts."

10. Anna Wilde Mathews, "Clear Channel Pushes One-Stop Buys," *WSJ,* May 22, 2002, p. B6; Lynnley Browning, "Making Waves on Air: Big Radio's Bad Boy," *NYT,* June 19, 2002, pp. C1, C6.

11. The share of each group's stations domiciled in a given state is expressed as a percentage, squared, and the squared percentages then summed. The HHI takes a maximum of 10,000 when a group's stations are all in one state. Its lower bound in general is zero, as the units (stations) are spread evenly over a very large number of geographic areas (a minimum of 196, given the fifty states plus the District of Columbia).

12. All data used in these tests were taken from *Duncan's Radio Market Guide* (1997 and 2000).

13. Similarly, when a different format is listed for a station's AM and FM signals, we took the FM format, since the FM band typically gets more listeners and is more profitable for the station.

14. Steven T. Berry and Joel Waldfogel, "Mergers, Station Entry, and Programming Variety in Radio Broadcasting," Working Paper no. 7080, National Bureau of Economic Research (1999); see also idem, "Do Mergers Increase Product Variety? Evidence from Radio Broadcasting," *Quarterly Journal of Economics,* 116 (August 2001): 1009–25.

15. They are Black, Adult Contemporary, Contemporary Hit, Album Oriented Rock, Talk, Oldies, Classical, Country, Soft Adult Contemporary, Jazz, Spanish, Progressive, Standards, Full Service, News, Sports,

70's, Gospel, Religious, New Rock, Business, Urban, Easy Listening, and Hits.

16. Browning, "Making Waves," implies that interactions in a national market for radio and related advertising involve, besides Clear Channel, only a handful of other large groups.

Selected References

Adams, William J. "TV Program Scheduling Strategies and Their Relationship to New Program Renewal Rates and Rating Changes." *JBEM*, 37 (Fall 1993): 465–474.

Ahn, Hoekyun, and Barry R. Litman. "Vertical Integration and Consumer Welfare in the Cable Industry." *JBEM*, 41 (Fall 1997): 453–477.

Atkins, David, and Barry Litman, "Network TV Programming: Economics, Audiences, and the Ratings Game, 1971–1986." *Journal of Communication*, 36 (Summer 1986): 32–51.

Auletta, Ken. *Three Blind Mice: How the Three TV Networks Lost Their Way.* New York: Random House, 1991.

Bae, Hyuhn-Suhck. "Product Differentiation in Cable Programming: The Case in the Cable National All-News Networks." *JME*, 12, no. 4 (1999): 265–277.

Banks, Jack. *Monopoly Television: MTV's Quest to Control the Music.* Boulder, Colo.: Westview Press, 1996.

Barrett, Marianne. "The Relationship of Network Affiliation Changes to Prime Time Program Ratings." *JBEM*, 43 (Winter 1999): 91–109.

Barth, David. "Assessing the Value of Vertical Integration in Television Program Supply." Working paper, Northwestern University, 2002.

Bellamy, Robert V., Daniel G. McDonald, and James R. Walker. "The Spin-Off as Television Program Form and Strategy." *JBEM*, 34 (Summer 1990): 283–297.

Berry, Steven T., and Joel Waldfogel. "Do Mergers Increase Product Variety? Evidence from Radio Broadcasting." *Quarterly Journal of Economics*, 116 (August 2001): 1009–25.

———. "Mergers, Station Entry, and Programming Variety in Radio

Broadcasting." Working Paper no. 7080, National Bureau of Economic Research, 1999.

Besen, Stanley M., and Ronald Soligo. "The Economics of the Network–Affiliate Relationship for Local Television Stations." *American Economic Review,* 63 (June 1973): 259–268.

Besen, Stanley, et al. *Misregulating Television: Network Dominance and the FCC.* Chicago: University of Chicago Press, 1984.

Besen, Stanley, et al. "Vertical and Horizontal Ownership in Cable TV: Time Warner-Turner." In *The Antitrust Revolution: Economics, Competition, and Policy.* 3rd ed. Edited by John M. Kwoka and Lawrence J. White. New York: Oxford University Press, 1999. Pp. 452–475.

Bielby, William T., and Denise D. Bielby. "'All Hits Are Flukes': Institutionalized Decision Making and the Rhetoric of Network Prime Time Program Development." *American Journal of Sociology,* 99 (March 1994): 1287–1313.

Block, Alex Ben. *Outfoxed: Marvin Davis, Barry Diller, Rupert Murdoch, Joan Rivers, and the Inside Story of America's Fourth Television Network.* New York: St. Martin's Press, 1990.

Blumenthal, Howard J., and Oliver R. Goodenough. *This Business of Television.* 2nd ed. New York: Billboard Books, 1998.

Brillstein, Bernie. *Where Did I Go Right?* New York: Warner Books, 1999.

Brown, Les. *The Business behind the Box.* New York: Harcourt Brace Jovanovich, 1971.

Bullert, B. J. *Public Television: Politics and the Battle over Documentary Film.* New Brunswick, N.J.: Rutgers University Press, 1997.

Cantor, Muriel G. *The Hollywood TV Producer: His Work and His Audience.* New Brunswick, N.J.: Transaction Books, 1988.

Caves, Richard E. *Creative Industries: Contracts between Art and Commerce.* Cambridge, Mass.: Harvard University Press, 2000.

Chipty, Tasneem. "Vertical Integration, Market Foreclosure, and Consumer Welfare in the Cable Television Industry." *American Economic Review,* 91 (June 2001): 428–453.

Chipty, Tasneem, and Christopher Snyder. "The Role of Firm Size in Bilateral Bargaining: A Study of the Cable Television Industry." *Review of Economics and Statistics,* 81 (May 1999): 326–340.

Christensen, Mark, and Cameron Stauth. *The Sweeps: Behind the Scenes in Network TV.* New York: William Morrow, 1984.

Christian, Tamber. "The Financial Interest and Syndication Rules—Take Two." *CommLaw Conspectus: Journal of Communications Law and Policy,* 3 (Summer 1995): 107–119.

Collette, Larry, and Barry R. Litman. "The Peculiar Economics of New Broadcast Network Entry: The Case of United Paramount and Warner Bros." *JME,* 10, no. 4 (1997): 3–22.

Covington, William G., Jr. "The Financial Interest and Syndication Rules in Retrospect: History and Analysis." *Communication and the Law,* 16 (June 1994): 3–21.

Crandall, Robert W. "The Economic Effect of Television Network Program 'Ownership.'" *Journal of Law and Economics,* 14 (October 1971): 385–412.

———. "FCC Regulation, Monopsony, and Network Television Program Costs." *Bell Journal of Economics and Management Science,* 3 (Autumn 1972): 483–508.

Day, James. *The Vanishing Vision: The Inside Story of Public Television.* Berkeley: University of California Press, 1995.

Dell, Chad E. "The History of 'Travelers': Recycling in American Prime Time Network Programming." *JBEM,* 47 (June 2003): 260–275.

Eastman, Susan Tyler, ed. *Broadcast/Cable Programming: Strategies and Practices.* Belmont, Calif.: Wadsworth Publishing Co., 1993.

Eastman, Susan Tyler, Jeffrey Neal-Lunsford, and Karen E. Riggs. "Accelerating the Flow: A Transition Effect in Programming Theory?" *JBEM,* 41 (Spring 1997): 265–283.

Eastman, Susan Tyler, et al. "Coping with Grazing: Prime-Time Strategies for Accelerated Program Transmissions." *JBEM,* 19 (Winter 1995): 92–108.

Economists, Inc. *An Economic Analysis of the Prime Time Access Rule.* Federal Communications Commission, MM Docket no. 94–123, 1995.

Engleman, Ralph. *Public Radio and Television in America; A Political History.* Thousand Oaks, Calif.: Sage Publications, 1996.

Ettema, James S., and D. Charles Whitney, eds. *Individuals in Mass Media Organizations: Creativity and Constraint.* Beverly Hills, Calif.: Sage, 1982.

Faulkner, Robert R. *Hollywood Studio Musicians: Their Work and Careers in the Recording Industry.* Chicago: Aldine Atherton, 1971.

Ferguson, Charles H. *The Broadband Problem: Anatomy of a Market Failure and a Policy Dilemma.* Washington, D.C.: Brookings Institution, 2004.

Fisher, Franklin M. "The Financial Interest and Syndication Rules in Network Television: Regulatory Fantasy and Reality." In *Antitrust and Regulation: Essays in Memory of John J. McGowan.* Edited by Franklin M. Fisher. Cambridge, Mass.: MIT Press, 1985. Pp. 263–298.

Fisher, Franklin M., John J. McGowan, and David S. Evans. "The Audience-Revenue Relationship for Local Television Stations." *Bell Journal of Economics,* 11 (Autumn 1980): 694–708.

Ford, George D., and John D. Jackson. "Horizontal Concentration and Vertical Integration in the Cable Television Industry." *Review of Industrial Organization,* 12 (August 1997): 501–518.

———. "Preserving Free Television? Some Empirical Evidence on the Efficiency of Must-Carry." *JME,* 13, no. 1 (2000): 1–14.

Gitlin, Todd. *Inside Prime Time.* London: Routledge, 1994.

Goettler, Ronald L., and Ron Shachar. "Spatial Competition in Network Television Industry." *RAND Journal of Economics,* 32 (Winter 2001): 624–655.

Goldenson, Leonard H., and Marvin J. Wolf. *Beating the Odds: The Untold Story behind the Rise of ABC.* New York: Charles Scribner's Sons, 1991.

Goldman, William. *Adventures in the Screen Trade: A Personal View of Hollywood and Screenwriting.* New York: Warner Books, 1984.

Guo, Karen, and Richard E. Caves. "The End of Fin-Syn and the Reorganization of the Television Broadcast Programming Market." Working paper, Harvard University, 2001.

Hamilton, James T. *All the News That's Fit To Sell: How the Market Transforms Information into News.* Princeton, N.J.: Princeton University Press, 2004.

———. *Channeling Violence: The Economic Market for Violent Television Programming.* Princeton, N.J.: Princeton University Press, 1998.

Hazlett, Thomas W., and Matthew L. Spitzer. *Public Policy toward Cable Television: The Economics of Rate Controls.* Cambridge, Mass.: MIT Press, 1997.

Hilmes, Michele. *Hollywood and Broadcasting: From Radio to Cable.* Urbana: University of Illinois Press, 1990.

Holmstrom, Bengt. "Moral Hazard in Teams." *Bell Journal of Economics,* 13 (Autumn 1982): 324–340.

Howard, Herbert H. "The 1996 Telecommunications Act and TV Station Ownership: 1 Year Later." *JME,* 11, no. 3 (1998): 21–32.

Hoynes, William. *Public Television for Sale: Media, the Market, and the Public Sphere.* Boulder, Colo.: Westview Press, 1994.

Hull, Geoffrey P. *The Recording Industry.* Needham Heights, Mass.: Allyn and Bacon, 1998.

Kagan World Media. *Economics of Basic Cable Networks.* Carmel, Calif.: Kagan World Media, 2001.

Kimmel, Daniel M. *The Fourth Network: How Fox Broke the Rules and Reinvented Television.* Chicago: Ivan R. Dee, 2004.

Krattenmaker, Thomas G., and Lucas A Powe, Jr. *Regulating Broadcast Programming.* Cambridge, Mass.: MIT Press, 1994.

Lashley, Marilyn. *Public Television: Panacea, Pork Barrel, or Public Trust?* Westport, Conn.: Greenwood Press, 1992.

Ledbetter, James. *Made Possible by . . . : The Death of Public Broadcasting in the United States.* London: Verso, 1997.

Levin, Harvey J. *Fact and Fancy in Television Regulation: An Economic Study of Policy Alternatives.* New York: Russell Sage Foundation, 1980.

Levy, Jonathan, Marcelino Ford-Livene, and Anne Levine. *Broadcast Television: Survivor in a Sea of Competition.* OPP Working Paper Series no. 37. Washington, D.C.: Office of Plans and Policy, Federal Communications Commission, 2002.

Litman, Barry R. "The Television Networks, Competition, and Program Diversity." *Journal of Broadcasting,* 23 (Fall 1979): 393–409.

Litwak, Mark. *Dealmaking in the Film and Television Industry: From Negotiations to Final Contracts.* Los Angeles: Silman-James, 1994.

Masters, Kim. *The Keys to the Kingdom: How Michael Eisner Lost His Grip.* New York: William Morrow, 2000.

National Cable and Telecommunications Association. *Industry Overview 2003. www.ncta.com.*

Newcomb, Horace, and Robert S. Alley. *The Producer's Medium: Conversations with Creators of American TV.* New York: Oxford University Press, 1983.

O'Gorman, Catherine. "A Behavioral Examination of Consolidation in the Radio Industry." Senior honors thesis, Harvard College, 2002.

Owen, Bruce M. *Economics and Freedom of Expression: Media Structure and the First Amendment.* Cambridge, Mass.: Ballinger, 1975.

Owen, Bruce M., and Steven S. Wildman. *Video Economics.* Cambridge, Mass.: Harvard University Press, 1992.

Owen, Bruce M., Jack H. Beebe, and Willard B. Manning, Jr. *Television Economics.* Lexington, Mass.: Lexington Books, 1974.

350 · Selected References

Owen, Bruce M., et al. *Economic Studies A–H,* Federal Communications Commission, MB Docket no. 02–277, 2003.

Pacey, Patricia L. "Cable Television in a Less Regulated Market." *Journal of Industrial Economics,* 34 (September 1985): 81–91.

Park, Sora K. "Determinants of Renewal and Adjustment of License Fees of Network Prime Time Programs." *JME,* 9, no. 3 (1996): 1–19.

Parsons, Patrick. "The Evolution of the Cable-Satellite Distribution System." *JBEM,* 47 (March 2003): 1–13.

Quinlan, Sterling. *Inside ABC: American Broadcasting Company's Rise to Power.* New York: Hastings House, 1979.

Rainey, Mark C. "The Cost Effect of Television Local Marketing Agreements." Working paper, Massachusetts Institute of Technology, 2000.

Ravage, John W. *Television: The Director's Viewpoint.* Boulder, Colo.: Westview Press, 1978.

Romeo, Charles J., and Andrew R. Dick. "The Effect of Format Changes and Ownership Consolidation in Radio Station Outcomes." Discussion Paper, Economic Analysis Group, Antitrust Division, U.S. Department of Justice, 2001.

Rosenberg, Matthew S. "The Television Broadcasting Network Affiliate Relationship." Senior honors thesis, Harvard College, 2002.

Schuessler, Thomas L. "FCC Regulation of the Network Television Program Procurement Process: An Attempt to Regulate the Laws of Economics." *Northwestern University Law Review,* 73, no. 2 (1978): 227–306.

Shapiro, Carl, and Hal R. Varian. *Information Rules: A Strategic Guide to the Network Economy.* Boston: Harvard Business School Press, 1999.

Stanley, Robert H. *The Celluloid Empire: A History of the American Movie Industry.* New York: Hastings House, 1978.

Sutton, John. *Sunk Cost and Market Structure.* Cambridge, Mass.: MIT Press, 1991.

Thomas, Laurie, and Barry R. Litman. "Fox Broadcasting Company, Why Now? An Economic Study of the Rise of the Fourth Broadcasting Network." *JBEM,* 35 (Spring 1991): 139–157.

Tiedge, James T., and Kenneth J. Ksobiech. "Counterprogramming Primetime Network Television." *JBEM,* 31 (Winter 1987): 41–55.

———. "The 'Lead-in' Strategy for Prime-Time TV. Does It Increase the Audience?" *Journal of Communication,* 36 (Summer 1986): 51–63.

Towse, Ruth, ed. *Baumol's Cost Disease: The Arts and Other Victims.* Cheltenham, England: Edward Elgar, 1997.

Twentieth Century Fund Task Force on Public Television. *Quality Time?* New York: Twentieth Century Fund Press, 1993.

U.S. Federal Communications Commission. *Annual Assessment of the Status of Competition in the Market for the Delivery of Video Programming.* CS Docket no. 01–129, 17 FCC Rcd. 1244, 2002.

———. *New Television Networks: Entry, Jurisdiction, Ownership, and Regulation.* 2 vols. Washington, D.C.: Federal Communications Commission, 1980.

Vita, Michael G., and John P. Wiegand. "Must-Carry Regulations for Cable Television Systems: An Economic Policy Analysis." *JBEM,* 37 (Winter 1993): 1–19.

Walker, James R., and Douglas Ferguson. *The Broadcast Television Industry.* Needham Heights, Mass.: Allyn and Bacon, 1998.

Waterman, David. "A Model of Vertical Integration and Economies of Scale in Information Product Distribution." *JME,* 6 (Fall 1993): 23–35.

———. "A New Look at Media Chains and Groups: 1977–1989." *JBEM,* 35 (Spring 1991): 167–178.

Waterman, David, and Andrew A. Weiss. "The Effects of Vertical Integration between Cable Television Systems and Pay Cable Networks." *Journal of Econometrics,* 72 (May 1996): 357–395.

———. *Vertical Integration in Cable Television.* Cambridge, Mass.: MIT Press, 1997.

Wegener, Richard James. "Vertical Integration in Basic Cable Television: Causes, Effects on Network Carriage, and Implications for the Entry of New Programming Sources." Senior honors thesis, Harvard College, 2001.

Wild, David. *The Showrunners.* New York: HarperCollins, 1999.

Wildman, Steven, and Kala Salomon Robinson. "Network Programming and Off-Network Syndication Profits: Strategic Links and Implications for Television Policy." *JME,* 8, no. 2 (1995): 27–48.

Wildman, Steven S., and Stephen E. Siwek. *International Trade in Films and Television Programs.* Cambridge, Mass.: Ballinger, 1988.

Williams, Huntington. *Beyond Control: ABC and the Fate of the Networks.* New York: Atheneum, 1989.

Woodbury, John R., Stanley M. Besen, and Gary M. Fournier. "The Determinants of Network Television Program Price: Implicit Contracts, Regulation, and Bargaining Power." *Bell Journal of Economics,* 14 (Autumn 1983): 351–365.

Zupan, Mark A. "Cable Franchise Renewals: Do Incumbent Firms Behave Opportunistically?" *RAND Journal of Economics,* 20 (Winter 1989): 473–482.

Index